UPGATE AND DOWNGATE

Ernest 'Boatie' Clark

Osberton Lock

UPGATE
and
DOWNGATE

Working the Chesterfield Canal
In the 1930s

Written and illustrated by
ERNEST 'Boatie' CLARK

Published by The **Hallamshire** Press Limited
in association with Ernest Clark and Friends

*To my daughter Sandra
for whom the story was originally written*

©2000 Ernest Clark

Published by The Hallamshire Press Limited
in association with Ernest Clark and Friends

Typeset by The Hallamshire Press Limited
Broom Hall
Sheffield S10 2DR
England

Printed by the Cromwell Press, Trowbridge.

British Library Cataloguing in Publication Data:
    A catalogue record for this book is available from the British Library.

ISBN 1 874718 54 7

CONTENTS

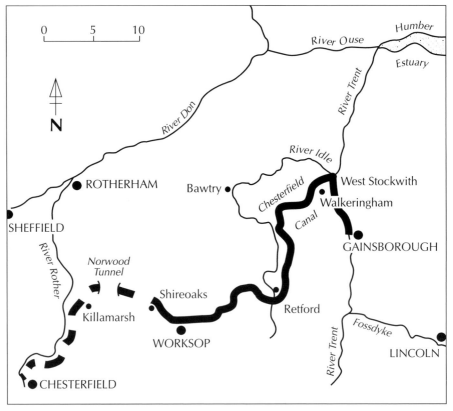

The route of the author's trips from Shireoaks Basin to Gainsborough on the River Trent.

INTRODUCTION

The title Upgate and Downgate may at first puzzle the would-be reader who will naturally assume that the book is 'something to do with canals' judging by the cover.

What, in fact, the book portrays is an insight into the day to day operation of navigating a horse-drawn narrow boat along the remote Chesterfield Canal from Shireoaks Colliery (Worksop) to West Stockwith from the early 1930's to the virtual end of carrying in 1946.

The Chesterfield Canal was opened in 1777, one of James Brindley's early contour canals, it stretched from Chesterfield to West Stockwith, where long distance cargoes would be trans-shipped into sailing ketches and keels to complete their journeys; the narrow boats being used, normally, for more local destinations on the River Trent.

In its heyday the 46 mile long waterway carried principally coal, lead, iron and steel from the Chesterfield and Staveley industries and stone, bricks and agricultural produce from the more rural eastern end.

Subsidence between Chesterfield and Staveley and the final closure of the similarly affected Norwood Tunnel, 1³/4 miles of it, saw the virtual elimination of all traffic between Shireoaks Colliery and Chesterfield in 1908.

This, then is the story of a boating family who worked the remaining 28 miles of navigable waterway from Shireoaks to West Stockwith in the 1930s.

The Chesterfield Canal craft also ventured on to the tidal River Trent, either to Gainsborough 4¹/2 miles upstream or Owston Ferry 3 miles downstream, at this time. However, in times past they travelled downstream to Keadby and upstream to Nottingham and even Leicester on occasion and via Torksey to Lincoln, Boston and very rarely to Spalding.

The trip to Spalding with coal; from above Worksop returning with agricultural produce entailed crossing the Wash for which a pilot would be taken on and then to Fossdyke and the River Welland to Spalding. The whole journey depending on tides would have taken from eight to ten days. Now a lorry could complete the trip in 4 hours! Such is progress.

But I digress. 'Upgate and Downgate' was the boatman's terminology for navigating uphill through the locks or downhill through the locks, the gate being the lock gate. Two very different operations with a horse drawn boat as the author describes in colourful detail.

Not only are all the various 'tricks of the trade' described in graphic detail but also are the people and their trades which are inextricably linked to the navigation, be they Company men, wharfingers, farmers or brick-makers.

Out on a limb when compared to other narrow canals, the Chesterfield boatmen learnt additional skills from the Keelmasters, that skilled body of men who sailed the Humber Keels into and out of Stockwith Basin and with whom they regularly rubbed shoulders in the 'Crown'.

Even the narrow boats had many of the features of a keel and it is not surprising that the terminology used in constructing and moving both types of vessel had its similarities.

Practically all Chesterfield Canal boatmen lived ashore and only stayed aboard in rather cramped conditions for 'the trip'. Consequently their children had regular schooling and, therefore, an advantage over their Midland counterparts in the job stakes when 'going ashore' for new employment as trading by waterway finished.

Ernest Clark's memories include many terms used, not only by the boating fraternity but also local miners and working people of North Nottinghamshire and the Glossary is provided should a translation be required.

The book reveals, for the first time, the complete story of the boatman and his family and will fill a gap on my bookshelf; I hope it will on yours also!

Richard Allsopp

LIST OF ILLUSTRATIONS

THE AUTHOR

Ernest Clark was born in Worksop, Nottinghamshire in 1917, the youngest son of Henry Clark.

His father, 'The Old Man' was a boatman and also his two elder brothers, Len and Bill. Ernie left school in December 1930 at the age of 13 after passing his entrance examination to attend the local grammar school.

Undecided what to do next, he joined The Old Man on his boats. Henry Clark was a Number One, i.e., he owned and captained his boats unlike most of the local boatmen who had sold their boats to carriers, R. Furley of Gainsborough.

The author aboard a modern narrow boat at Morse Lock, Worksop on 11th April 1998
shortly after the section of canal from Stret Lock to Haggonfields was re-opened to traffic
after lying derelict for around 50 years.
(Sid White)

Ernie's attention to detail earned him the nickname 'Mustard' by the other boatmen and 'Jellicoe' by the local fishermen, (after Admiral Jellicoe").

Leaving the canal in 1946 when 'the writing was on the wall' for carrying by boat, he was offered a job at the Albion Flour Mill in Worksop and remained there until his retirement aged 72.

He has lived up to his name of Mustard throughout his life from becoming a proficient boatman and fishermen, winning numerous trophies, he turned to art and painted the canal scene where he had worked, with accuracy and flair. Some of his paintings have been used to illustrate this book.

Music was another of his interests and he played the piano and later became an accomplished saxophonist, playing in the band at the Worksop Palais de Danse for many years.

He also became popular as an after-dinner speaker, amusing the diners with his more humorous boating activities.

Nowadays he spends much of his time in his greenhouse and has one of the best gardens for miles around!

Ernie Clark's 'Upgate and Downgate' has been written with a delightful blend of history and anecdotes and as such should appeal to canal enthusiasts and students of social history alike.

CHAPTER 1

THE CANAL COMMUNITY

Misterton Low Lock

I am always meeting people who say, 'I'll bet the old boaters were a right lot of characters' and everlastingly being asked, 'What kind of people were they?' Obviously a leading question, calculated to draw from me an amazing recital of funny or interesting incidents, accounts of the lives of a people different from the run of the mill simply because they worked on the narrow boats. This may well have worked when I was young, raw and guileless, but now opinions have a certain maturity that gives the impressions of my youthful days a fuller meaning, the wisdom of hindsight as it were. I do not accept that the Chesterfield Canal boatmen were some kind of a freakish community. They were ordinary human beings, people who followed in the footsteps of their elders and reacted exactly as any average person would to the everyday experiences of a life that was a little out of step with the regular hours and predictable events of shopkeepers, factory workers and similar daily jobs. The boatmen learned their trade by experience and example. The work had no timetable, other than daylight and darkness, a freedom of sorts, where the needs of the job were the only consideration. This made the boaters independent, allowed them to do the job in their own individual way, and be their own gaffer within the needs to earn a living for themselves and their families. They had to know the mysteries of caring for their horses, (a boat skipper always owned his horse), caring for themselves when away from home and look after boat and cargo at all times. This way of life could quite easily give a unique status in the eyes of the general public.

All this doesn't answer the question however. People have a habit of wanting answers to be what they would like them to be and many writers try to fit in with this and give the public what it wants. This I cannot do, my impressions of people are mine and mine alone, I don't say that I am right or wrong but I invite the reader to agree or disagree with my findings. So let us forget the romantic 'Roses on the water can' type of canal writing and talk about the Chesterfield Canal Community.

The canal that remained navigable was short—only about twenty-eight miles from Shireoaks to Stockwith. The numbers of boats and consequent crews, were small. Most of the crews had homes ashore and lived afloat only for the short repetitive journeys that the limits of the canal and trade imposed upon them. I knew young and old skippers who took their families with them. Their wives became mates and the children were accommodated in the confines of the tiny cabins. They managed all right, they had to, but it was very different from the impressions given by stories of canal families who lived in the narrow boats of most canals. These familiar craft had a large cabin when compared with the Chesterfield Canal Boats. The much longer journeys on the Midlands canal network made living aboard the sensible and practical thing to do. On the Chesterfield Canal, the journeys were usually of three of four days, sometimes less and so a home 'ashore' was sensible and practical to them. Apart from a very few man and wife crews, we were always father and son, skipper and mate, or just relations such as my brothers and myself. Once again, being such a small waterway, we were familiar with all the other crews and little happened to anyone without it being common knowledge to everyone else, we lived in each other's pocket as it were. On the limited length of waterway we had, we would travel the whole canal once or twice every week and so we could not call the community complete without the whole population of the waterside, we met them regularly on the many regular trips we made. Lock keepers, lengthsmen, canal labourers and tradesmen; men who worked on the canal, and who we met often in our daily voyaging. Cottage folk who lived on the waterside, farmers and farm labourers, brickyard crews, landlords, publicans we tended to call them, we certainly knew them. Then much less often, the landowners and their gamekeepers. All these, with village folk, the skippers and mates of the Humber Keels, shopkeepers. These people all knew and had daily contact with the boatmen and so have to be included in the Canal Community. So what do I say when I am questioned about characters? They were there all right, one could almost say they were all characters by today's standards. I could point to the family aspect for boating seemed to run in families, and so we had a situation where the surname was not enough. Cousins, uncles, brothers, nephews and sons, all of one family gave us a similar problem to that of the Welsh villages with their 'Jones the milk' situation. We couldn't very well say 'Jones the boat' as all were boatmen, so nicknames and physical peculiarities were used. I can recall clearly one family which had a 'Fat Jack', 'Fussy George' and 'Deaf Bob', another member of this family was very tall and so he was automatically called 'Long Jack'. This tall skipper's son grew taller and broader than his father and became 'Big Bob',

Haggonfields Lock was the shallowest lock on the canal in the authors boating days and it is not clear to this day whether it was necessary as a result of a mistake in the construction of the canal
(R. Allsopp)

so you can see the surname became superfluous. In the absence of physical inspiration we had nicknames—I can recall 'Tippy', 'Smash', 'Ginger', 'Smiler', Kingy', among others. My family name, Clark, inevitably made the old man a 'Nobby', his father was 'Kingy'. I was undoubtedly the shortest boatman on the whole canal and so I was 'Little Nobby'—in my absence, or when I had given offence, I became 'Shortarse', all's fair in love and nicknames. I remember an older member of the Worksop United Anglers who always called me 'Little Jellicoe', doubtless after the famous World War I Admiral, and for years I was called 'Jellicoe' by older Worksop anglers who regularly saw me on my journeys. I admit that I was called much more than that if our boat ruined a well baited spot when the fish were feeding. I have a soft spot for those old anglers, and they also had their nicknames. It is a sad fact that I shall never again see 'Twit' Turner, 'Tinner' Smith, 'Bricky' Taylor, 'Juddy' Wilkinson, 'Killer' Marshall or 'Mazzie' Marsden, to name a few. They will always be parts in my canal memory jigsaw.

When I left school, and even before then, the Skippers appeared to be huge, kindly, red-faced bewhiskered men, just as policemen seemed to be tall, wide, moustached Coppers and not the skinny boys they now appear to be. Of course, time, that great worker of wonders, soon revealed the true picture. The deference to my youthfulness disappeared and I now saw revealed a much more accurate picture. Here now was the whole cross section of boaties—mean, generous, kind, cruel, selfish, tolerant, illiterate, intelligent, soft spoken and plain filthy mouthed—all were there. They are everywhere, and so we had to have them on the canal I suppose. The pleasant or unpleasant characteristics were only seen occasionally and for most part a level, civilised pattern of canal etiquette prevailed. A sort of unwritten law covered most situations. A few inter-family type differences were there but these only appeared when drink, horse trading, or something similar 'rocked the boat'.

When we had another boat following us, we did all we could to leave the locks as handy as possible, when we met other vessels we had priorities which we observed automatically, if another crew was in trouble, we helped them. Simple, necessary and basic, these unwritten laws worked.

Within this little world of Chesterfield Canal 'boaties' there emerged some who reacted in predictable manner to situations and these habits soon made them unique among their fellows, and so they became characters. I can recall a number of such individuals. The sons and daughters of these people still exist and consequently I am loath to name names. I could not possibly risk giving hurt or offence to people whom I still occasionally meet, and in most cases respect, therefore I can only loosely call them boaters. We had a large skipper, 'Fat Jack', his huge frame emerging from the tiny cabin hatchway was a sight we saw regularly, and so the absolutely ridiculous picture was lost in the familiarity of it. To me it seemed it was not so much that he was leaving the cabin as that he was shoving the cabin down over his ample hips, but he was as nimble as a kitten on the narrow gang-planks. Mind you, why these planks did not collapse was a mystery to me. This skipper's mate was called Bob, short-sighted to the extreme; he wore thick lensed spectacles and had an owl-like way of peering at you. He always wore knee length breeches and 'leggins', some disrespectful mates even insisted he slept in them. The trousers had shiny, greasy folds in them and along with the battered leggings certainly saw some wear. Given an equally worn flat cap and ageless muffler, he became a perfect team-mate to his huge, fat skipper. They were straight from the pages of Charles Dickens. Despite all this, short-sighted or not, Bob drew horses for a pastime. His drawings were very good—traditional racehorse type stance, laboriously coloured, named and lovingly turned out on any paper he happened to get hold of, and often by smoky cabin lamplight. We had the childish cruelty to call him 'four eyes'. I have seen him, crouched over the cross-plank, stub of pencil in his hand, his ample frame casting grotesque shadows on the cabin sides as he moved in the flickering oil lamplight, and with the effortless ease of long practice, draw the lovely outline of his latest horse. What a pity it is that we rush through our early life to grow up as quickly as possible, the emergent years can have so many lovely memories if we gave them time to happen. I cherish the memory of 'four eyes Bob' and his treasured 'hosses'.

A certain 'Walt' sported a gold earring, and a pair of specs. He also had a type of profanity that was unsurpassed in its class. He swore so naturally and comprehensively that you didn't even realise he was using filthy language—a kindly, skilful boatman. He had the insatiable desire to sing when he had a few drinks. I was only a boy when my brother Len was married but I recall the vision of 'Walt' (who was invited to the function) complete with earring, and held safely upright by other guests, singing in a great voice 'I'll be with you in Apple Blossom Time'. I suppose it was his release, it put the wind up me, crouched in the corner with my lemonade. He was kind and helpful to me when I 'went boating'. The list is endless, wonderful horse keepers, skilful poachers, scrupulously clean boat handlers, all were there. Some slow, some nimble, strong men, weak men. We didn't have many sick men—I can only suppose that you just couldn't be sickly and endure a 'boaties' life as well. While one may think of boating as a slow, placid, peaceful journeying from place to place, such a vision is only part true. With the total absence of power outside of horse and manpower, a lot of cargoes needed sheer hard work to load and unload.

In these days, when schoolchildren are stuffed to the gills with free handouts, when music has been transformed into a deafening noise, lights flashing and blaring day and night, and the face of our fair countryside beribboned with roadways choked with traffic of every shape and size, when an ever increasing supply of money has eroded the value of our possessions, the vision of the old 'boaties' fades insignificantly into their paraffin and gas-lit shadows along with many other relics of those pre-war days of the fourpenny loaf. As I read that which I have already written, I find it increasingly difficult to breathe life and interest into the canal dwellers of my childhood. I found their lives only have dimension when set in their own time, I can understand the humour, and the meaning of their many reactions to their environment. After all, I was born and lived and worked with them. Then I looked in envious awe at the many examples of skilful horse care, boat handling and the tireless energy of physical cargo handling. The thought of being a skipper myself someday with the responsibility of boat, cargo, horse and mate seemed a worthwhile ambition to aim at achieving. I find it difficult to share this understanding with anyone reading this account. I suppose the way of life of bygone boaties is of interest to some who have a feeling for yesteryear. With the revival of the old Shire horses and the desire to paint the modern narrow boats in an alleged traditional manner and when old wooden cartwheels are treasured ornaments for the drives and gates of the little boxes we now build everywhere, and now this mentality has turned to reviving old canals, someone will surely remember that once upon a time, these derelict waterways had human occupants.

The popular conception of crafty boatmen living off the land amuses me. Certainly some farmers and landowners labelled us pilferers. We were judged and found guilty without trial, so to speak. Some misguided people likened us to gypsies. At that time we occasionally met some of the old 'diddycoys' and we found them decent enough, so the comparison didn't bother me in the least. They were entirely different from the present motorised, scrap and car-dealing traders you see today. Well of course we fiddled a little—but what could we fiddle? Most of the canal side was cereal or grassland, the occasional fields of fruit or other delicacies such as peas, carrots, spuds and other vegetables were few and far between, although a few such fields did exist in places like Hayton

Mossy Lock or Guesty's Lock as the author prefers to call the lock with its small cottage formerly a tool shed. The photograph dates from around 1905. Note the footbridge across the top gate. This characteristic feature of the Chesterfield Canal is perpetuated to this day.
(M. Jackson collection)

or Clayworth common. We looked upon mushrooms, blue stalks, and eggs of duck and waterhen, eels and a few other things as perks of the job. My Mother-in-law had a fish and chip shop; she also sold pickled cabbage, onions, etc., which she made herself. Now if I was passing a field of red cabbage in the middle of an icy winter night I would probably acquire a few for the old lady. I never took many—they were so huge and solid I couldn't carry many anyway. They pickled best of all when they had been in a few hard frosts. I have seen people buying the rich, dark red pickles and I have often wondered if the buyers had ever been in the middle of a cabbage field around midnight on a frost crackling night.

A few sweepings for the lockkeeper's hens, or a bag of coal for the grate in his damp little lockhouse sometimes 'fell of the back of the boats' so to speak. I suppose we had an occasional dishonest boatie or the odd poacher, but then these were in all walks of life weren't they? The cargoes my family carried were English wheat, oats and other cereals grown near the canal. We collected these on behalf of the Albion Mill at Worksop who purchased it from farmers on local market days. Thus we came to know all the waterside farmers, and from this relationship we could obtain all the vegetables, eggs and other farm produce we needed free or so cheaply that we had little need to raid the fields at all.

One form of pilfering I enjoyed was when we wanted holly and other evergreen for the old fashioned Christmas. Osberton and Wiseton were the best places and we filled the house with these traditional decorations. I wonder what a present day child would think if he got a stocking with an apple, orange and a bar of chocolate in it along with a sugar mouse with tiny eyes and long candlewick tail? I would think we were not more or less honest than any average citizen in any walk of life. As the Old man said, 'Honesty is the best policy, thank the Lord we've never had to use it'.

I do know that the 'boat-boys' were handled with more discipline than the youngsters of today. Our skippers and elders saw to it. We were kept in our place all right and learned respect thereby. My view nowadays is that respect and discipline is a desirable condition to start your introduction to adult life. Respect for your parents spreads until you respect other people's views and property. Lack of respect and you have the seeds of vandalism and other social evils which beset society today.

The stories of boatman's language did have some truth in it. I had always heard it so I didn't find it unusual—I used a bit myself (when my father wasn't about). Boatman's language, like 'pit talk' was over exaggerated and not as general as popularly believed. I knew one 'boatie' who really shocked me with his violent rages and filthy language. He was probably the best man I knew with the horses, with a vast knowledge of their wants and care and he always kept his horse in wonderful condition.

At West Stockwith was a man who helped loaden the boats. He could not say the simplest thing without a flow of invective. He was tall, with malevolent features, immensely strong and a hunchback. I used to be nervous of this huge, evil looking man, but he was a very skilful man at his job. His advice and knowledge was freely given and I came to like the man. With youthful cruelty we call him 'humpy' (behind his back of course).

Not all encounters, however, with the contemporaries were so pleasant. One evening I was walking ahead of the boat, tired of the slow gait of the deep laden craft. I sometimes did this as you could often see more things going on if the horse hadn't gone first and disturbed them. Just below Man Face bridge a lady accompanied by a young spaniel was quietly fishing. She was spinning, that is, she was casting a lure and probably hoping to catch a pike, chub or possibly a bristling perch. The waters were well stocked with these fish in those days. She had a fine cane rod and a tackle box that represented about a year's wages at my level. Now I had caught pike in Stockwith Basin, roach, perch and chub along the canal and many eels when using the 'Auger' and so I thought I knew all about fishing. Being young, I wished to impart this knowledge to the good lady, and tried to do so. That was a big mistake. Carefully retrieving her lure, she called the spaniel to heel and politely asked me in a voice similar to the one Marie Antoinette must have used when she made her famous remark, 'well let the peasants eat cake then', 'Will you please go away'. Later I realised I had intruded on the privacy of one of the ladies of the family who owned all hereabouts at Wiseton. The Old Man was highly amused at this encounter—I thought the French Revolutionaries had the right idea. Now if this incident had involved one of the old Sheffield anglers the outcome would have been somewhat different. A typical 'Sheffielder' of that period would probably have a silk neckerchief knotted at the side of this neck, a faded serge suit with the waistcoat weighted with a heavy watchguard, usually of solid silver and hung with various medals, denoting previous fishing match successes. His seat would be a squeaking wicker fishing basket surrounded by a litter of flask, bait cans, brolly, landing net and waterproof coat. His rod would almost certainly be a little 'three-piece' Tonkin cane with Lancewood top-piece and carrying a walnut Nottingham reel. He would most likely have listened to me politely and then said, in that never to be forgotten old Sheffield accent—'Don't dee woory di heerd owd luv, Ah were gerring dees bleedin roach afore dah were bawn'. I would have found him a lot easier to understand than 'Marie Antoinette' and spaniel.

In life we meet many people, most of them are soon forgotten. Now and then we have contact with someone and this becomes a memory durable for a lifetime. People do not become notables, cards or characters because of their occupations but if some otherwise ordinary person leaves a lasting impression on people they meet, then I feel that person is well on the way to becoming a character. One such very ordinary person was George Montague. He was foreman of Hill's Brickyard at Gringley Shaw Lock. Always clean, sensibly dressed, he discharged his duties in a manner that made me at least believe in the dignity of labour. Quietly spoken, absolutely intolerant of profane or obscene language and a kind man under all circumstances. My father said he was a Christian who didn't need any Church. George modelled skilfully in clay and when the brick kilns were 'drawn' you would sometime see baked clay images of animals, birds and fishes of exquisite quality. A modest man, I only discovered this talent by accident.

Once I cycled from my home to Gringley Shaw Lock to meet my brother and the boat. I arrived before they did and waited patiently, seated on the top gate balance pole. Mr Montague could see my predicament. I was courteously but firmly invited into his home and there I was given home-made bread, spread with farm butter and cream cheese, sprinkled with chopped chives and covered with crinkled lettuce. I have since had elegant and expensive meals galore and have forgotten them, but the memory of that tea in the Montague's cottage and the kindly people who invited me, I shall never forget.

Human behaviour and reactions can be fairly predictable although stress can alter them. The pattern of behaviour of the long-suffering horses, which hauled our boats, was honest. Lazy, reliable, hard working or vicious, the horse is what he is, their human controllers have to adjust to whatever type of horse they have to get the necessary obedience required for the work, and some most unlikely animals became remarkably good 'boathosses'. We did not use huge horses such as Shires and the like. A noble sight indeed is a Shire. Little wonder these lovely creatures are having a revival in popularity. Unfortunately they were too large to be handy along the narrow paths and low arched humpbacked bridges and too slow for the empty boats, strange as that may seem. We needed more of a medium horse that had good shoulders and four good feet and we probably had 'Heinz's varieties' among the collection of breeds and crossbreeds we saw daily. I am biased enough to believe horses are very high in the intelligence stakes for animals and the high degree of skill and sheer craftiness among some boat horses was truly astonishing. Heaven knows, there was little scope for them in the long hours of work under all conditions but some of them became real assets or as the old man said, as good as a second mate. We had two of these assets in our family. Other horses came and went, but Tiger and Ginger seemed to go on forever. Tiger was not lovely; he was in fact, ugly. Dark brown, roman nosed, ungainly, he had a deformity known as 'swung in the back'. I never could find out what this really meant, but it caused an ungainly, clumsy way of walking with the hind legs, and when he tried to gallop it was a cross between comical and pathetic. With plenty of scars on knees and shoulders a well as everything else, he was no oil painting. But he was a darned good boat-horse and all skippers admitted it.

At Drakeholes tunnel, which had no towpath, the horses 'went over'. After getting the boat on its way into the tunnel, we took the animals over the tunnel and waited at the other end. Tiger could take himself over. He knew a friendly crust of bread awaited him at the cottage on the tunnel entrance. This was a gatehouse cottage and stood by the road from Bawtry to Gringley. The kindly Mrs Walker was a 'soft touch' and Tiger knew he was in with a chance for a titbit if he waited there. We encouraged this as it meant we could rely on finding him there when we needed him, and if Mrs Walker hadn't a crust handy she would give him a penny chocolate biscuit (she sold these to anglers) knowing she would get her penny when we saw her. This was a good system when we were travelling 'upgate', until Mrs Walker became ill. On this occasion she was nursed by her sister who came to stay at the cottage for this purpose and of course she was unaware of Tiger's private arrangement with his friend. By the cottage door was a small table. In the fine weather, on Sundays, this table was a stall for lemonade, fruit and biscuits, on sale to the many anglers and their families who fished there and the very popular cycling clubs who used this road in great numbers at weekends. One day during Mrs Walker's illness, her helpful sister had a baking day and in country fashion, dishes of jam and lemon tarts were placed on the little table to cool. It had to happen, Tiger arrived, he couldn't believe his luck or his eyes. He must have had visions of a horsey birthday party! When I arrived one dish was broken on the ground and Tiger was a daub of lemon and jam up to his eyes. The very frightened lady was trying to 'Shoo the naughty horse'. The Old Man had to dip in his pocket, dishes and pastries had to be paid for but later we had a good few laughs about it all. We travelled a long way that day before Tiger stopped licking his whiskers and looking for 'tags' and remnants of jam and lemon curd pastries sticking to his chops.

A mere recital of people and incidents, funny or unusual, cannot do justice to the boaties. These incidents are in every walk of life, the distance of the past can and does lend enchantment to the view. For the most part, boatmen were too busy earning a crust to be any other than honest and hard working. Exceptions to every rule exist and a mere recital of interesting anecdotes could not give any fair and unbiased account of the men and women who lived and worked in ancient conditions, lagging behind a world that was changing and incapable of competing with the changes. When I left school, the signs of these trends were in evidence and the end of commercial navigation was only a matter of time. In the thirties you could still bring 'a hundred quarter of wheat upgate', by the forties, 'eighty five quarter' was about the limit in summer conditions on a badly silting channel.

The diminishing cargoes led to traditional boating families seeking alternative employment, and a new and less dedicated type of crew took over and, of course, we now knew that the 'end was nigh'. I still meet the odd figure from the past days and am still called 'Boatie' by a few older residents of Worksop and Retford.

I well remember Mossy Lock as local people call it; we called it Guesty's Lock. Big Walter Guest, gravel voiced, blue twinkling eyes over a fine moustache and his little short sighted wife, who despite poor bespectacled eyesight could always find a minto or pullets egg for 'little Clarky'.

We had one of the old boats that wouldn't 'go in'. This was 'Gerald', skipper one George Newton, and so poor old Georgie never had a bonus return load of Shireoaks coal to boost his meagre wages. George died after having a nasty accident with a lock-key, I believe at Misterton Lock. His very popular son, Norman, skipper of the 'Perseverance' died not too long afterwards after an accident on the football field. I have always felt particularly sad about the loss of friendly Norman Newton as I was an inadvertent part of the unhappy affair.

It happened this way—my brother and I had delivered a cargo of flour and offal to the warehouse at Retford. It was Friday and after George Newstead had wheeled away the last bag we decided, in view of the onset of the winter night to lay below Retford Lock until morning. All we had to do next day, Saturday, was to go down to West Stockwith, six hours, for an empty boat with a horse like Tiger. Later that evening Norman Newton, his mate Collie and the good ship Perseverance arrived 'upgate' with a wheat cargo. They failed to clear the lock which was locked up at six o'clock by Bert Rossington, the keeper. It would not be opened until six in the morning. Norman had planned to leave Retford very early, make the six hour journey upgate to Worksop and still have time to bike home to West Stockwith and play for the local football team versus Townrows Mill Team at Gainsborough. This now was impossible, time would not permit it. After we had suppered up the horses, we all sat over a pint in Peggy Davison's taproom and came up with a solution to the problem. I would be mate to Collie on Norman's boat and go 'upgate', although this would mean I had to bike the twenty odd miles to Stockwith early on Monday. Norman would go down with my brother Len and an early start would have him home at Stockwith before dinner with plenty of time to play for his team at Gainsborough. This he did, and an unfortunate clash of heads, and the subsequent fatal concussion, and friendly reliable Norman Newton was dead. I have often thought of the chain of events of this sad occasion.

If one of the new boatmen had gone up the locks to Shireoaks, he would have seen the sealed off Lady Lee Cut and pondered on its possibilities and gone through the deepest lock on the canal, Deep Lock with its bridge and steep unhandy flight of steps at the lock-tail. Our old chestnut horse Ginger, crafty,

A Shireoaks Colliery Co. boat, possibly 'Evelyn', at that companies wharf in Worksop having brought coal downgate from the colliery for the local coal merchants. Note the wooden chimney or 'parson' situated under the dark band on the tiller.
(M. Jackson collection)

knowledgeable, reliable Ginger used to keep hauling the boat and go up those awkward steps like a mountain goat. Above Deep Lock was the length of one George Allwood, he was the keeper at Shireoaks Lock and when the mood took him, he was the most helpful lock keeper on the canal. He would help you down his whole length; his long swinging stride, legacy of his service in the First War, made sure the locks would be full and the gate open when we reached them. With a real 'Nelson Touch' he would turn a blind eye to canal regulations and give us a welcome, if illegal flush, to help us out of the locks and then with a farewell wave he would walk back home. In all the years of trips to Shireoaks, this helpful man's wife never failed to give us a jug of cocoa when we reached their cottage. The cheerful blaze in the fireplace of Shireoaks Lock House was more than earned. Just above the lock house was Shireoaks Basin—then the head of navigation. It was here, in the brick walled basin that coal could be loadened, tipped and shovelled from wagons into two primitive chutes and into the boats. In the hands of careless or inexperienced boatmen the balanced pans of the chutes could severely splinter the wooden 'combings' of the boats. Some boats carried 'combing irons' for protection on such occasions.

The basin, its hut and the chutes were his kingdom. Officially Wally worked on the pit top. When boats put into the basin he was the one sent to cope with them. He was a slight man, shoulders rounded with physical work, a religious man who spurned bad language, he had a temper when provoked, a man of his time, few such exist today. In the cold wet dark winter mornings, or the mother of pearl gleam of a summer's dawn he walked, yes, walked to Shireoaks from his home at Worksop, and he had a early starting time. Utterly reliable, he ruled his little 'Basin World' and never favoured himself in so doing. The coal cargoes were shunted along a loop line over the chutes. Although a lot of coal ran out of the bottom and end doors of the wagons, quite a large amount had to be shovelled by hand into the chutes and from these the boatmen trimming it into the boat's cargo holds. Wally very rarely had help, and sometimes he had two, three or even four or five boats to loaden. He uncomplainingly carried on even when he was in a bit of a temper. His aversion to bad language caused some little amusement, for pitmen and boatmen ran high in the profanity stakes. The doors of the coal wagons could be temperamental and sticking or jammed doors could be dangerous. The door catches were released by blows from an iron bar and fingers and knuckles were at risk if extreme care was not taken. One bitter, icy morning, whilst he was releasing a sticking door, poor old Wally took the skin off his knuckles, very painful indeed in the biting cold. Wally was soon stamping about with bloody knuckles in his mouth, muttering darkly against fates. The Old Man, my father, said to him, 'Shall I give it a proper cussing for you Wally? That would ease it'. 'No! No! No!', spluttered the unfortunate Wally, spraying blood, tears and snot in all directions, 'No, you flopping well mustn't!'

I can see how easy it would be to give the impression that the canal was peopled entirely by kind, hard working crews and others. Unfortunately we had our percentage of evil men, selfish men, and spiteful men, we had our skivers, cadgers and smart guys. Of course, skiving was in no way as rewarding as nowadays, it had not the scope you find in our great Social Security based society. Some boatmen I avoided as much as the confines of our little world would allow and doubtless there were those who had little time for me. Today the Wallace Kelks and George Montagues etc., would be labelled 'Thick as two planks', mugs and balmy by able bodied men living on the state with a standard of life that Wally would never have dreamed could exist. Disagreements and feuds did occur, bad blood between skippers happened occasionally. Sharp dealing in horse trading and drinking brawls, were ever present, but for the most part these were sleeping dogs which we allowed to lie, and generally we were pleased to pass the time of day whenever we met other crews during our journeying. After probably hours of not seeing a living soul to talk to, we were keen to swop titbits of information and gossip during the brief encounters of the day, or when we shared moorings at night. The Old Man loved to gossip, and I was amused at all he found to say, questions he asked in the few minutes it took to pass another boat. When he met an old mate, it was positively amazing what he found to talk about, it was like a dam breaking with all the pent-up news he wanted to impart or receive. We talked little to one another on the trip, perhaps we had 'talked ourselves out' anyway there was little discussion needed about the job as we had few new situations and the everyday running was handled automatically, the consequence of constant repetition. This situation could often be amusing and I vividly remember one such occasion. We were crossing Clayworth Common one day when we met an 'old mate' of my fathers. We had seen him coming for some time across the wide spaces of the common and as we were 'downgate' I had to be ashore to slack for the approaching craft and allow the horses to pass safely. As soon as they could, the two old mates 'got at it'. Their state of health, the weather, details of cargo, condition of the canal, likely place or mooring that night, news of other crews who may be nearby or following, all this was discussed and done with, as the gap had between the craft was widening. Then, and only then, the Old Man asked the question he had been dying to ask all the time. 'How's your youngest daughter going on George?' Now George, the other skipper, had a good looking young daughter and in the manner of his generation he had warned this young lady of the dire consequences of 'bringing any trouble home' and all the shame and disgrace that would accompany it in those days of strict morality. Unfortunately the young lady had a bit of bad luck and outraged all the Victorian attitudes to pre-marital experiences. Today this situation is just a laugh and anyone 'caught' is just careless, nothing more, in fact it nearly seems to be accepted and arranged for. Poor George however, was in an agonising position, and knew the girl's condition could not be hidden for long and something had to be done about it. By this time the two boats were quite some distance apart and the conversation had to be carried on in a loud voice— shouting in fact. The echoes rang around the wide expanse of Clayworth Common as George replied, 'I went to see that farmer chap who caused it and he's agreed to marry her but keep it dark Harry, I don't want it getting about just yet'. The thought of that anguished father, 'keeping it dark' at the top of his voice, from a range of over a hundred yards distance, has caused me many a chuckle over the years since.

Humour along with most human attitudes has changed and the droll humour of the canal community almost has to be explained to the modern quick fire, slick presentation, overdressed or perhaps more likely not dressed at all, type of comedy. Any evening on TV or radio, we get endless variations of old situation comedy proudly acclaimed as though it was new. Mother-in-law, Irish, Scottish and personal domesticities have been joke material, which by now is worn threadbare. Celebrities pop up like mushrooms after a warm summer rain. Comedians today, seem to spend more time selling brand commodities with the endless television jingles than the old craftsmen of my generation who probably only had a bowler and a loud suit for props. This is how I saw the funny side of the canal community. I would like to emphasise that this is my personal opinion and whether anyone agrees or otherwise with my views, then I respect theirs. I feel that the anonymity brought about by provided overalls, safety boots, safety headgear and donkey jackets, has changed the props of the working class funny man. After five years of battle-dress it was easy to accept the standardisation of working attire. My canal humour could not be arranged, it happened spontaneously and in the most unexpected situations, such as with old Herbert. Herbert was a stonemason. He cheerfully laboured along with other labourers if his special skills were not at that moment required. On one such occasion we had to empty a cargo of cement, neatly stacked in the boat in one hundred weight paper sacks.

A band of workers complete the laying of a substantial service pipe at Woodcocks Bridge Retford before the widening of the bridge. An interesting maintenance boat is moored on the far side of the bridge. The two policemen were possibly on traffic duty as the workmen's hut is restricting the width of the A620 road to one lane. **(Bassetlaw Museum)**

At the place of delivery there was no proper wharf. No crane, no way of standing any 'legs', we just had our usual crude barrow and plank situation. Today it would have attracted all the palletisation; containerisation and stacker trucks need for the modern handling of goods. We were left with the old answer to it, 'hand-balling' the sacks. Now Herbert had a long, creased face, watery eyes, and what stumps were left of his teeth, completed his unhappy appearance. The canal inspector was present and he and Herbert gazed at the cement. The inspector, tall, well shaven, neat cap and wearing a 'railway mac', clutched his notebook and prepared to solve the problem of the cement cargo logically and precisely. His underlings waited patiently for his comments—Herbert stepped forward and faced the inspector. 'Mister', he said, 'I feel the situation calls for the skilful deployment of brute strength and ignorance'. Incidentally Herbert played the piano quite competently. I was privileged to hear him play on occasion and envied him his talent. Today he would have National Health spectacles, National Health teeth and boiler suit and would not even be noticed in a crowd.

My father, the Old Man, had a native wit—it was a bit 'earthy' and when I was young I would see him with a group of cronies all laughing their heads off. The hush, which my approach always caused, was a mystery to me at first—I soon learned the old jokes, and laughed as loud as anyone when I was deemed old enough.

The White Swan Public House, Drakeholes, a favourite overnight stop for the author and Tiger; the scene of the crime where Tiger devoured the home-made scones and jam.
(R. Allsopp collection)

One Sunday morning we were painting the boat at Piggot's Bridge. It was a beautiful summer's day and the bells of the Priory Church were crashing and clanging their joyous Sabbath message. The Old Man was 'cutting in' the white stroke which finished off all painting on the bends of the boat. This white line needed a steady hand and the Old Man was giving just that, with squinting eyes and tongue stuck out of the side of his mouth with his supreme concentration. A nicely dressed passer-by said to him, 'Isn't it a lovely morning with the beautiful bells and the warm sunshine?' 'Eh!' said the Old Man out of the free side of his mouth. 'Aren't the bells and sunshine beautiful?' repeated the passer-by. The Old Man slowly and deliberately eased his brush from his beautiful white stroke, looked at the passer-by and said, 'Yull etta speak up Mister, I can't 'ear owt fut bloody row them bells is mekkin!'

The old boaties were not a collection of half-wits or bumpkins. I liked and admired many of them. Some were very intelligent although they had little academic qualifications. I numbered quite a few friends among them and learned much from them which helped me for my academic qualifications were also very limited. I have recalled their wisdom many times since, when I had problems of my own. The older type of boatmen would invite you into their homes when you were staying nearby, and the gesture was reciprocated by my parents when these friendly people were at Worksop and the amiable relationship reflected in our meetings on the voyages. With few exceptions, I liked the genuine boaties and their willingness to 'give and take'. I surprisingly found an unexpected side to a camp of gypsies—these much-maligned people were wintering in a lane near the canal. My brother Len and myself met some of them in the White Hart at Clayworth and after a few drinks my brother gave them a couple of bags of coal for their caravan stoves. On our return journey we were given a supply of clothes pegs that lasted my mother for years, and a hedgehog baked in clay. I daren't sample it but Len said it was passable. When it was broken open all the quills and skin came away clearly and apparently this was the 'way of the Diddycoy'. We had 'common ground' with these wanderers, for they lived as their conditions decreed, much as we did, and just as misunderstood.

Despite being 'born' to boating, living among boatmen from birth, expecting to be a boatman when I left school, I never really liked boating. For a while I enjoyed the new freedom from the routine of school life, but that soon wore thin. The long hours, constantly away from home, when my contemporaries were experimenting with all the adolescent adventures of fledgling teenagers, the girls, the billiard hall, and the new excitements open to youth of my age. I felt deprived, felt I was missing out and blamed boating for it. In retrospect it was amusing, at that age everything is new, all the generations in their turn seem to think they are the first in the field when of course all they are experiencing is as old as life itself.

My canal connections were tied up with the Albion Flour Mills at Worksop. We had the coal cargoes, English wheat 'pick-ups' at waterside farms and warehouses and regular flour and offal cargoes to Retford. Along with these, we had the Canal Company trade—taking repairing materials all along the canal, providing horses to move 'Company' boats and the old Steam Dredger, and handling any job that turned up. Furleys fleet of boats transported the foreign wheat from Stockwith, but we often got cargoes from them if we were empty at that end of the canal. In spite of all this, the Mill was the basis of our trade.

With the outbreak of the 1939 war things began to change. The coal from Shireoaks Colliery was rationed and alternative supplies of fuel were allocated by the Local Fuel Officer. This meant road and rail were soon involved, and worse still for me, it also meant hired transport. By now my brothers had been called up or were in reserved occupations, so I was alone, apart that is from having my ageing father who struggled along with the rheumatics that were a legacy of his lifetime of boating. He willingly helped steadying the tiller when I used the boats. To cope with coal allocations that could not be brought by boat, the Mill Manager had side and end doors put on an old platform lorry and I used this to supplement the water transport. Thus I became a 'driver–boatman' and my links with the canal were beginning to weaken. I found the lorry a welcome change from the slow ponderous narrow boats and this despite the sheer physical work that was needed to load and unload the same. The Old Man made valiant efforts to cope with the 'Bloody Lorry' but his ailing, stiff joints finally won the battle. Along the canal things were also changing—a good many of the old faces disappeared—age and the attraction of 'War jobs' took their toll of the traditional boaties along the failing waterway and the mixture of skippers now were a load of 'odds and sods' compared with the originals.

Chequer House Bridge

CHAPTER 2

THE BOATS

Drakeholes Tunnel

On the shelves of libraries throughout the cities, towns and villages of our land are a fascinating host of books dealing with canals and canal customs and people. In them, in glorious colour, are photographs of flights of locks, 'legging tunnels', viaducts, bridges and boats and boatmen. The attention is drawn especially to the traditional décor of the narrowboats with an endless emphasis on the scrollwork, roses and skilfully painted cabins, tillers, mops, cans and buckets and even the chimneys. We see the generously proportioned family cabins and the little flared heads in front of the high watershed of the cargo hold covers. One author even called them 'gaily painted slugs on their silver trails', his approach only emphasises the tendency to dwell on the supposed romantic aspect of the subject, and I suppose it could be accepted on some inland waterways. I feel it may be part of the flexible poetic licence needed to make a publication fit a little nearer to what the public wants—or think they want.

To the eyes of a young man who was totally involved with the Chesterfield canal, all the above was a Utopia completely and utterly different to his own existence. So I leave the romantic canal historian with a final view of a smiling boatman, ruddy cheeked and friendly, with his hand on a gaily-painted tiller, with him would be his equally ruddy-cheeked wife in spotless white apron and 'flat cap'. With her would be a gradually flighted cluster of equally ruddy cheeked offspring bunched around the entrance to a cabin bulging with glass, brass and traditional family heirlooms, in short, all the ingredients beloved by author and reader alike.

This was not my experience, I found the boat people of my canal to be just ordinary everyday people reacting in their individual way to their environment and thereby I suppose becoming unique but still containing the usual proportion of saints and sinners. On the library shelves I found little information on the Chesterfield Canal boat. Perhaps we can fill a few missing chapters on the style and nature of the craft used on my waterway, the Chesterfield Canal narrowboat.

Imagine the tasks of the boat builders who created the first of these craft. When you think of building a boat, you think of the practical and artistic scope involved, beautifully proportioned curves and lines, to embrace the water with natural grace, to be able to glide on, and through the water with little turbulence, to ride with effortless ease on stormy seas. Balance and proportions to remove all stresses, the perfect marriage of beauty and function. With sail and later, engine, to give control of the elements, and ability to travel when and wherever the craft is required to go. Now think of the complete and utter difference that lies in the building of a Chesterfield narrowboat with its sole source of power, the boat horse. The narrow boats of my waterway were no mystery to me, they had always been there from my earliest memories, to my boyhood calculations they were included in the past, the present, and I fully expected them to be part of my future. Little changed in those days, traditions were observed, sons followed their fathers in family affairs, a large loaf was only four pence at Christmas (old money) and it would still be four pence next Christmas. No one could see or anticipate the dramatic, violent changes hanging like the Sword of Damocles over our heads. Scientific discoveries of incalculable magnitude, untold new stores of energy available, the cow was actually going to jump over the moon it seemed. The war years and the aftermath brought the inevitable casualties along the way, our old wooden boats were among these casualties.

One must be left somewhere, no doubt converted into some of the weird hybrids one can see today in Basins and Marinas. I know where my families' boats finished up, but I lost track of the other privately owned boats, and the working fleet of Furleys, the old firm of Carriers by Water. I remember the last boat they had built, a fine narrowboat called 'Ruth'. She contained features hitherto untried on our canal.

After the initial excitement of leaving school and becoming a fully-fledged mate had worn thin, I started to see the narrowboat as it really was, with the limitations and shortcomings I hadn't had time to notice before. I made many repetitive trips up and down the canal and occasionally in the River Trent, and after making comparison with drawings and photographs of boats on other inland waterways I developed a personal theory about 'our' boats. It was entirely my own theory, unproved, unsupported by anyone else, but it was, and still is, a firm belief of my own. This idea of mine was born when I started to tie alongside, and go aboard the old wooden keels which then came laden into West Stockwith Basin and whose cargoes of hard foreign wheat and other grain were transhipped into our narrowboats for passage to Retford and Worksop. It needed five or six boats to empty one of the keels.

At that period of time a number of these fine old boats plied the River Trent. In my reckoning they were the 'high-water mark' in the development of wooden barges which needed the ability to use wind and tide to function. This was a product of the days before a successful mechanical means of power propulsion was available, and the principal materials were timber and ironwork fashioned by blacksmiths and founders. I like to think it was a progressive creation evolved by generations of rivermen who improved and developed on the earliest craft until they could improve no more. Men who had no powerful engines to tame the unpredictable moods of the tidal river and the wide tortuous windswept estuary where the river met the sea. These men, with the accumulated knowledge of their fathers and grandfathers knew they had to use the natural forces they could not change, and in the Humber Keel they had the ultimate instrument for their purpose.

The only variation I saw in the old wooden boats was a craft I once went aboard at Owston Ferry, this fine boat was 'Sloop-rigged' instead of the traditional square rig of the boats with which I was familiar. The wise old warehouseman at the jetty where we were moored told me that this type of craft was associated with the trade from Barton-on-Humber and could sail more accurately than a 'squares'l'. In conclusion, the old man said that a 'Barton Bulldog' could sail into the 'eye of the wind'. True or not, I loved that name, and believed the story, mainly because I really wanted to.

Nothing resists change, and iron keels had already started to supplant the timber built boats. At first the iron boats followed the dimensions and design of the originals, and more and more they relied on a growing fleet of powerful tugs to make their trips up and down the Trent. Even this change was not to last, for today most boats on the Trent have their own engines and most of the original sailing and 'driving' days rigging and fittings have gone forever. I was fascinated by the old time keels, my youthful eyes couldn't see enough of them and to clamber aboard one among all the varied confusion of gear ('dunnage' my father called it) was sheer poetry. The powerful mast with its taut shrouds, and fore and aft stay, the huge sail lashed to its spar and carefully covered against the elements, built-in carefully sited windlasses at vantage points to enable feeble man to control and handle every function necessary in the navigation of the boat. Derricks to handle the cargo, sturdy wooden windlass built in the bows to handle the heavy anchor which hung from the porthole either side of the stern; how the ratchet and pawl used to clatter when the crew used the two handles of the anchor winch. Sensible hatches, strewn with cordage covered the fat, wide, deep cargo holds, timber-heads, blocks and tackles, and we cannot forget the shaped 'lee-boards' which hung from the vessel's sides. Having seen some paintings by old Dutch Masters, one could almost imagine the influence of Dutch boatbuilders in the design of the wooden keels. The beautifully shaped counter with wide varnished aft rail, huge rudder, and the large heavy tiller needed to work it, the wide bluff bows so suitable for the Trent with its powerful 'springs' and surly muddy 'neaps', a boat completely at home in its environment. Here on board the old keels was born my theory. The Chesterfield canal (or

The maintenance boat 'Norah' known to the boatmen as 'Norahboat' at rest in the 'Company Yard' in 1958. Almost at its birthplace.
(M. Jackson)

34

what was left of it) debouched into the river at West Stockwith. Our narrowboats used the Trent as an extension of their sailing range if and when necessary. Gainsborough, Owston Ferry and other riverside places were in reach of our boats, which however unhandy they were, did have a way of coping with the tidal river. My own experience of the Trent was limited, but tales told by the 'Old Man' of days and nights on the Trent filled me with wonder and envy. I saw enough however to make me begin to believe to my own satisfaction that when the canal reached West Stockwith, the boats it needed were built by men who also built the shapely old keels. I believe they built the narrow boats to use the Trent as well as the canal; that they adapted the Trent way of doing things instead of concentrating on custom built 'green water' narrow boats designed specifically for the man-made canal.

The old craftsmen, skilled in the use of razor sharp adze, long draw knife, every shape of gouge and chisel, and long handled augers. Patient, efficient, competent men, probably sons or grandsons of boatbuilders capable of choosing timber and working it with the confidence of the master builders they were. I suppose that some form of narrow boat was used by the canal builders themselves as their navigation extended along its route, and before it even came near to the Trent, but I do know I have not seen any narrow boats built like a Chesterfield Canal narrow boat that I lived on and spent my early working life on. They were unique in their design, and that some reason for this must exist. Imagine the task given to the builders of boats, the inflexible dimensions of the narrow lock chambers, the restriction of headroom by the little humpbacked canal bridges, the depth of the canal that required a boat to carry one ton of cargo to one inch of freeboard, and with all that, the ability to turn in its own length in the twisting tortuous channel of a contour canal. Seventy two feet by less than seven feet; in this cramped space was needed room for cargo; room to store loose gear and supplies for journeys; room for at least a two man crew to find shelter, warmth, a kitchen, a bedroom and all that passes under the heading of living quarters. Give the boatbuilders all these requirements, and restricted dimensions in which to fashion them, and immediately away goes everything beloved by the traditional boatbuilders, no lovely clinker build, no neat carvel hull, no shapely counter or transom, no proudly flared stern, nothing to 'fashion with pride', what we had left was the Chesterfield narrow boat, disproportionate length to width ratio, stark 'hard chine' section, any curve or 'flare' restricted to the few steam-bent timbers of the 'bends' fore and aft, having no way to turn to avoid the inflexible fixed dimensions, the builders did what they could. In deference to the custom on keels in which the captain slept aft and the mate slept forward, the builders put a cabin at each end of the narrow boat, and they even put a narrow fixed bed-board in the fore cabin. I suppose a mate could use the 'forrend' bed if the captain's wife was aboard, but if the Captain had his lady with him the mate would be unnecessary, for all the boat women I knew could do the mate's job fairly competently. I never saw an iron narrow boat, at least not on 'our' canal. I have seen rusty iron lighters on other canals but the Chesterfield canal boats were all timber. I listened with great interest when the old hands were discussing or even arguing about the merits or otherwise of Ash, Oak, Red Deal, Pitch-Pine and Elm, also less well known woods such as Teak, Greenheart, Hornbeam and various imported timbers. I could only come to the conclusion that each part of the boat needed a special wood. The great variety in the natural qualities, strength, durability, not forgetting the cost, made it sensible to have a mixture of timber used in relation to stress and wear of specific parts of the craft. The variety of ironwork used was largely hand-made by blacksmiths, but certain fittings such as beam irons and windlass ratchets, and the strong 'knees' which reinforced the box-like sides of the hold were usually castings. The blacksmiths made the many 'drawn' spikes which effectively pinned the timbers together, and an endless arrange of dogs, hooks, staples, cleats, tholes and the protective ironwork of fenders and stem. Little wonder that the boatyard echoed to the incessant hammering of the smiths and the hissing of hot iron being staunched.

The hull of the boat between the bulkheads of the fore and aft cabins was just a long box and had none of the curve or 'belly' we associate with wooden boats. The narrow length of the cargo hold was 'hard chined' with its square section and the width and depth were almost uniform except for a bit of lift towards the aft deck which gave a little extra head-room in the cabin. The boatbuilders were not deterred by the unattractive and featureless craft they had on their yard, they knew the important thing was to turnout a workmanlike job. They knowingly selected the timbers for the bottom and the sides of the boat, and individually tailored each piece for its place with the slight bevel needed to give a correct entry for the caulkers with their 'Oakham twists' which were tightly driven into the seams until the hull was waterproof. The side planks of the boat were called 'strakes'. (Boatmen called them 'strokes') and as they were built up they were 'pinned' with long blacksmiths' spikes, and careful scarf joints were used in the horizontal journey. The upright position of the sides was stoutly and necessarily reinforced by iron knees which were placed at regular intervals along the inside of the hold. The curves at the head and stern were 'steam bent' and strongly rebated into the sturdy bowed 'stem' and the straight sternpost, boatmen referred to this part of the boat as the 'bends'. The strokes, which were called low stroke, first stroke, second stroke and top stroke, were strongly stiffened by the addition of strengthening pieces strategically placed fore and aft at the obvious collision points. We have to remember that a boat steers from the aft end and when the rudder went 'hard over' the stern of the vessel had to move first before the head could answer, something like a car in reverse, this resulted in that the stern of a vessel could and did get a fair share of bumps along walls or in aqueducts and bridge-holes and this also made the end strengtheners very necessary. The top stroke was given extra thickness for its whole length to form a gunwale or as was much more usual the erection of a 'combing'. For combings were essential if a boat was going to carry cargo that needed 'sheeting down'. Boats have been built for specific cargoes such as coal, stone and bricks etc., which needed no protection from the weather. As these cargoes gave a lot of wear and tear to the boat's timbers they had a wide strong gunwale to cap off the top stroke, and were known as 'Gunnel boats'. When a combing was fitted it was simply a low wall of timber securely spiked to the top inner edge of the top stroke and formed a 'rebate' with face of the combing and the 'sill' of the wider top stroke. The rebate so formed gave the essential space for the heavy tarpaulin sheets to overlap the boat side without being 'proud' and chafing on locksides and such. The covers were supported by 'bottom lashings' which passing over raised cargo or centre planks formed the important watershed that prevented pools lying in sagging hollows and seeping through overlaps of the sheets. The bottom lashings were held in place by evenly spaced 'dogs' in the combing 'face'. 'Dogs' were simply square spiked hooks driven into the combing at regular intervals the whole length of the hold and faced downwards against the pull of the lashings. The carefully adjusted covers overlapped the combing and the 'dogs' and were held securely in place by 'top lashings'. In their turn, top lashings were held by 'S' shaped hooks which were fixed in the gunwale ledge by large staples which allowed the cover edge to be held tightly out of harms way in the combing rebate. However hard we tried to get the covers taut we usually ended up with a bit of 'sagging' and in persistent rain we had to regularly 'sweep the covers' to prevent heavy pools forming, which in turn made the sagging worse.

It is easy to imagine the difficulties faced by the builders when they had the problem of keeping the long relatively thin sides of the boat rigid and parallel, they effectively managed this with heavy iron 'knees' and cross beams. The side planks lay horizontally along the boat and were 'lined' inside by a layer of thinner perpendicular boards nailed securely on a 'seal of chalico' which made an effective watertight finish. (Chalico was a paste made of tar and fine flocks, or dried horse manure, seasoned in a 'Chalico tub'). The 'knees' were simply iron angles, they were tailored to fit the particular part of the boatside they were used in, this was very necessary as the inside of the boatside had various shapes caused by the addition of the strengthening pieces. The knees tapered from the 'heel' both ways, and were securely bolted to the boat timbers with the flat taper of the bolt heads countersunk slightly in the face of the outer hull which had to be 'sheer' and have absolutely no 'proud places'. The cross beams gave a final 'stiffening' to the boat's sides, the fore and aft bulkheads gave strength on the shoulders of the boat, and three cross beams gave the long length of the hold nicely spaced support. The dominant factor in the use of the beams was the fact that they were dovetailed into the 'top stroke' of the boat and thus prevented inward, or more important still, outward movement of the boatsides. The dovetailed crossbeams were very effective, but even with the beams in position, when an empty boat collided or twisted, a visible ripple ran down the sides. The beams were far more important than their simple appearance indicated, sited strategically, they were a great source of strength, a ready made form of partitions for the cargo hold, and absolutely necessary to the gangplanks that were our only way of getting about the boat when empty or loadened (laden) with cargoes that could not be walked upon easily. The beams were not evenly spaced, even that simple requirement depended upon other factors. There were three main beams, 'foremiddle' or 'lutchet', middle and aft. The middle beam was also sometimes called 'aft middle'. Just in front of each bulkhead were narrow beams which simply carried the ends of the planks and were not dovetailed. The position of the fore middle beam was important, here was the hauling point of the empty boat. This beam was different to the others in that it was also built to hold the 'lutchet'. This was the name given to the upright seat of the mast. It was pronounced as in 'judge it'. I haven't the faintest idea of how it came to be so called. I have seen similar constructions in other craft named 'tabernacles' but we called it the lutchet and the beam shaped to hold the lutchet was always called the lutchet beam.

The masts were squared at the bottom half to fit the lutchet and I was always amused at the names of the long-mast and the short-mast, for there was only about two feet difference in them. The short mast was just about two feet long, give or take a few inches. There was, as always, a sensible reason for this short-mast. An empty boat had to haul from the lutchet and the bridges in some instances were so low that any longer mast would have not been able to clear them. The long mast was for loadened hauling. A loadened boat could haul from the fore timberheads, but the laden boats were very low in the water and in times of weed and ice, the skippers used to haul from the long mast to give maximum clearance to the long swaying hauling line and avoid the irritating clearing of the cotton line every time it 'trailed'. Hauling an empty boat was always from the short mast and the lutchet had a few essential features for the job. The lutchet fitted in a seat in the beam facing 'forrard', it was practically free standing in that it was held upright simply by short-chain, staple and pin. It could not move forward because it was behind the beam, it couldn't move sideways for it had extensions of the beam to hold it in position and the chain and pin prevented it from falling backwards. The foot of the lutchet fitted into a slot in the floor of the hold. A sloping 'toe' on the bottom of the lutchet prevented the lutchet foot from swingback when the line tightened during hauling. It could happen that sometimes a hauling line fouled and the empty boat would run ahead with its own momentum until the fouled line tightened and caused a backward check to the boat. This misfortune could cause the line to break or much worse, smash the lutchet beam but for a simple failsafe precaution. The toe of the lutchet was sloped to accept forward strain on the line. If reverse strain was applied, the heel of the mast was allowed to slip out of the seat and then the lutchet could swing backwards and hang on the chain and pin from the beam. The loose mast would then simply pull out of its slot in the lutchet and instead of a disaster we just had a nuisance.

A loadened boat, low in the water, had no difficulty and could haul from the mast, or from one of the fore timberheads, but once again we had a specific problem to solve to allow an empty boat to be hauled by a horse. As usual the boat builders solved the problem, and that was why the position of the lutchet beam in the boat was so very important, it was the true hauling point, and it was the reason old skippers would knowingly say 'She'll go up if she's true'. If you took a wooden rail and tied a string to it somewhere in the front half and then trailed it along a waterway, you could by experimenting with the position of your 'tie' find a point when the rail would trail along 'holding station' and not dragging into the water's edge or veering wildly away from the side, then you would have found the hauling-point. The old boat builders didn't have to experiment, they put the lutchet beam in the right place and we soon learned the little habits of the boat's steering qualities by usage, most had their individual characteristics, some good, some not so good. Some boats were 'handy', and would follow the horse, some were bad steerers, all had their individual 'trim' when loading and we needed to know these, for an inch or two by the head or stern made all the difference in the world when we had to steer and haul the boat. An empty boat didn't haul straight for long, it either started to 'drop' or 'run up'; when the boat ran towards the opposite side to the towpath, it was 'going up' and if it drifted towards the towpath side it was 'going down'. The towpath was always called the 'inside' and of course the other bank was called the 'outside', and an empty boat either 'ran out' or 'dropped in', some boatmen said a boat was going up or dropping down which meant the same thing. When we steered, we called it holding her steady, or steadying the tiller, and we checked the running up and dropping down before it hardly began and by the feel of the helm we held a reasonably even progress. To steer an empty boat into narrow places such as locks, aqueducts and the narrow bridge holes required a proven strategy. When an empty boat ran up, it ran at an angle and when you corrected that angle with a touch of the helm the boat would briefly run straight. Approach

An unusual view of a Chesterfield narrow boat but one which shows the exposed
steering position and the high freeboard, useful when navigating the tidal River Trent
with a full load. It is believed that the location is Manton Viaduct and James Chambers is steering.
His son James is sitting with his wife Mona.
(C. Mitchell collection)

any narrow place, we 'ran her well up' and at precisely the correct moment we 'held her in' and the boat would then be in a straight line for entry into the narrows. The timing of this manoeuvre made all the difference between good and bad steering and between bumping her or a smooth entry. In these conditions, an empty boat could not 'run up' into a lock or such, it had to be dropping down to gain control of the 'entry-line'. Gale-force cross winds which blew towards the towpath made empty boat steering a nightmare, and could be damaging to the boats where a hard bank chafed the bottom timbers when the wind 'blew a boat down'. Several notorious places of ill fame existed where the canal was exposed to high winds and we treated these with fear and respect as we approached them.

The cargo rested on the 'shutts'. Shutts was the name given by boatmen to the boards which lay crosswise in the floor of the hold. The actual bottom of the boat lay below the shutts and the fore and aft 'scantlings' lay on the bottom and supported the shutts which gave a few inches of clearance between the true bottom and the shutts and so formed the shallow 'bilges' which allowed any water to lie on the boat bottom without reaching the cargo. The shutts were lightly nailed to the supporting scantling but were mainly held in position by laths laid along the edges of the hold, something like mouldings. The shallow bilges were very necessary to keep cargoes dry but they also had their own problems which we had to take into account. We did not cover the holds when empty and so a time of heavy rain could 'put a sup' in the bilges, and some boats had a leak or two which also 'put a drop under the shutts'. This situation could be controlled easily by regular attention to the pumping, and in addition to the pump in the 'forrend' we had a pump in the hold just behind the lutchet beam. This pump amidships had a collar which formed a spout that passed through the combing to allow the water to escape overboard safely. This pump was situated in the best position to pump-out when the boat was laid level in the water, but badly silted bilges with slow drainage sometimes meant that some water was not 'up lifted'. To get a boat really dry we finished off with the fore pump when we loadened the boat. We traditionally loadened head-first, that is, we started with the 'fore-box' and this meant the boat head would go low in the water as the cargo weight increased, the stern would actually rise, and the boat would lay at a steep angle down by the head. Any water in the bilges would 'run-forrard' and could be dealt with by the 'fore-pump'. When a boat had 'middling of watter' in the bilges, we had to pump immediately the head started dropping or the water running down the length of the boat would flood up through the shutts and the forrend floorboards with dire consequences to a perishable cargo or anything stood on the forrend floor. A good old skipper hated to get his forrend floorboards soaked, but much worse, he hated to load or unload 'wrong way round' and get his cabin oilcloth and rug wet. If we had to 'drop her stern' we always pumped as much as possible beforehand with the middle pump, and deliberately 'listed' the boat to the pump to get maximum drainage. Leaking boats meant constant attention to the pumping, a leak was most troublesome when a boat was deep laden, and one can suppose pressure was greatest then.

Wise skippers soon learned to live with the odd leak, they knew the best places to 'rub her' on the muddy shoulder of the channel and effect a seal against taking water in or they would use fine ash, wet sawdust, or similar materials and dump them down the boatside where they knew the 'weep' was situated. The finer sediment would be sucked in the leak and form a plug.

Boating tended to be a constant attention to detail like leaks and other little problems and the list of 'don't do that's' must have been bewildering to a newcomer to the cut. The long narrow cargo hold with its strengthening beams was sealed fore and aft with stout bulkheads, the joints in the bulkhead boards were covered by narrow laths of timber to make an effective dust and draught and watertight wall. Beyond the bulkheads the ends of the boat were handily formed with the two cabins, the one situated in the forepart of the boat was called the 'forrend' and the one aft was always called the cabin. The 'forrend' was smaller than the cabin for it was just the length of the 'bends'; i.e., the curve of the bows. This compartment was theoretically the crew's quarters, but as the full muster of a narrow boat on 'our canal' was only two people—Skipper and Mate—the forrend was rarely if ever used as accommodation for either of them. A bed-board was built in the forrend, just a narrow shelf like platform that was fixed and could not be folded away when not in use. It was always called the bed-board—but it was always used as a shelf. The interior was sometimes decorated, but as its usual use was that of a storeshed it was never carefully 'grained' and varnished, as was the cabin. The limited space was further restricted by the 'legs' of the timberheads, for all boats had at least one pair of timberheads forrard, and some had two pairs. The timberheads protruded through the deck timbers with an inward tilt and the carefully shaped 'legs' ran in a taper down the inside of the curved bends to which they were firmly fixed. Where two pairs were used it gave the small cabin an even more cramped look. A strong iron knee was set in the stempost and a small timberhead was fashioned at the head of the stem. This compartment had no seats or other fixtures and no stove, although one boat I knew had an exit built in the forepeak for a chimney pipe to go through if needed. This boat always kept the unused chimney pipe well covered for all boats foredecks were repeatedly drenched with water from the leaking top-gates of locks which allowed the pressurised water to enter the lock chamber in the form of curved fountains and these fountains sprayed over the foredeck when the stem of the boat reached the 'bump-board'—a wooden fender in the centre of the lock sill.

These 'leks' in the top gates of the deeper locks could be troublesome when travelling downgate particularly when a boat was deep laden. In really deep locks such as the one opposite the Chemical Works alongside the Worksop-Shireoaks road, the loadened coal boats lay well below the sill and beautiful feathery arcs of water could, and did cascade over the aft deck of the boat. In most cases the closed hatch was ample protection for the cabin interior, but in these extreme conditions, the real trouble was caused by the descending spray going down the chimney which was right aft, and as boaties usually had a nice fire going the result was an explosion of steam and ash which made a right mess of the cabin and its carpets and fittings. We did sometimes get caught out, usually by an unexpected leak, but we knew only too well where the problems were likely and we would slip a bucket over the 'Parson' until we got clear, preferring a cabin full of smoke instead of water and the scattered remains of our fire. In the forrend we traditionally kept the 'snap-basket' for although it was a poor sort of larder, at least it was the coolest place for our victuals. The basket could of course stand on the bed-board, but the safest place was to hang it from a hook fixed in the cambered deck beams, for there it could swing in comparative safety when we had the occasional bump or two. In the absence of a fire, the forrend could be damp and musty—regular sweeping up of the spilled horse feed and careful use of the hatchcover helped keep the forrend sweet and aired. The really serious risk of damp and wet came from the bilges. When a boat was down by the head when loading or unloading any water in the bilges ran down the whole length of the vessel and careless attention to pumping out by the crew could lead to water rising above the floorboards of the forrend with unpleasant results. With this eventually in mind, the wise old boatbuilders installed a pump in the forrend just clear of the bulkhead and this pump emerged through the deck in the corner formed by the 'headledge' and the end of the curved screening. This allowed the water being pumped to drain harmlessly overboard. The pump itself was a crude hand operated affair, just a square wooden sleeve which rested on the boat bottom with access vents at its base to allow the water to be sucked-up. The pump was sealed in position as it passed through the floorboards and again as it emerged about an inch or so through the deck timbers so allowing the pump

A loaded upgate boat at Leverton Road (Claters Bridge), Retford.
Apart from the lack of commercial traffic little has changed in this scene.

to be used without wetting any part of the forrend interior. The pump 'sucker' was merely a square block of wood which loosely fitted the sleeve of the pump, it had a good sized hole through the centre and a weighted leather 'clapper' formed a hinged seal against any lifted water. The sucker had a leather collar around its top to effect an airtight fit and helped the suction and the whole affair was worked by a long upright handle with a cross grip at its top. It was an unpopular pastime was hand-pumping, a half bucket of water was emptied into the pump for a 'primer' and then vigorous pumping accompanied by throaty gurgling sounds as the pump took hold and then you had a nice regular flow— as The Old Man said—'good for the boat, bad for the back'. In other vessels, the romantic names like 'the chains', the 'forepeak', or the fo'castle graced the forward compartments of the craft, we always called it the 'forrend' and all I ever saw it used for was a store shed—not very romantic.

Aft it was an entirely different story—to paraphrase a great man's words, 'Never in the field of human boatbuilding, was so much done by so little, in so many ways'. This was the cabin—never called anything else. It was the centre of our narrowboat world, here we lived, slept, and prepared our food, here was the sole source of warmth and shelter, and any and all of the meagre comforts we had whilst on our trips. The cabin could be stifling in the summer heat and smoky when the warming fires were buffeted by winter's icy blasts, especially when we were forced to use the hatchcover for protection against snow and rain. Despite all this, it was our haven, we acclimatised ourselves to it, we found by regular usage that we could adapt to the low headroom, the hard wooden seats, the limited stowage space that meant everything had to have its place and had to be kept there. We even got used to the simple bed that was only a 'flock' mattress laid on a wooden base. On stormy nights, the creaking of mooring lines, the soft nudge of the hull against the wharf, and the drumming of the rain on the deck timbers just above our heads even made our little home seem snug as we lay in the narrow spartan bed, often in the soft glow of a fire which was being kept in all night. All this, in the pitifully small space available was 'the cabin'. It was larger than the forrend, the bulkhead was set further away from the sternpost, and the rough triangle formed was used completely by the builders. The more generous use of 'lift' aft gave us a little more headroom than in forrard. A shelf, coathooks and one or sometimes two drawers under the bedboard were all that was needed to give us our wardrobe, kitchen and storage place necessary for our clothes and 'bits of things'. We were completely at home therein, but in the 'depression years' before the Second World War, we occasionally had an unemployed acquaintance along with us just for the ride or as a welcome break from being fed-up, spent-up and bored with standing around out of work. Their many bumps on the deck beams as they got used to the little cabin gave us a few, if unsympathetic laughs, especially when we let them sleep next to the bulk-head directly below the shelf, for when they 'made a put' to get up they fairly made the pots jump off the shelf.

The shape of the cabin was formed by the aft bulkhead and the two curved sides of the boat which met in the sternpost. The only feasible place for the very necessary stove was in the apex where the boatsides met and formed a triangle 'smack in the stern'. The stove was almost a free standing affair. It was a four-sided cast iron construction, the wide face of this stove contained the grate bars, in the mouth of the stove and a very efficient drawplate which could be slid up and down with a brass knob and create quite a draw. A removable hob gave a safe 'stand' when we used saucepans and other cooking utensils. An arched cavity beneath the fireclay lined back and sides and bottom bars of the 'fire-hole' held a shaped ash tin with wide brass edged front and drawer like back extension which caught the falling ash and cinders. The face of the stove had ornamental scrollwork and was very decorative. When we 'black-leaded' and touched up the brass faced ash tin and draw-plate knob, we had a smart looking fireplace. The top of the stove followed a shallow taper into a pipe which loosely fitted inside the fixed iron pipe and ran through the deck timbers. The stove could be easily removed by sliding the bottom away from the stern. A fixed iron plate on the floorboards formed a stand for the stove, and when standing in position, the bottom of the stove was prevented from sliding on the plate by plating nails sited either side of the foot of the stove face. We emptied the ashes once or twice a day—sometimes on the bank, sometimes over the side.

The bed had to be at the widest place, along the face of the bulkhead. The bed-hole took the form of a horizontal cupboard. The bulkhead was the back wall of the cupboard, the pot shelf was the top, and the base which was about two feet wide, and flush boarded to stand just on the back-seat. The door of the bed-hole was hinged to the base of the bed and held by catches to the front of the shelf and when it closed it had a nice back slope to the narrower shelf and so formed a handy backrest when used as the back seat. The door was called the bed-board and was simply a batten door, with the battens inside and thus under the mattress when in use. The door did not completely span the bed-hole. It had slightly tapered ends which fitted snugly into fixed sides and thus the door could then open downwards and outwards without its top corners fouling the iron knees of the inward curving sides. Rolled inside this horizontal cupboard was the mattress, the pillows, and sheets and blankets for our bed. When the bedboard was down, supported on the side seats, the bedding was rolled out and the bed 'made'. It was adequate for two grown men, although a very tall man would be 'nipped for length'. I have often slept three in a bed, cramped but manageable, if in an extreme case we exceeded three, then we slept 'athwarts the bed' and if it was winter, wriggled our feet in front of the fire.

When the bed was folded away and the bed-board safely fastened shut, the living cabin was revealed. At the foot of the bed-board for the full width of the cabin was the back seat. On its narrow length, with the aid of a cushion formed by a tightly rolled overcoat in one end corner we could have 'a quiet five minutes on the back seat' in somewhat cramped and dubious comfort. In addition to the back seat, a side-seat ran along each of the cabin sides, which was joined flush to the backseat and extending along the curve of the cabin walls as far as the leg of the twin timberheads which extended well down the cabin sides a bit aft of the hatchway. At the timberheads, the side seats, which were tapered, finished with a nice rounded end. Resting on either side seat was the cross-seat, a loose seat with ends tapered to match the sides curve which was the step when entering or leaving the cabin. The cross-seat could be pushed up to the bed board when it was down and supplement the width of the bed a little. The cross-seat was not too bulky being made of suitable timber so as to be strong and 'spring' without being clumsy.

We had no steps or ladder and you dropped onto the cross seat when entering the cabin, most of your weight being taken by your arms on either side of the hatchway and so I suppose lowered would be more accurate than dropped. The hatchway was about two feet square and lay in the middle of the deck line just forward of the two timberheads. Leaving the cabin was the opposite of entering in all ways. You placed a hand on either side of the hatchway gripping the hatch carlins—the raised collar of the hatchway that prevented deck water drainage entering the cabin—and with a gentle spring on the cross seat you lifted yourself smartly upwards until you could get one knee on the hatch carlin and clamber to your feet on the deck. Some older and less able skippers got a bit red faced and 'puffy' with this gymnastic requirement and often 'hutched their arse' on to the deck edge and drew their legs after them. I saw some 'rum faces' being pulled by crews with rheumatic joints, but the operation was so everyday, one didn't even notice it. So we had a folding bed, back seat, two side seats, one cross-seat and a shelf, one or two drawers and an open fireplace. On each timberhead was a clothes hook and other hooks were spaced along the short length of the sides. A mirror and a watch usually graced two of the hooks although most boats had an alarm clock on the shelf. The Old Man hung his watch on the cabin side for safety when he wasn't actually wearing it, and it never seemed to take any ill effect from swinging and bumping occasionally. I still have it and it still goes. The hooks were only suitable for caps, scarves and lighter jackets. Heavy overcoats were folded tightly in the corner of the seats unless we were forced to dry them. When our overcoats were thoroughly soaked we sought any fine spell to dry them out on top of the cargo, or if empty, on an improvised clothes line and then aired them in the cabin. Bulky overcoats seemed to take all the seating space when hung on the side-hooks and so we avoided this whenever we were able. Even in the narrow gaps either side of the stove, the limited space was used. We kept kindling in neat little heaps on the floor by the side of the stove knowing it would always be handy and dry. (How often had the Old Man said to me, 'Never seek kindling or watter in a morning'.)

If the frying pan was clean of grease we hung it by the stove. The frying pan was a really heavy iron affair; it had to be to cook on an open fire, and always had a hole in the end of the sturdy handle. Leather hoops were fixed to the cabin sides by the stove and here we kept our lock keys dry and rustless, for they were vital to our journeying. Between the timberhead and the stove, we hung the lamp; simply a stable-lamp used for all and any occasions. It hung safely from the roof beams by the stove. We had one or occasionally two drawers situated centrally beneath the back seat. These held our 'bits of best clothes' and were usually padded tight with our oddments. Pots, tea caddies and any of our utensils that would squeeze into the limited headroom of the shelf were stored thereon, large saucepans, spare boots and other clumsy gear were stored beneath the side seats usually in the corner at either side of the drawers.

The cabin was always decorated. The sides were lined with neater precision than the hold or forrend and usual grained and varnished. The bed-hole and deck timbers or ceiling were painted with light colours such as pale grey or light buff. We felt that the darkness of the cabin was helped by the paler colour. Most boats had oilcloth fitted and a pegged rug for floor covering and generally the skippers were very clean and tidy in their little cabins. We found no fault with the cabin, we were brought-up in them, lived in them all weathers, we knew no different. What little difference was possible in the cabins could only be in minor details such as the decoration and placing of individual items such as the soap-dish, kettle and similar small objects. Basically the fixed dimensions enforced a standard design, that was the way it was, that was the way it had to be and the best way—tried and proven. Comfort was the least of considerations; we had to be as comfortable as we were able; the cabin was part of narrow boating.

I remember with amusement the antics we performed when the early wireless sets were the rage. The whole country seemed to be a forest of wireless poles with their sagging aerial wires and white insulating pots. Out of every back window an earth wire found its way down to the ground. We caught the fever and had weird and wonderful results with improvised aerials on boat hook poles and earth wire hanging over the side weighted with the spare lock key. (The Old Man would have gone berserk at such sacrilege.) We had little luck but occasionally we heard a bit of scratchy atmospherics mixed with some snatches of music. The skipper used to like the 'top ten' of that period, tunes like 'Did you ever see a dream walking?' 'Please', 'Love is the sweetest thing' and the old melodies of my youth. At least they had a melody and words that made some attempt at rhyming. Even with the little help he got from the 'musical evenings', the skipper still never managed to learn the lyrics and continued to assault the quiet night with amazing versions of his own creation. With the demise of the old Cossor three valve set with which we experimented, we gave up the struggle, and peace returned to our little cabin.

The decks of our craft were just as simple and functional as the rest of the boat; the aft deck was larger than forrard and was simply the roof of the cabin. A raised 'head ledge' separated the deck from the hold and the sides of the deck were bounded by a curved screening which ran down the deck edge from the stern-post to the head ledge with a narrow gate left in the corner thus formed for drainage purposes. The sternpost was two or three inches higher than the deck and the screen was a matching height to it. The hatchway was in the centreline of the deck and slightly nearer to the sternpost, around the edge of the hatchway was a low, raised collar called the 'hatch-carlins'. This prevented water draining down the deck entering the cabin. The hatch cover had a matching wall along its underside which fitted round the outer edges of the carlins and effected a weather seal when the hatch was in use. Immediately aft of the hatchway were the twin timberheads, one either side, just inside the screening rail.

In the corner formed at the stern was the 'parson', a wooden chimney which fitted over the stovepipe as it emerged through the deck. The parson was usually constructed by tapered faces forming an octagonal tube. It had a slope at the tip and we could turn the parson to suit the wind and try to prevent smoke backing down into the cabin. The parson was not very high, it had to clear the low bridges when we were travelling light and the curved tiller had to pass over it as we steered and this made a dirty, sooty place on the tiller.

The rest of the deck was clear apart from the coal-box, which stood against the head ledge immediately in front of the windlass. The coal box was not large, it held about enough coal for two or three days in winter and roughly for a round trip. My family had a lot of coal cargoes to handle and so we could always have a few bags of spare coal for any emergencies such as being frozen-up or to bribe lock-keepers and warehousemen into making a special effort on our behalf.

The coal box always stood smack in front of the aft windlass, it was in the centre of the widest part of the deck, and left uninterrupted access to the gangplanks on whichever side they lay. It also made a step to the planks when they lay down the middle of a bulky cargo. Sometimes we moved the box, for instance when we needed a clear deck during trips in the River Trent or perhaps when we swilled the box out and used it to store eels in when we had good auguring conditions. The box with its lid made an ideal eel trunk for our little

Narrow boat 'Lena' rounding Parsons Bends or Howden Turns, Misterton. The boat was owned by R. Furley & Co. and captained by Jack Hewitt in the 1930s.
(Mrs Smith)

bucket wouldn't hold the wriggling eels of all sizes. If they got loose on the shutts the small ones would find a way through into the bilges with unpleasant results when they died and rotted. A decaying eel could give off quite a pong in hot weather.

The windlasses themselves, one forrard and one aft gave me much food for thought. They were of extremely simple design, just two upright posts within a wooden roller in between. The posts were lap jointed and bolted on to the upright head ledge with the legs of the posts running down the bulkhead into the hold. The roller had a metal collar at one end and a ratchet and pawl at the other and the central spindle passed through the tops of the posts sufficiently for their squared ends to take the lock key. The windlass was ridiculously low for winding requirements, but it couldn't be any higher for the empty boats had scant headroom in many of the bridges, indeed we had to lower the tiller and get down on our knees when we steering through some of the smaller arches. The windlasses on the boat I most often sailed on were simply ornaments. They were so low that even our normal lock key hadn't the clearance to turn although we had a silly square lock key which we used for dropping slides that would turn the windlass roller. The only use we had for this windlass was as a handy place to hang the bucket or to lay the ends of hooks and stowers in a convenient place ready for instant use in any emergency. We could also use the windlasses as a stand for the planks when loadened with sacks and the gangway needed to be in the middle. On some old boats the windlasses were as tall as could possibly be achieved and had cleats placed strategically on the face of the posts and it must be accepted that the old boat builders would not have included windlasses in the design without some good reason. Somewhere in the two hundred years of the canal and boats existence, a form of cargo handling had to be available at places where there were no wharves and cranes, and that derricks and windlasses were the likeliest form. I never saw any built in 'holds' for shrouds and other supports for derricks. On the keels the sailing mast firmly held by shrouds and fore and aft stays was the natural place for the derrick boom and one can imagine a mast being made to fit the lutchets of the narrow boats and that it would need provision for supporting shrouds and stays but apart from a ring or a cleat on the head ledges, I never saw any sign of such fittings. The windlasses on the foredecks of the Humber keels were very efficient but the primitive windlasses I saw on the narrow boats had no form of bearings or sleeve to hold the windlass ends, they simply ran through holes bored into the posts. The short bulk roller had no flanges to hold the heaving line and must have been far more efficiently designed if and when they were used by the crew in routine operations. I often wonder if some form of portable winch existed that could be rigged and dismantled as required and thus solve the ever-present problem of headroom that seemed to limit all things on a narrow boat of the Chesterfield Canal. Perhaps a workable windlass has existed and as the need for them declined so we were left with a situation where the windlasses were included to make the boat 'look right' or simply out of habit from the times when efficient and regular use of windlasses was a normal function. I sometimes gazed at our little ornament of a windlass, too low to take a normal lock key and a humorous thought crossed my mind. One of the skippers on our canal was extremely tall, his son was crewmate for him and he was even taller and far broader than his father and it occurred to me what a sight it would be to watch them working with our windlass. Can you imagine two huge, tall men, with their bottoms in the air as they wielded the tiny handles of a windlass not up to their knees? I could easily imagine the language they would be using and the colourful comments of other crews who saw them.

The only time I ever used our aft windlass was when I was young and felt that the world of narrow boats was just waiting for me to come along and improve it. I made a sail, my mast was a pole that fitted the lutchet and had a built in pulley at its head, and the sail itself was a discarded lorry sheet mounted on an old cut down boathook shaft. A worn hauling line was my lifting gear and I had a small key to turn the windlass. My sheets were cover lashings. My enthusiasm was boundless; I used my little square sail with mixed results, humorous and otherwise and on one notable occasion nearly sailed with it on the Trent. The effort and trouble involved outweighed my trifling success that after a series of catastrophes I conceded that the canal could carry on without my helping genius and the windlass was allowed to slumber again.

The aft deck was not only the roof our little cabin; it was where a high proportion of navigation was conducted and the helmsman needed all the space

In this view of West Stockwith basin loaded and 'clothed up' boats wait to leave 'upgate'.
It is most likely a Sunday when the Gringley Locks are closed otherwise the captain's
would be keen to get away to be first in the unloading stakes.
(M. Taylor collection)

he could get when navigating some of the tortuous bends, or particularly when, as in the River Trent, the aft oar was vital. The huge oars for Trent work were supported on 'crutches' which stood in specially prepared holes in the screening rails, one either side of the deck about midway between the hatchway and the head ledge. On the aft deck we used 'long-crutches' and the oarsman had to stand up to use the long unwieldy oar, and possibly steady the helm at the same time thus needing all the deck space he could get.

On the top of the stern post, was fixed a strong square staple which held the gate-line and usually a 'helm-strap' for that most important fixture of them all hung from the sternpost, I mean of course the rudder. True boaties called it the 'Hellum' just as they called a bulkhead the 'bullocks heered'. The helm was a most important feature of a narrow boat, without one we were helpless, 'like a fish without a tail' as the old saying goes. The long narrow boats had little elbow room. Narrow channels, low bridges, and shallow water in the sides of the limited winding track of the canal; in these circumstances the helm was a vital part of our operation. Our rudders were 'up to it', they could and did 'put her where she should be', when capable steerers handled them. Having a level deck meant we could use a long tiller and with the leverage this gave the helm, could really be thrashed about if necessary but good timing was always better than brute strength and good crews had good timing. On some canals, the large raised aft cabins of the boats only left room for a small cockpit and consequently the tiller arms, being shorter, had less leverage. We could put our back to the tiller and steer with little movement about the deck except in tight bends and in cold weather; a man of average height could stand on the cabin crossplank and steer with most of his body inside the warm cabin. The Old Man's comment on this form of steering was, 'If your arse is warm, you're warm all over' and truly when you steered from the crossplank, your backside was smack up against the stove. The helm itself was another example of the thought and experience that went into the apparently simple details of the boats. It was probably a bit large in proportion to the general dimensions; it needed to be, we only had horsepower and a powerful thrust of the helm was needed to keep in the channel and hold against the pull of the hauling line. In this situation the stern had to move first, to alter the angle of the long hull and allow the head to go about. The helm had a 'head', a 'lead', and a 'web' and a little scope did exist for the builders to include a limited curve and flare in the construction. It hung on the sternpost and was not in any way at all fixed to the boat and it could, and often did, jump off, usually at the most inconvenient time. The head stood higher than the top of the sternpost but not quite as high as the parson did. The strong sturdy 'hellum head' sloped away at the 'cap' and a slightly tapered square hole was cut through fore and aft, this was the 'eye' and was where the 'nub' of the tiller was inserted. The eye was slightly angled so that the tiller and its upward curve could clear the parson before it levelled off at the steering level. Below the eye was a bored hole still going fore and aft and this was to take the 'hellum iron' or 'hellum hook' as it was often called. The hook was securely held by a large nut behind the head and in front the hook, curved up and over the top of the sternpost and formed a straight downward pin which fitted into a matching hole in the sternpost. A strap or iron strip came up the trailing edge of the sternpost and lapped over onto the sternpost head, the hole for the hellum iron was cut through the strap and this then gave the essential strength needed for the considerable wear and tear of continuous steering involved. Running athwart the head and below the iron hole was the smaller hole which enabled us to thread the rope strap. The strap was simply a spliced rope loop, usually made from discarded hauling line and the strap just passed through the hellum head and on through the square staple in the sternpost head. The only function of the strap was to secure the helm to the boat if and when we had the helm off, for without the security of the strap, the helm could part company with the boat when anything caused the helm to lift and lose its anchorage to the sternpost. The broad 'blade' of the helm was held securely by jointed cross pieces which sloped up from the helm post to give a nice artistic appearance, the trailing edge of the blade was called the 'web' and the whole wide face of the blade widened downwards to give maximum purchase below the water line. The bottom of the helm blade had further cross pieces fixed for extra strength, where it was definitely needed, for the helm extended for a few inches below the true bottom of the boat hull and while this improved the helm's efficiency, it also invited constant risk when the empty boat came close under the bank with its stony bed. The helm blade boards passed between the top cross pieces and were finished in a flowing 'swan neck' curve which gave a nice line and at the back of the helm head, between the eye and the cross pieces the back corners of the helmpost were scalloped out in two very decorative half-moons which were always painted with a vivid 'best red'. The bottom of the helm was fixed to the sternpost with a 'pintle'. Just above the empty water line the helm had iron straps either side of the blade and these straps met on the front of the helm post in the form of a very strong eye, that is a down facing hole. Matching straps were fastened to the sternpost also with a downward hold and these were certainly arranged so that the eye on the helmpost was immediately above the hole of the sternpost ironwork. Secured to the helm face by a length of fine chain was the heavy iron pintle with a flange at the top. The pintle passed downwards through the matching 'eyes' and a loose hinge was formed. No permanent fixing was involved with the helm, it simply hung on the sternpost with its own weight and the boatman approved of this for it was better for the helm to 'jump clean off' than to drag and damage the ironwork. This was why the strap was most important for the helm could come adrift and just hang in the strap from where it could easily be hung again even when travelling. In the River Trent, wise skippers would have the helm loosely secured by a mooring line to the aft timberheads, this was a good idea for if we had the helm off in the Trent, the added safety of the mooring line eliminated the chance of disaster if the strap was chafed and weakened. I don't know if a helm would float on its own, but I suspect that it enough ironwork to sink it and therefore if we lost the helm in the canal it could be a 'bloody nuisance' but in the Trent it could be catastrophic for we were helpless to be able to retrieve it even if it didn't sink. The extra precaution of a mooring line round the helm meant boatmen didn't give accidents room to happen. The narrowboat tillers were strong, sensible affairs and we could even sit on them when steering. When held hard over they could be outside the line of the boat and we did have the odd accident with careless handling and some tillers had the telltale bolts through their middle which spoke of such incidents. We usually had a spare tiller aboard for emergency. Crews trusted the tillers, both for strength and for holding in the helm eye and they would lean on them even when outside the deck limits. A firm slap when putting the tiller in gave a very good hold and the tillers 'wore to the eye' and fitted so snug and tight that we often had to give a good shake to remove them from their seat.

At the other end of the boat was a smaller deck, the fore deck. It was shorter than the aft deck and the space between the head ledge on the bulkhead and the stern was loosely called the 'boats head' or as the boaties pronounced it 'her heered' or 't'boorts heered'. The foredeck was similar to the aft deck basically but a few differences did occur. Although it was shorter, it had an identical hatchway and hatch and a windlass stood behind the head ledge with its legs down the bulkhead exactly as on the aft deck. Some boats had two pairs of timberheads forrard but in fact one pair was sufficient for all normal usage and all boats had a smaller timberhead built in the stemhead. The windlass and the timberheads on the head could be fouled by the hauling line when travelling light, the line swinging from the short mast often dropped behind them and we had to go forrard and clear it, a tedious situation if we were busy with a meal or something equally important. Of course, we found a remedy for this and when we travelled light we would bend a line from the stem timberhead over the head of the main timberheads and up and across the tops of the windlass, fastening the line tightly and firmly. When the hauling line swung inboard, and this was always when we were in a tight inside bend, then the line would ride on our safeguard rope and drop safely overboard again. The stem timberhead was actually formed by part of the stem itself and the stem was a really strong affair—it needed to be. Unlike the straight sternpost, the stem had a quite a lovely curve which put its strongest part in the most likely place for a bump, and a reinforcing iron 'bar' ran from top to bottom of the stem. Usually the stem bar was built with a slight taper both ways from the middle and with the strongly curved stem and similar pattern stern-post, a boat could absorb quite a nasty bump when head on. A head on bump was called 'stemming up' but more damaging than these were the considerable bumps we gave the 'shoulders'.

The 'boat's head' and to a lesser degree the 'boat's arse' got quite a few bumps on the curved shoulders or the 'bends' as boaties called them. To minimise this type of damage the boats had built-in fenders, two pairs forward and one pair aft. These fenders were simply wide strong ledges reinforced for their full length with an iron 'strap'. The fenders forrard comprised of one wide pair just above the loadened waterline and a smaller pair just clear of the empty line. The top pair were very wide, they came out from the stern in a lovely curve and gradually curved back again towards the back of the bends so as to be inside the line of the boat sides. These wide fenders soaked up minor collisions and were very necessary, the lower pair were primarily for empty boat collisions when the top fenders would be too high to be of much use, and the single pair of fenders aft were wide sturdy affairs about in the same position aft as the 'top-fenders' were on forrard. Although the top fenders both fore and aft were ideally placed to be used as stepping places when getting aboard, good boatmen rarely put their nailed boots on them, preferring to have them painted a bright red and well varnished and spotlessly clean. The small low fenders forrard were tarred along with the hull.

Little space existed between the fenders and deck screens but this was the only place a Chesterfield Canal boatie had to indulge in any fancy paint work, even this space was restricted for it could only be on the actual bends of the boat where it was safe from the rubbing and chafing of the outsides of the hull. He had little room for poetic licence with the scant areas at his disposal, first and foremost his paintwork was functional and protective. The paint areas were fairly standard on all boats, they painted the decks, windlasses, screens, head ledges, top of the helm, bucket, water can, coal box, nose tin, lutchet and all the shafts of hooks and stowers, etc. The only paintwork on the sides was between screenings and fenders in the curve of the 'bends' all else was tarred. One skipper I remember painted the protective plating between the fore fenders a nice deep pink and gave a distinctly different look to his boat. All boats had a light protective plating around the shoulders of the boat and a little amount of plating protected the 'chine' of the hull. When this bottom plating became worn or damaged it caused nasty snags when the hauling line trailed down the sides or when we passed over sunken lines of other craft. Damage under water was serious for we had no dry-docks— we had to go to the slip at West Stockwith—with loss of time for cargo carrying in addition to the boatyard expense. The dock at Retford had been filled in long ago.

The colour scheme of the boats was equally standard and as older boaties and boatowners did their own painting an 'under cover' rivalry existed in the quality of the colours. The basic colours were blue and red, blue was for screening, for fenders, stern and sternpost and the 'half moons' on the 'hellum' and the 'name-holes' cut in the bends. The colours were exclusively used on the above-mentioned places, the remaining area, that of the bends between the screens and fender sills were always grained. The graining was important, it had to be just right, not too dark, not too light and skippers experimented with various yellows and buffs for the base colour and different strengths of 'scumble' until they achieve a nice balanced finished, warm and alive. A passable finish with graining brush and combs completed the job. A few were professionally grained and I often tried to capture the lovely effect of knots and wide grain of skilful old Mr Grant, the well-known Worksop signwriter and painter who occasionally did a bit of wonderful graining on our best boat.

Every do-it-yourself skipper had his idea of a good blue or a true red and strove to achieve these lovely shades by mixing their own colours. You have to remember that in those days, paint had lead and linseed oil in it and blue, red and the full colours had a habit of drying out a lighter shade than when applied and this had to be allowed for along with allowance for the effect of a thick coat of carriage varnish which always finished off the painting. The paintwork had to stand wear and weather and the finish with varnish was essential protection to all paintwork other than the walk about parts of the decks which usually were a sensible pale colour such as light grey or stone or buff; the light colour was helpful at night. The Old Man loved a good blue or a good red and strove mightily to achieve them with changes of undercoat and such methods. He knew exactly the right sort of orange you had to put under a good pillar box red without getting it 'more like a tomato', and he knew exactly where the blue had to be to dry right. He once experimented with mid-green in place of Royal Blue and I quite liked the change. All painting was completed by a white stroke

The winch and slipway at Tomlinsons Boat Yard, West Stockwith in 1966
capable of hauling a keel out of the water.
(M. Jackson)

on the actual edges of the deck and this gave a pleasing boundary between the rich graining and the blue screens and ambitious skippers included white half-moons at the end of the bends with a nice effect. All the ironwork was 'blacked off' and the ends of the paintwork finished with black paint to prevent damage by coming in contact with tar which immediately discoloured the lead paint. The final coat of carriage varnish 'gave her a bit of bloom' and completed the job. We like to paint and varnish early in the year to repair the ravages of a long winter and this gave time to wipe her down and give her a booster coat of varnish for the next winter.

To be able to reach the angle of the bends when painting we used to lay 'Katy-cornered' across the canal and the Old Man usually painted in front of the Albion Mills at Worksop—here he could use both banks with ease but it had to be at the weekend to be rid of all the dust which 'swilled' about here. It was here on a famous Sunday morning that the Old Man was finishing varnishing, he always said you had to varnish while the sun was 'going up' to get a hard finish and it needed one teaspoon of clean paraffin to a pint of varnish to prevent later blistering. Rightly or wrongly he had achieved a good flowing finish clear of brush marks and dust and was happily standing back admiring his handiwork. The pale blue smoke of 'thick twist' cheerfully curling from his pipe, brush and varnish kettle in his hand, a friendly gentleman passing by on his way from the Priory Church, no doubt with the strains of old hymns still in his ears, paused and said to the Old Man, 'What a lovely job you have done, it looks beautiful'. With a satisfied look on his face the Old Man said, 'Aye! She stands as proud as a Leeds whore!' It may well have looked beautiful to the passer by—what is beauty? We are told it is in the eye of the beholder. I didn't reckon our boats were beautiful, they were simply the tools of my trade, used by me and all the other crews and just an essential part of the job. Is the factory floor beautiful to a production line worker? Beauty, I find has a habit of being influenced by personal interest. To a farmer, warm growing rain on his developing crops is beautiful, the sodden campers holidaying on his land would have a vastly different name for it. To a boat owner such as my father, the sight of his boats laying deep with cargo in the holds was sheer beauty that was undoubtedly helped by the thought of the payloads and ensuing gain thereof. To my youthful gaze, the sight of Piggot's Bridge, homeward bound after three or four days of cold wet decks, muddy towpaths and soggy feet was sheet poetic beauty. Of course it meant home again and all the comforts of a good home and so I find beauty to be fickle and lay in seeing that which you want to see. Beautiful boat, no, I found them to be functional or even honest for they did what they had to do only just as well as the crews would let them, looking as clean and shipshape as their occupants made them, and in general reflecting the pride or otherwise of owners and skippers.

I often thought of the possible chicken and egg situation. Did the canal come first, or the boats? Did the canal have to fit the boat or did the boat have to fit the canal? Of course I know we had boats long before we had canals but even then, a special boat had to be developed for the new navigation. The daunting dimensions involved were on every side. A chain is as strong as its weakest link we are told. A canal was only as long as its navigable channel, as deep as its shallowest part, as wide as its narrowest part or as high as its lowest bridgehole.

When we painted the boats we usually had a signwriter to do the lettering, although I tried my hand at the difficult task and became quite handy with a writing brush. I remember watching with youthful envy the effortless ease with which old Mr Grant swiftly wielded the lettered brush. One year he did a really delightful shaded scrollwork on the stern of our old boat Lillian. I never managed anything so elegant as that, although I tried. There was little writing involved, in the small 'name hole' forrard we just put the boats name. In the longer name hole aft we had the owner's name and homeport and on the face of the lutchet, we had port of registration and number. I ended up doing all our own signwriting and sometimes helped some other owner with his lettering. I made one, and one only attempt at some form of fancy decoration. In a magazine I saw the silhouettes of birds of prey, and with the help of these I painted the silhouette of an eagle with spreading wings and tail on the lutchet and also on the coal box. I was quite proud of my handiwork, no other boat had anything like it and the eagles bravely spread their wings to my great satisfaction. Alas not for long, for one day in the Basin Lock at West Stockwith, little 'Cock' Farr the lock-keeper said to me, 'What's that on the coal box Clarkie?' I proudly told him it was a Golden Eagle and asked him what on earth he thought it was. He answered, 'I thowt it wor a likeness o' that bloody Turtle we caught in't lock t'other week'. I didn't renew the eagles when we painted again.

The remaining parts of the boat after we finished the 'bit of paintwork' were all tarred. The glutinous smelly stuff was plastered everywhere and repeatedly slapped on any parts that had chafed bare until it stopped soaking in. Tarring was a job for a warm dry day and the boat would have to be clean and dry in the bilges and with all loose gear ashore to have the boat riding as high as she would; we could only tar down to the water line of course but we could 'list' each side in turn to gain a few inches and scrape any weed fringe that had formed on the hull. Beneath the aft fenders where the boat never rubbed, we could get a build up of tar and ugly layers of old tar would sometimes be scraped to form a bed for the new coat. The actual tar was applied by long handled tar-mops, the heads of the mops were angled to enable the user to work easily the whole length and depth of the boat's sides. Tar was naturally too stiff for brushwork and had to be prepared. The method used for preparing the tar was simple and effective. We laid a collar of house bricks on the side of our mooring and lit a fire within the bricks. The tar bucket was placed on the bricks and the contents heated until they became as 'thin as watter'. The hot smoking tar was easily applied in this condition and a good result obtained, we quickly and easily 'slormed it' everywhere. We had to be extremely careful not to splash the paintwork with tar for it soon made dirty brown stains on the fresh paintwork. For a long time after tarring we would get tar on our hands and clothes, particularly when 'sheeting down'. On the combings and gunwale of the boats lay the 'dogs' and 'hooks' for the sheeting lashings and when the hot tar mops scrubbed over them an excessive amount of tar was squeezed all around them and left a slow to dry build-up which glued the hooks to gunwale and made a dirty sticky job of lashing down. Hot sunny days also softened the thick tar and allowed the hooks to embed in the warm mess for weeks after actual tarring time. So it was that for a few brief days she was 'flashed up' and when she'd had a lick of tar the boat would look smart. I just cannot bring myself to say beautiful, but for a few trips the newly painted boats would be handled with a little extra care and under the critical gaze of the Old Man we had to 'look where you put your bloody feet'. We had to avoid scratching the newly painted screenings and fenders with our nailed boots and when we came aboard from a dirty towpath we had to wash our footwear thoroughly with the mop for the skipper didn't want you to be 'clartin up the deck wi' yer mucky boots'. The extra care and attention lasted about as long as it took for the smell of varnish 'to go off her'. Most crews had a standard of respect for the paintwork and this was observed at all times, almost out of habit you might say.

Painting took time and some of it could be done while we were using the boat, however, when the nice weather came the canal inspector would be looking to major repair work and we usually had a stoppage when part of the canal would be closed for navigation and during the enforced inactivity, we had a good chance to 'flash her up'. Occasionally during a stoppage we took time to take the shutts' up and clean the deposits of mud and cargo remains which accumulated in the bilges. The lifted shutts would be cleaned, reared up to dry and tarred during the process; any damaged or broken shutts could be repaired or replaced and the whole cargo space could be given a gleaming black coat of the preserving tar. Sometimes we had the ill fortune to load the boat with a cargo of sacks of grain etc., and the natural fibres of the sacks would stick to the new coat of tar leaving ugly regular patches of loose sacking hairs in places along the hold sides and these disfiguring scuffs would remain a very long time. The Old Man like to organise a cargo of coal for a first trip after tarring for the coal dust took the newness off the tar without any discolouration—dried her up so to speak and a regular lick with a clean water mop to harden the varnish was as good a start as any with a newly painted boat. We tarred all the crossbeams but never put anything on the gangplanks. The planks were our footpaths fore and aft and anything that could make them slippery was avoided. We found the most effective way of having a safe walking (or running) surface on the wooden planks was simply to keep them clean. To this end we washed the planks or better still scrubbed them if they had any slimy accumulation of dirt on them. A favourite method was to use the occasions when we were travelling light upgate in the single lock sections and then as the boat rose in the lock we could drop a plank in the gap between lock-side and boat. As the water level rose the last few feet we would vigorously scrub both sides of the plank with the hold brush. We usually scrubbed our planks up the Forest Locks. There were four locks and four planks so it was just right. If the planks were cleanly scrubbed they dried quickly any time of the year and gave a nice feel to the feet and a non-slip surface. We also used these occasions to scrub the rebate of the combing and gunwale. It cleaned and hardened the residual tar and made the use of the hooks and dogs much easier when lashing down. All these many knacks and foibles the Old Man drew our attention to were used regularly and I found them occasionally tedious but I must admit that it was only the patient and constant attention to these usages that maintained a 'well found' boat.

See the Appendix for details of a typical Chesterfield narrow boat.

Cross Cut Bridge

CHAPTER 3

CARGOES

Albion Mill

When James Brindley and his contemporaries beribboned the countryside with waterways, they used the title of navigations. Popular legend has it the men who toiled with the tools of the day digging out these navigations became known as 'navvies', a name which has been with us to this day. These artificial waterways were constructed for the cheap transport required by industry and when suitable boats were put upon them, we had a fully operational inland waterborne transport system. This grand title was well earned and industry had a cheap reliable means of moving coal, stone and the many goods of the industrial revolution. The craft involved were tailor made for the waterway they used and a variety of boats of differing shapes and sizes came into being. It may well be that the disregard for standardisation may have helped in the decay of the system although the railways have taken much of the blame.

As for the cargoes, we would have liked the chance to have a go with diamonds, topazes, emeralds and the 'sweet white wine' of Masefield's fantasy but we did have the coal, iron, pig or otherwise, so I suppose the Staveley area trade was ended at one blow when the Norwood Tunnel collapsed. The Old Man used to relate at length stories of limestone, 'gas-lime' and other commodities in the 'top end' but we had Shireoaks as head of navigation. The canal had been declining steadily well before I came on the scene. The boatmen were of the original stock however, steeped in the canal tradition and ways of doing things. I am always thankful I got going on the boats before all this was finally over. Coal cargoes were still a worthwhile trade and a fair volume of traffic was involved in carrying wheat to the Albion Flour Mill at Worksop. This wheat trade was in fact the main activity of the ailing canal. The Albion Mill had a constant need for the hard foreign wheat which entered the country at Hull, came up the River Trent to West Stockwith and our narrow boats completed the delivery. This trade was the concession of Messrs Furley & Co – Carriers by Water—or so said the ambitious heading on the firm's official notepaper. I recall seeing some old bill headings of the Albion Mill which had a centre piece depicting the Mill's well-known outline and fully rigged ships lying along a fine waterfront—so much for the poetic licence of the Edwardian designers on such business notepaper. All's fair in love and office stationery! I well recall this sphere of activity—the grain came up the Trent in the elegant bluff bowed, stoutly built Humber keels. These fascinating old craft with their graceful counter, sturdy helm, lee boards, beautiful aft rail of varnished oak or ash and fat holds bulging with grain beneath a wealth of top hamper were a fine sight to 'cargo hungry' narrowmen. (The keelmen called us 'narrowmen'). These keels were dumb-boats, having no mechanical power. They sailed beneath a fine square rig sail with lowered lee boards to give a 'hold' when laid across the wind or drifted with the ever constant tides controlled by hand windless anchor and a fine 'eye' and 'feel' for the tide. This was called driving. These were the options of the keelmasters. Unfortunately these methods relied on nature in its whimsical moods and needed help to meet the regular demand for cargoes, a timetable so to speak. This help came in the shape of the old river tugs—coal and oil fired boats with powerful engines and a list of names such as Trentman, Riverman, Englishman, Welshman and so on.

With the help of these old work horses, a string on tow of five, six or more of the keels could leave Hull and on one tide reach West Stockwith or Gainsborough, these being the handling ports for the Furley's grain traffic. The busy little tugs came pushing up with the tide—the long straggly tows strung out behind them— and on fair days you could stand on the lock-tail at Stockwith Basin and see the plumes of smoke from their funnels advancing across the flat Trent Valley for quite a long time before they came into sight at the bottom of Stockwith Rack. The casual swinging of the tow could be misleading as the helmsman carefully eased their craft into the correct position to allow the leading vessels to negotiate the tight bends hereabouts. The tow would be arranged according to destination and any keels due in at Stockwith would 'knock off' at the precise moment and lay into the lock tail, round up, and get a line ashore. Then the busy little lock keeper, one Cock Farr would soon be warping the heavy craft into the lock. It was usual to wait for high water and in the brief spell of dead water the lock keeper could easily slide the keel into the lock. When a boat had to 'come in' on a running tide, a good deal of skill, sweat and careful use of fenders and windlasses was essential. On the other end of the tide—low water—there was sometimes insufficient water in the lock to float the incoming vessel and you simply had to wait for a 'flow of tide to give water in'. Once in the lock all was under control, the squat keel was now out of the muddy swirling river and in the green, weedy still canal water. In fair weather the keels would be deep laden, with water over the decks amidships and I used to marvel at the nerve of the keel masters who had to bring these boats over miles of the Humber in such condition. At this stage, the narrow boats became a part of the job. It needed five or six narrow boats to shift the cargo of one fully laden keel and these would soon be easing alongside the keel like badly proportioned chicks around a mother-hen.

The Company (Furleys) had a regular loader for these occasions and he was a tall, humpbacked man with malevolent features and a ready tongue but he was a tireless worker and knew his job thoroughly. He would be on one handle of the derrick windlass and the other handle was manned by one of the keel's crews, usually the mate. The windlass had ratchet and pawl and a brake which needed skilful handling. I vividly remember the operation of loading. At first light the keel crew would remove the hatches and covers and then the derrick would be carefully lined up for the job. To save the sweat of the windlassmen this was very finely gauged to give a 'straight up—just off the combings' lift. The hanger on would dextrously whip his 'snotter' round the heavy sack neck and steady the bag from swinging with the lift. The handler would then take charge of the bag, holding it off the keel's combing until high enough (it was a crime to allow the rising sack to foul the combing). Then swinging it over and as the windlassman let go, depositing it on the combing of the narrow boat alongside with a swift release of the snotter hook. The bag was then shouldered by the 'stower' and stacked in the hold of the narrow boat.

At that time all grain came in large heavy sacks—eighteen stones to a sack— two sacks to a quarter. The sacks were usually LNER or 'Chisholm'. A good load was one hundred quarter which, with the sack weight and other bits of equipment, meant the load was about twenty three tons. I dreaded the handler's job. When the keel was 'deep down' the combings of the narrow boat were too high for me and when one end of the keel was high the narrow boat was way below and I hardly ever got a good level from which to work. The long wire spring of the derrick usually had a heavy weight clamped just above the snotter hook, this helped the wire to 'run down' and prevented it whipping up to the pulley at the derrick peak when an imbalance of line occurred in derrick 'setting'. This weight was pear shaped usually and could be bolted on in two halves and was positively lethal. A clip on the 'lughole' by this weight was a never to be forgotten experience and we were extremely careful of it especially in bitter weather.

In the winter the basin was a very cold place. The lock had buildings either side of it and the gap between was a wind tunnel for the biting Easterlies. The cold was pitiless on a winter dawn and I well remember the Old Man saying 'You've nobbut to get over't fost hot aches and yu'll not be starved agearn'. The tall, evil looking loader used to make the most obscene remarks concerning the dire consequences of such weather on a delicate part of a brass monkey's anatomy.

Shireoaks Colliery basin in 1956 seven years after the last boat load left for Misterton.
The shutes are still in place however and the water is free of debris. This colliery provided return
loads of coal for many of the boats carrying general cargoes to Worksop.
(M. Jackson)

When we had sufficient cargo transferred to the narrowboat we were on our own. The keel crew would move skilfully among the orderly confusion of sail, piles of heavy ropes, shafts, hatches and all the dunnage which these fine old craft needed and adjust the derrick, remove more hatches and generally prepare for the next empty narrow boat to come alongside. The crew of the loadened narrow boat would now divide, one would fetch the 'hoss' and the other would 'slack off' and start to push the deep laden craft away from the keel and across the Basin to the 'bridge hole'. We used a long pole called a stower to do this job. The loader would wish you 'Good-bye'—looking down balefully from the foredeck of the keel, he would most likely say, 'Get the bugger out of it, there's other bloody boorts to loaden'. As I have previously remarked he was a likeable chap! I liked those lovely old wooden keels, but even then they were being replaced with iron keels, these iron boats were built to the dimensions of wooden keels at first and were quite nice craft but somehow they lost a little character in the process. I remember the newer keels well—Dux, Lex, Pax, Noe and similar names were chosen for them. The wooden boat names were my choice Ella, Fama, Wembly, Aureola and such lovely sounding titles.

Nowadays boats on the Trent have their own power, cargo carrying power boats started to pull the tows and were called Packets and then solo power seemed to take over and much of the towing was gone forever. I feel there is much to be said for a navigable river which makes direct contact between sea and inland towns. When I saw those old 'tows' rushing along on a big tide, carrying hundreds of tons of cargo fifty miles on one tide along, swishing and churning the muddy river into a froth of 'chops and whelps' as they surged along, I felt they would always be needed.

The loadened narrow boat would be prepared for the monotonous trip to Worksop. If it was fine weather the sheeting down of the cargo would be probably undertaken later. For the present the deck would be cleared, the boat trimmed evenly by moving a sack or two, hauling line paid out and all in readiness for the arrival of the horse. Soon we would hear the animal's hooves. If it was a Stockwith crew the horseman would have the 'snap' basket with him—large butcher's basket, clean, well-scrubbed and filled with victuals for the days ahead and covered with a clean tea towel and a personal towel and when needed, a change of sheets and pillowslips for the boat's bed. The basket would be hung in the fore end for safety and coolness, the knotted hauling line would be hung in the strap on the horse's 'cobblestick'. With a friendly slap on the horse's rear, along with a loud 'goo on then', the animal would walk to the end of the line, take the strain and the voyage was under way. West Stockwith was a small, reasonably isolated habitation, with few entertainments other than the pubs and purely local activities. I noticed the Stockwith lads seemed to look forward to a night at Retford or Worksop for these towns must have seemed quite lively places in comparison to Stockwith, with picture houses and lighted shops and most of the things missing in their village. A night at the pictures and a greasy bag at a 'chiphole' afterwards was living it up to the pleasure starved boat lads, and if the boat was nearing one of these towns around time for the 'first house', a swill in a bucket, clean trousers, best cap and scarf were all the preparation needed for the night out. I noticed another attraction at these stopping places. A number of young ladies would stroll by to see which boats were moored of an evening. The obvious interest of the older mates in these lipsticked, high heeled, artificial silk-stockinged damsels puzzled me at first, but not for too long—and another sweet mystery of life became an open book. I got to know a number of these 'ladies' despite dire warnings from the Old Man. I suppose he had his moments in his day, after all it is a very old pastime.

We allowed sixteen hours for a loadened trip from West Stockwith to Worksop. A well found boat with a good horse and experienced crew could clip an hour or two from this time. Unless forced, we never did a straight through run, the whole journey at one go was hard on the horse. It was far better to break the trip at Retford or Forest Lock and rest the animal. In this way you could keep going all the week without making the horse 'leg tired'. Good boatmen cared for their horses' welfare even if they didn't care for themselves very well. After all, the horse was vital to the operation. The old 'boaties' were well organised, clean cabin, well kept horse, although it was difficult to get any weight on the horses by the very nature of their calling.

The frying pan was the main cooking utensil but a heavy iron saucepan or stewpot could be used to good effect and indeed some crews could certainly do marvels on the little coal stoves with stews, spuds, dumplings and plain filling fare preferred by these independent characters. A couple of harvest rabbits stiffened with a cow heel and you had a saucepan full, fit for the healthy outdoor appetite of a boat lad along with a few spuds and a hunk of bread.

While being the main cargo to enter Stockwith Basin, grain was not the only commodity. We also had cement for the depots of Retford and Worksop. Pollards, a low grade wheat offal, Brushwood, the lengths of Birch poles needed for the woodyards at Worksop. At that time a market boat used to operate along the Trent. This was an old keel which made a regular service run with mixed commodities for riverside warehouses. The variety of its cargoes was exciting, it seemed to have a bit of everything. There was never any lack of volunteers to get this old keel into the Basin—who knows, a case may get damaged and you could finish up with a battered but free supply of imported jam or some such bonus. A half bag of sweepings of cow cake or linseed cake were a welcome supplement to the horse's monotonous diet. Boatmen were not pickers up of unconsidered trifles but the inflexibly tight budget of the time made any little pick-up a welcome bonus. Used sparingly linseed was a wonderful conditioner for the horse's hair and skin, especially when the winter coat was falling away. The horses were usually bellied; that was when the hair was sheered away from the lower half of its body to avoid sweating, lathering and tagging up of its coat. Used carefully, linseed put a gloss on the horse's coat. We would give the animals purloined cow cake, boiled wheat and other delicacies but one had to be very careful with high concentrate foods because of disastrous side effects if abused or overdone. The market boat sometimes gave us unusual cargoes for places like the North Notts Farmers at Worksop. Freestones, the Bakers, well-known in

Worksop had supplies of Ranks 'As you Like it' flour. Another unusual cargo in the market boat was locust, a dried bean like commodity which was feed-stuff but we would chew away at the tough husks whenever we could get a handful. One could assume that the market boat was a last relic of the days when the whole riverside communities relied on the waterway, before the coming of the much handier vans and lorries of the petrol age. Although Furley & Co had their own fleet of narrow boats to handle the Trent cargoes they sub-contracted to 'by boats'; privately owned and eager for work—this would help avoid payment of demurrage which occurred if the keels were laid in the basin too long. This generous practice was resented by some of the Furleys skippers and we would hear dark mutterings of 'tekkin the bread out of wi mouths' from these disgruntled gentlemen. The Pollards were an unpopular cargo—being low grade wheat offal, they were very light and came in sewn bags of about six stones, and having no neck to put a noose round they were handled by a 'Pollard Hook', a lethal twin hooked pickup on the end of the hoist. If the sacks ripped, the hook became an uncontrolled danger to anyone who was unfortunate enough to be in the way. I knew one skipper who was very badly torn by such an accident, very unwisely, he held the chain above the bag to steady it when the hoist lifted. Unfortunately the bag tore and the hooks dug into the man's wrist and he was lifted bodily by the cruel claws. Poor old George Wolfenden had a clawlike stiff hand for the rest of his life. Apart from the awkwardness to handle, Pollards had another disadvantage. Being light, we had to stack them much higher than the heavier grain cargoes in order to get a full cargo. This usually meant the boat would be top heavy and list badly and roll like a barrel when sailing. Steering such top heavy loads was a nightmare and sheeting the bulky cargo which had to be kept dry was a particularly difficult kind of operation.

The narrow dimensions of the boat did not allow any form of gangway other than planks laid along the craft. When we sheeted down, lashings were tightly pulled across the boat held by square hooks, called dogs, just square hooks, upside down to hold the light ropes in position and these lashings passing from side to side, spaced by the dogs and crossing the raised centre plank gangway, gave a watershed character to the sheets when they were laid over them. The sheets were held secure by further lashings, known as 'top lashings', just as the underneath lashings were called 'bottom lashings'. The top lashings were held by longer, curved hooks fixed by 'square-tined' staples nailed into the flat ledge of the gunwhales. Unless the boat was in a bridge hole or a narrow lock, fixing these numerous lashings both top and bottom was a very acrobatic task with a swift dip in the canal being the result of careless or awkward footwork. The crews were very adept and agile, qualities that were achieved by regular use of the narrow gangplanks and under conditions where you had to put your feet right and have a fine sense of balance.

Another unloved cargo that came into the basin was called Brushwood. This was not the light twiggy growth we call by that name when we push our way through a wood or hedge, it was simply lengths of birch poles, about six inches in diameter and about eight feet long. This white, close grained timber was ideal for making brush heads in the local wood yards, hence its name. We have all seen photos of timber ships in port with their decks stowed high with the bulky wooden baulks or poles and listing all over the place. In a much smaller way this was our problem. The brushwood poles were too long to stow across the boat or 'athwarts' as we called it and had to be piled 'fore and aft' in regular heaps. Once again we had a top heavy situation and a really safe job of lashing was essential, although fortunately we didn't have to sheet down. The trip to Worksop was tedious with these ungainly cargoes, and handling the poles could find muscles you didn't know you had. I have unloadened these white barked poles on to the drays of Tomlinson, Smith, Godley and Oates, all well known wood yards of Worksop, usually at Piggot's Bridge which is also known as Priorswell Bridge. There was also a wood yard where the laundry now stands and one at the end of Garside & Shelley Streets. Their tall wigwam like stacks of long poles drying out were a familiar and welcome sight to my youthful gaze when we returned from a round trip. I was not very happy when I saw the keels with their cargo space piled high with imported Scandinavian and Russian Brushwood cargoes. I knew what was coming.

A modest traffic in cement existed to Earles Depots at Retford and Worksop. It was only a limited trade and I didn't see much of it and actually handled more cement for the Canal Company repair work than I did as a warehouse cargo. The cement had its own particular characteristics. It was packed in tough paper sacks of one hundredweight each. These had no neck for hoisting, hooks could not be used and only careful use of slings and battens could lift them. We had our own way when we had to unloaden into ground floor warehouses, we just handballed them over the gunwhale and on to the sack barrows of the warehousemen.

A small flour trade from the River Trent was carried to the warehouses at Retford and Worksop. The flour was usually from J. Ranks, the Hull based millers and as my family had the handling of flour and offal from Smiths Flour Mill at Worksop, I was filled with youthful resentment when I saw these rival cargoes of flour. I can remember the carts and drays of local bakers collecting loads of this flour from the depots at Retford and Worksop. The popular varieties from 'our' mill were Albion Patents and S.S.S. or as they were called, Supers. The North Notts Farmers had a limited amount of imported cattle feed, low grade offal and the S.G.O. or Sussex Ground Oaks, and these usually came into the Basin at West Stockwith in the market boat. These cargoes were but a small part of Furley's activities and were just an occasional addition to the main trade, the imported grain.

The flour for Retford warehouse was uplifted by means of a hand crane on a turntable. The heavy jib was long enough to reach the top floor of the building if you had the dire luck to have to use it. With a chain for lifting and the gears enclosed in a metal case it was a noisy grinding clanging monster that awoke the morning echoes around the wharf. The warehousemen would painstakingly oil it, bring out the single large iron handle, test the brake and hand you the sets of two ring snotters. All was now in readiness, four bags at a time swung out of the boat across the towpath and twisted until the bags were facing the waiting sack barrow awaiting, then with a right roar, the whole lift would be struck on to a specially made stage which allowed the barrows to function. The stage was kept leaned against the warehouse wall when not in use and made a nice corner for courting couples on a dark night. It was also used very extensively by dogs which strayed or were taken along the towpath which was a public footpath hereabouts. The fly in the ointment however, was the fact that the crane had to be worked by the crew of the boat involved. It was back breaking work, detested by all, dangerous to any inexperienced handler. When the sacks had been lifted we were supposed to remove the handle after taking over by the handbrake and then lowering slowly, we hadn't the time for this. We bolted the handles on to the drum with a stud–bolt and when ready, we let the lot go as fast as it liked using the brake only to prevent an overrun of the lifting chain. The furiously whirring handle and rattling chain amplified by the drum casing caused a roar like thunder and was a veritable death trap to passers-by. Mr Newstead, the warehouseman was a tireless methodical man, let him have his own way and you were soon unloadened and in fact I never remember an accident during all the many cargoes I delivered there. Similar hand cranes existed at West Stockwith and Worksop. We had no funny tricks with these, the lockkeeper was in charge at Stockwith and little 'Cock' Farr brooked no nonsense with any of his charges. The one at Worksop was in the company yard and thus under the stern gaze of that very important man, Mr Bagshawe, the Canal Inspector, who lived in the yard. This crane was used when someone with a cart or dray was collecting directly from the boat.

A loaded narrow boat approaches Shireoaks Top Lock c1905. The lock cottage is the white building on the right and the double gabled house on the left was the colliery engineer's house.

When the cargo was to be stored in the warehouse an entirely different lift was used. The warehouse spanned the canal on a bridge and the cargo was lifted through the trap doors beneath the bridge and on to the first floor upstairs. The crane was a collector's piece even in the days of my boating. It was made of wood and a thick rope was used and instead of the clangs and bangs there was a horrible squeaking and creaking from the wooden gears. It was terribly slow being highly geared and almost as difficult to get the empty slings as it was to heave up the load which was usually two bags on this crane. On warm days we were glad of a visit to the nearby Gas Tavern during the dinner break.

Nearby we had the North Notts Farmers warehouse. This also was built over the canal just above Worksop Lock and the long dark bridge formed by the building was permanently damp and slimy. I had little experience of cargoes to this place but what few I did handle were either unloadened into the dark recesses of the ground floor or alternatively by a hoist, through the trap doors onto the first floor. This trade was mostly handled by Furley's boats and we usually had the trouble of easing past them in the dark narrow bridge when we were bringing loads of coal down from the colliery at Shireoaks.

Most of the traffic was upgate, that is to say from the West Stockwith end upstream towards Worksop. Unhappily most of the boats which emptied at Retford and Worksop, had the unprofitable trail back to West Stockwith light. Not all however. A small but regular supply of coal was needed by the brickyards at Walkeringham and Misterton. Wiseton Estate had a load occasionally and some cargoes went to a few steam powered irrigation pumps and factories along the River Trent adjacent to the lock at Stockwith. These cargoes were welcome additions to the normal trade of Furleys skippers and were in a way a sort of bonus.

Cockings Brickyard at Walkeringham had two boats of their own, The Lord Milton and the Lady Milton and these boats usually handled the brickyards coal requirements. They also had regular cargoes of the wheat from Furleys and so some coal was handled for Cockings by the regular Furley fleet on occasion in a sort of one good turn deserves another situation. A little barley was carried to two maltings at Claters Bridge and Gashouse Bridge, Retford but it was only a small trade. The larger malting at Worksop was too handily sited by the railway sidings to have any call for canal help. And so we had a fleet owned by Furleys that handled practically all the cargoes that came into the basin at West Stockwith. The Company was far-sighted enough to allow by-boats, that is non-company craft, to have a part in this trade when work was abundant and a happy relationship was created and the goods were handled in fair rotation and reasonable speed if such a description could be used in this type of work.

In times of slack trade, when keels did not reach the basin because of gales or for any other reason, then of course it was Company boats first unless of course expensive demurrage was likely. We had no unions, no handouts and the basic need to earn a living was the first priority; principles, differentials or demarcation were not the beloved phrases they are today and a reasonable pecking order was maintained with a lot of give and take along the way. Any other trade was a different matter. Little enough downgate commerce existed and what there was tended to be allocated to certain privately owned craft and was jealously looked after by the skippers in question. Furley's boats got a share of the brickyard coal trade, their constant travelling up the canal loadened with grain meant one of them would be handily placed to pick up a cargo for the return journey. Some skippers were preferred to others by the employers for instance when the Wiseton Estate needed a coal cargo, they usually gave it to their own particular Captain. Very little regular work existed outside of the Stockwith trade. One such example was the Chambers family who handled the coal cargoes for the wharf just above Worksop Lock. At this wharf a weighbridge and agent were present and Messrs Milner & Lazenby conducted a thriving household coal business. Old Harry Chambers, the head of the clan, so to speak, his sons, Dave and Jack and later on his grandson kept the wharf well stocked with the various grades of coal needed. They were industrious and equally at home with boat or cart as well as barrow and shovel and handled all these with the ease born of long practice. They had two boats, Ida and Evelyn, and when occasionally the coal business was slack, they would fetch a cargo of grain from Stockwith, checking by telephone first to be sure of a load. On these occasions they had to use Ida, the other boat was a gunnel boat and had no combings to enable cargo to be sheeted down. This kind of narrow boat was occasionally called a 'quarry boat'. My father acquired Evelyn from them and renamed it Valour.

I liked old Harry Chambers and his family. His son Jack used to greet me when we passed their boat as they were unloading. 'Nar then Little Mustard' he used to call to me. I saw him not long ago in hospital. I was in there myself and poor Jack was nearby, desperately ill. Ill or not, he managed a poor imitation of a smile and whispered 'Hey up Little Mustard'. Happily he recovered.

The clop of horses' hooves no longer echo along our streets as domestic coal was delivered. Central heating and smokeless laws, have cancelled out the function of those tireless men and horses. Many people accept their milk, newspapers, letters and in those far off days their coal, without giving a thought to the early rising all weather, regular service entailed, just as the workaday miracle of pure water from a tap is too common to be appreciated, until it dries up.

We had a friendly rivalry with the Chambers. My father had a coal concession for the local flour mill which needed two loads of coal at least each week. This meant a bit of jostling to be first at the Colliery Basin. We loved to get in front of each other and had about equal luck in doing so. At the flour mill we had a winding hole adjacent but being above Worksop Lock, the Chambers used to haul 'arse fost' as far as the Lady Lee crosscut bridge before they could 'swing'. Hauling stern first is a very unhandy operation and it was very easy to really damage a boat this way. David Chambers was however very good at this type of sailing—he got a lot of practice.

The other regular trade, which must come to my mind, was the family business in which I was involved. We had a reasonably wide base to work from, the main part being the Albion Mill coal, flour and wheat trade. The Old Man also had the Canal Company work which was a useful volume of cargoes, also a bit of private dealing in manure and anything which would turn up a bob or two for in his day; the Old Man was a 'forager'. Our boats were always stained with coal, clay and even manure—to our Old Man muck was money.

With the arrival of the thirties, much of the character of the waterways was disappearing. Many of the old skippers would naturally vanish and the decline of the canal trade would ensure that son following in the father's footsteps tradition would vanish with them. The work available for these canal families was less certain and therefore less attractive to the younger members and it was only the depression which affected the whole industrial scene which caused many of the traditional boaties to continue with the life although some had already taken jobs ashore. Work was likewise to change, very little scope remained for the owner-skippers and what work was available was easily handled by the Furleys fleet, which travelled empty most of the time when making the return journey to West Stockwith. My own family was able to survive longer than most because of the concession the Old Man had with the Flour Mill trade and the canal company work. In these we had a steady flow of cargoes, sufficient to the time in hand. When younger, the Old Man had worked ashore in wood-yards and with his brother on the railway but he was a boatman and usually came back to boating. He owned his own boats and employed men to suit the requirements of the time. I worked four of his boats but one of these was merely a spare to have a cargo of coal in hand when handling the Flour Mill coal contract which had to be regular and reliable. The requirements for coal to run the engines of the mill were about eight tons per day give or take a little allowance for a run of dirty coal or extra output by the mill. These occasions could cause more coal to be needed and any weekend working would do the same. This simply meant about two boatloads of coal per week and sometimes five loads in the fortnight. The Mill ran twenty-four hours per day, 7.00 am on Monday until noon on Saturday. Weekend running was almost unknown and in common with practically all the local works and factories, everything stopped with the twelve o'clock 'hummer' at mid-day on Saturday and as the Old Man said, 'You could hear the silence'. The coal work was upgate work and the rest of our trips were downgate work, and we had to plan carefully to manage the downgate work so as not to be in danger of letting the necessary coal supplies fail. The use of the spare boat to hold an extra cargo was very helpful in this planning. The coal wharf at the Mill was very much a home made affair, simply a low retaining fence made of planks ran across one end an along the water's edge copings leaving just room to walk between the moored boat and the coal heap. The other end was open to allow access for the boiler fireman and his barrow. The boiler house and pumphouse building formed a back wall to the wharf against which we piled the coal. The whole affair was primitive by today's standards, simply a heap of coal slung as high as possible against the boilerhouse front and prevented from sliding into the canal by the retaining wall which was two planks high and held in position by old steam pipes driven into the wharf brickwork. The boat was not allowed to lay 'snug' along the wharf coping because of a water intake to the boilers which would be choked and so the boat had to be held clear of the wall usually forward and a narrow gap for the intake was then formed. To prevent spilled coal getting into the canal through this gap, we had 'spillboards' which leaned against the hull of the boat and were held in place by metal clips which hooked over the combing. So once again we had a classical brute strength and ignorance situation. We could, by using the 'long swing' build the heap high enough to get twenty five tons of coal ashore and as this was in no way sufficient to last for a week, it needed replenishing constantly. In addition to the regular supply of 'two inch nuts' needed by the boilers we had a regular wagon of Clowne Hards for the fleet of steam lorries which replaced the horse drawn transport used by the mill. As this type of coal was very hard and came in huge lumps it had to be wheeled ashore in barrows and stacked using the better shaped lumps as walling and filling with the 'slack'. New smoke regulations put an end to this and the popular Clowne Hards were replaced with smokeless Anthracite, a shiny coal much given to shattering easily and making a lot of slack. Being Welsh coal the anthracite came by rail and as a boy I used to try and figure out how long it would have taken us to fetch it from the 'Valleys'. Being the shortest boatman on the canal I had quite a long throw to get the coal high enough to reach the wharf. People passing by along Canal Road wondered where the coal was coming from as I was completely out of sight below the combings. In fact it was a bit of a local joke. We had a store of coal about one hundred and fifty tons, piled roof high in the cellars of Ellis' Maltkilns at the bottom of Union Street. This building had a door opening onto the canal at waterline and when the canal was closed by ice or for repairs, this was our emergency supply. A similar quantity was stored against the mill boundary fence and in cart sheds and so we could cope with several weeks of freeze-up or some other stoppage.

In addition to constant coal handling, we had a reasonably regular weekly cargo of flour and offal for the warehouse at Retford and the local bakers, horse and pig keepers. This was a tedious cargo, needing to be kept dry and clean so we had to sweep out thoroughly, pump any water out of the bilges and put a layer of chaff over the 'shutts' to prevent accidents with any water coming in when listing or such. Most boats had damp places in their sides and we had to load with extreme caution near such places. The Old Man used to reckon that the 'sharpes' and meals we carried used to 'draw the damp through' and we had to avoid this by not allowing the sacks to press tightly against these 'weeps' as we called them. In winter gales and storms we had some hairy incidents with flour cargoes but surprising little in the way of accidents although we did occasionally get a little damage.

One cargo that did have its share of problems was the English Wheat Trade. At that time, wheat was made 'in the stack'. Mown by the binder, carefully kneed into open stooks and left for so many clear days to dry. Then it was 'led' and stacked. These stacks were very skilfully made, 'head-in' carefully built overhand and then beautifully thatched and completed into a living granary. The next time these stacks would be disturbed was when the thrashing machine arrived and the grain would be thrashed and stored in the heavy sacks ready for delivery to the miller. This process could spread over the winter and into the following spring as farmers waited for the threshing contractor or improved prices for the grain. When I say English Wheat cargoes I refer specifically to the corn grown by the canal-side farmers. To many of these places the boat was the traditional form of transport. When the mill horses were replaced by heavy steam lorries, the narrow muddy farm lanes were unsuitable in winter for these iron monsters and my family carried on as before bringing in the grain by canal. The grain buyer for the Flour Mill was a very familiar figure with the farming community for miles around and had a weekly office in various local cattle markets. When grain was available he examined samples for quality and concluded the business of buying on behalf of the mill. When all was satisfactorily settled he then gave my father the details of the purchase, where it was, approximately how much there was, and when he wanted it collecting.

The mill had nowhere near the silo capacity of today and grain intake was regulated by storage space available at the time. If it was expedient to buy grain in quantity it had to be stored in the sack in any space available. The process lasted all through the winter and well into the spring and I identified this particular cargo with the worst weather of the year. Along with the weather we had other problems to overcome, the actual lifting of the grain when we arrived at the collection point. The collection of foreign wheat was straight forward enough, wherever it was loaded we had a degree of mechanical help available. The steam

A very early photo of Shireoaks Colliery and the Shireoaks Low Lock taken from the original road bridge. The balance beams appear to be roughly fashioned from tree trunks. Note how little the colliery spoil heap has encroached into the surrounding land.
(L. Godlewski collection)

crane at Furleys wharf in Gainsborough could lift four, five or even six of the heavy sacks and other Trentside warehouses had hoists to lower the cargo into the boat. We even had a warehouse at Owston Ferry where wooden chutes were laid down a specially constructed passage in the wharf and the bags slid down on to crossplanks on the narrowboat. These chutes were in handy lengths and were lashed in position, overlapping and regulated to suit the state of the tides which had a considerable rise and fall in this part of the river. On very low tides the chute was fully extended and we had a long chute down which the sacks came. The first row of bags came reluctantly but soon the chute became drier and more polished and then the bags began to 'sled' down to the waiting boat with ever increasing speed. As the loading proceeded it became quite hazardous at the bottom of the chute as the bags fairly whizzed down and then we needed the mop. With it we could wet the end section of the chute and this acted as a break to the descending sacks and offered some relief to the catchers on the crossplanks.

When loading foreign wheat from the Humber Keels we had the use of windlass and derrick. The well sited derrick efficiently handled and the well maintained windlass in the hands of competent winders gave us a reasonably good service even if it needed manual handling. Sometimes the keels could not enter the Basin at West Stockwith, perhaps for insufficient water on the neaps or the keel was too big for the lock, then we had to pen the narrowboat through the lock and lay alongside the keel at the lock tail.

English wheat did not have any mechanical help at all and every phase in the chain of events from the field to the hoists of the Mill was the muscular power of man or horse with the possible exception of the binder and the threshing machine. Our problems with English wheat concerned getting it from the farm to the mill. The horse transport and later, the steam lorries were not as suitable as the boat when it involved the canal side farms with poor roads and in some cases just muddy lanes and a busy trade ensued. In some cases the wheat came to the canal in horse drawn drays from quite a distance away, thus when the heavy steam lorries were replaced with a fleet of small petrol vehicles, many farms could be better served by the new lorries and so the amount of cargo declined and just involved a few farms actually on the canalside. Quite good moorings existed at Osberton Hall, Osberton Lock, Wiseton, Gringley and Misterton. In those places wharves or suitable moorings could be used and other access places were used usually where a good road or lane to a bridge existed. Some bridges had a provision for carts to get to the waterside and these were considered sufficient if not perfect. When we had a decent wharf, the only thing necessary was strong shoulders to carry the heavy sacks of wheat to the combing of the boat and the waiting arms of the boatman who would stow it. Such occasions were the exception and when it came to using bridge-holes, the problems increased. You could not get the carts very near to the loading point. The actual bridge hole could be very small and slippery and it was not too easy to moor the boat in a stable fashion. With a long carry, and an unstable boat the farmers were very unhappy if the boat moved whilst a farmer with a heavy sack on his back was leaning against it. The situation became fraught with possibilities.

When any particular boatie was noted for his clumsiness we used to call him 'a farmer' so you can see what I mean.

The situation was even worse where we had neither wharf nor bridge. Two such places come to my mind vividly—California Gate and Hayton Castle Farm. Here we had nothing, nothing that is to say, except the brute muscle power of men and horses aided only by any idea or suggestion by the unhappy boatman or farmer. California Gate Farm lay below Gringley Shaw Lock. A lane from the lock ran to the farm and an arm from this lane joined the canal nearby. The short lane to the canal was poor but the main problem was that there was no mooring or solid bank, in fact the canal simply happened to pass by so to speak. We just got as close as possible with the cart and laid spare planks across the towpath and with a mixture of weight lifter and balancing act the reluctant farmers would carry the wheat along the planks to the boat combing. When the boat became lower in the water we had to lay further and further from the bank and then we put a trestle, borrowed from the farm into the water to support a plank bridge to the boat. The farmers didn't like the look of this at all, especially as the trestle was on mud and tilted alarmingly at times. To finish off this unbelievable situation the two farm men who usually had the job of bringing the corn to the boat consisted of one very tall one and one very short one. They were funny, awkward, unhappy but willing. Their language and comments matched the situation perfectly.

I have never forgotten Cuckson's farm and California Gate. It was probably the last of the English wheat pick-ups. At the end of the lane was a mound, overgrown with grasses and hawthorn bushes and also there was a colony of cowslips with the longest stalks I can ever remember seeing. I suppose they grew so long in competition with the lush grasses and their cheerful creamy yellow faces were a harbinger of the better weather to follow. I tried bring some to my Mother's little flower patch at home and sadly they languished in conditions they couldn't tolerate. I believe this was the first sign of deep love of wild flowers I now have and my eager desire to see provision made for the preservation of the threatened species. What more natural place than the banks of a rural canal?

I also remember old Mr Cuckson with some warmth. He used to let us 'bait' our horses in a 'loose box', up to the belly in hay and he always gave us a 'bag of chop' to supplement our horse feed supply. I churlishly repaid his kindness by nicking a few swedes and getting caught at it. 'You like swedes then sonny?' was all he said and I observed that sheepishly, 'A pile of mashed swede and taters wi' a pat of butter on needs a bit of beating'. From that day on, whenever we picked up at California Gate, on the last cartload of grain would be a few spuds, a couple of swedes and a pat of farm butter. The sad loss of his son in an accident with a horse, aged and saddened old Mr Cuckson and so I suppose that real life stories do not always have happy endings.

Just downgate of Cuckson's Farm was the farm of Mr Barron. Here we had good lane and a bridge with good access and we could cope reasonably well. The worst of all pickups was at Hayton Castle Farm. Older boatmen called it Hayton Brickyard—I knew it as Crow Trees. It could well have been the site of a brickyard, heaven knows there was a lot of greasy clay there. When I went there it was a boggy, muddy pit full of slimy water and a fine stand of spreading poplars which was the roosting and nesting site for a huge colony of crows—hence the name. I also remember a lovely patch of 'Watter-blobs' (Marsh Marigold) which flourished in the boggy bank. It was a cruel place for horses and men alike and I will always associate the Hayton Castle pickup with thick clay apparently without any bottom, inadequate mooring, foul language, lost tempers and all that was the worst in 'pick-ups'. Where we had wharves the wheat collection was better, I liked it then. You were always in with a chance of a bonus—a few eggs, spuds or any of the finds you could make on a farm. We rarely ran short of butter, cream cheese, vegetables and farm eggs, especially duck eggs, seemed to have a special flavour. It may seem trivial, almost pathetic, in these days of two car families and £20,000 per year workers, but labourers were on forty nine shillings (£2.45) a week in many cases—a full week mind you—and we hauled cargoes from one end of the canal to the other, boat, horse and crew of two, for little more than three pounds, so any 'odd bob' we picked up was a boost to our meagre spending money. Money was not sufficient to be given away—but many of the canalside people were generous to a fault with gifts in kind—and there were others who were not so generous with anything at all.

When I started with the boats the English wheat trade was dwindling, petrol lorries had replaced the heavy steam wagons, and these lighter vehicles could get into the farm yards where wheat loads could be picked up by them when they were returning from flour deliveries and with greater speed than any boat. I don't think the lorry drivers were very keen on wheat collections—the grain was often in sheds, barns or lofts and the heavy bags could be quite a problem when on the floor and needed to be lifted on to the lorry platform. Another dislike was the fact that the farmers had their own routine and when a lorry driver arrived he could find the farm deserted of menfolk and thus have the choice of walking across fields looking for help, or loading the grain single handed—a heartily detested situation. We had a taste of this situation ourselves— often we would arrive at a farm after dinner and find that feeding or milking time would prevent any loading taking place and then we had to restrain our impatience and wait until next morning. Then we would have to wait until the morning chores were attended to. The Old Man used to get really frustrated with all the delay—you have to remember we needed all the time we could get, particularly in the short winter days. Our travelling speed was very slow—that we had to accept—but we liked to 'bundle in' and hurry the loading and also the unloading—to save as much time as we could for travelling. This seemingly casual way the farmers kept us waiting until we could be fitted into their routine, we found most trying.

On these occasions I envied the lorry drivers, their mileage was in minutes to our hours, twenty miles was nothing them—to us it was twelve or more hours—in winter a lot of that time in wet or darkness. I also envied their having 'sack winding barrows'. These they would bring with them when picking up and with them could lift the heavy sacks to what height was necessary. These barrows were large clumsy affairs but they had a built-in winch which, operated by a handle, were much better for lifting than the more common 'topping sack'. When you saw a lorry leaving the mill with a 'hicking barrow' tied on top of his load you knew that a pick up was laid on for the return journey.

When heavy sacks needed stacking two or three high, we had a 'topping stick'. These days most packaging is in paper sacks and much lighter units. We had much heavier units—flour was always in ten stone bags—offal in twelve stones, wheat in eight or sixteen, oats, barley, rye usually sixteens. Rolled oats and bran being of lighter bulk came in ten and eight stone sacks respectively. Palletising has arrived and a much quicker and easier way to handle everything prevails. We had just a sack barrow to move the old heavy sacks in and out of sheds and warehouses—that and 'elbow grease'. To use a sack barrow—we called them 'running barrows' the sack needed to be upright—not laid down and a good man with a running barrow could wheel two at once if they were two high and upright. When they were stacked two high it was called 'topping them up' hence the name topping stick. This was, as its name implies just a stick about two feet long—any longer than that could be clumsy. There was a good joiner made one at most depots but they could easily be improvised from brush shafts, pick shafts and any such materials cut down to length. Simple to use—all you needed was for two people to face each other either side of the sack, grab the neck of the sack with hands behind the direction of lift, then one man would slide the stick low down, behind the sack and other would grab the free end of stick and with a concentrated effort the bottom of the bag would be lifted onto the bag it was to stand on and then with a heave by the other arm the bag would be pushed upright to stand on top of the first one. A good topping team could stick the bag apparently effortlessly and very neat and tidy and unlike to sag or fall. Of course, a really crafty topper could 'lay the stick' and give his companion the heavier lift—the wrong end of the stick so to speak.

Being a boat owner the Old Man needed regular reliable work to keep a cash flow for the everyday expenses of running and maintaining his little fleet. The Albion Mill connection was a valuable source of such regular work. He also had the Company work and this was an equally important part of his operation. By the company I mean the LNER Company who maintained the canal and had a works yard and office at Worksop. This yard was the nerve centre of the canal labourers and tradesmen's teams which carried out the work. Here lived the canal inspector, here also was a Company Office, a blacksmith's forge, a joiner's shop and sheds and stores for stonemasons and bricklayers. A warehouse spanned the canal on a bridge and a primitive hand crane stood with its jib pointing to the sky and an ancient wooden hand operated hoist could lift cargoes from boats moored beneath the trapdoors into the first floor space of the warehouse. Stores of sand, timber stone, gravel, bricks and the necessary miscellany of materials needed for the endless variety of jobs which occurred lay all about the place in orderly confusion. Beneath the stern gaze of the canal inspector, these workmen carried out their tasks, travelling to the various places along the waterway wherever their skills were needed. As an indication of the capabilities, I would like to mention that it was in this yard I saw built and launched, the only boat I saw on our canal with a cabin similar to those usually seen on narrow boats of the midlands network. This boat was named Norah and was launched sideways into the canal from the Company yard with due ceremony. I include this craft in my reflections of cargoes because my family along with carrying cargoes for the company also provided horses for them when needed by their boats, the dredger, the ice boat and now of course, the good ship Norah. We were commissioned when journeys were too far for hauling by the Company workmen, a practice much used and known to boatmen as 'bow yanking'. I worked Norah on a number of occasions and I soon found the advantage of the large cabin was only for the accommodation value. It was very roomy after our own little cabins but there the attraction ceased. The huge bulk of the cabin made a swift nip forward nearly impossible and the ridiculous little deck aft left no room for one of the long tillers we normally used, instead we had a short silly upcurved tiller. Being short it was very stiff to use and the Old Man said it was about as much use as a 'copper stick'. The absence of a good sensible, proven, timberheads made gate-catching and bearing away almost impossible and I soon realised that except for a few feet of cabin space, we had a far more efficient design for the handling involved.

Narrowboatmen called this craft 'the Norahboat' and I had the pleasure or otherwise of a number of trips in her. The new inspector, Herbert Bagshawe,

Albion Mill under construction in 1906. The photographer has caught a loaded horse-drawn boat gliding past heading downgate.
(Roz and Ian Davies collection)

who arrived on the scene about the time I started, was a very efficient man. He came from the Macclesfield Canal at Marple and we soon had his new ideas being sounded out in a strange accent. He instigated work requisition sheets, and the Old Man used to gaze in awe at the list of cargoes for the period beginning etc., etc. Form or no form, the welcome cargoes of materials for repairs to banks, locks and other works meant a flow of work. The cargoes were of such materials as clay, ashes, sand, gravel and cement, 'jacks' and stone. Before the Norahboat was built we also handled timber and wood fabrications for lock repairs and the more skilled jobs handled by the tradesmen. Now this side of the work was handled by the Company boat, which became a mobile workshop, shelter for mealtimes, bad weather breaks and was a good arrangement for distant jobs away down at the other end of the canal.

When we took cargoes for the Company, help was given by the Company labour for the loading and unloading. The main bank repair material as far as the towpath was concerned was ashes and clinker. We had a regular cargo of this material from the coal fired boilers of the Albion Flour Mill who were glad to get them taken away especially when the heap was piling up beside the boilers. We usually loaded these on Saturday morning and all spare labour would walk down from the Company yard with barrows and shovels to help us. I liked this job, it meant I would be at home for the weekend and could catch up a bit with my social activities and we always had a laugh or two from the characters in the Company team. Of course, if it was during the 6.00 am to 6.00 pm lock up period, we had to take the boat below Bracebridge Lock in order to get away at a sensible 4.00 am start on Monday. The Old Man thought 6.00 am starts were a waste of time and used to say 'it's never as dark in a morning as it is at night'—the truth of course was that we could use the moon's phases and have its welcome help morning and evening as it passed through its quarters each month.

The ashes were always soaking wet, being drawn hot from the fire-holes they were quenched by the fireman using a hose-pipe and a lake formed in the bed of the heap, this was a situation we did not mind. The canal inspector stipulated that company loads would be approximately 24 tons. Now the Old Man knew to a hundredweight or so, or a fraction of an inch, to where his boat wanted to be loaded down. In view of the condition of the canal at the time, we used to load a 'fair load' somewhat less as twenty four tons was a bit on the heavy side and everyone should have been happy. However, the Canal Inspector occasionally came with his labourers to the Mill and used a 'loading gauge' before we commenced operations. This gauge was simply a long flat stick marked off in inches from the bottom to the tip or hand grip. At the bottom was a short arm at right angles to the leg. The gauge was slid down the boat side and hooked the short arm beneath the bottom of the boat, then you could easily see how many inches of draught the boat drew. This was usually done somewhere near the middle pump and the spot marked with a lump of chalk. If this process was repeated at the mark when the boat was loadened you soon had the number of inches the boat had dropped during the loading and as our boats drew one inch to the ton you can see that a pretty accurate estimate of the cargo weight could be obtained. The gauge made casual loading a bit difficult and this is where the wet ashes helped, having pumped the boat dry to get a good empty reading, the wet ashes soon drained into the bilges and were sometimes helped a bit with the hose-pipe. With the ashes and the water to help, the labourer would read what he was expected to off the dipstick and everyone was happy including the canal inspector! I can still see the crafty smile on the Old Man's face as he thought of the tons of water we would pump out before we slacked off and my brother and I were ruefully thinking of all the pump strokes needed when we did it. The Old Man said the inspector was a bit of a new broom but he certainly swept well, longer than most brooms although he did eventually go off the boil and we rarely saw the loading gauge then.

The canal was getting generally worse in condition and wheat carriers were cutting loads down. The canal inspector read the signs and let sleeping dogs lie insofar as insisting on a twenty four tons capacity for company work. Another cheap useful material used in the maintenance of the cut bank was 'Jacks'. Now Jacks was the local name for a type of pit waste tipped on the high slag heaps of Shireoaks Colliery. At the time of which I write, this waste came to the surface and was carried by wagons into a siding and a team of horses and carts carried it up a sloping bank into the tip. Prominent among this material was a smooth black type of waste which I am told was found in a layer between the actual coal seam and the slatey slag or stone in which the coal seam lay. Sometimes these Jacks formed a high percentage of the wagon loads of waste destined for the tip and a very important feature of them was their combustibility. Given a good draught and making allowance for a lot of ash, these Jacks made a good alternative to the true coal in one's fireplace and were every bit as hot. The locals knew this and an amazing assortment of prams, barrows, bikes and home made transport of every description to pick Jacks on the slag heap and cart them triumphantly away to their waiting fireplaces. A benign official eye was blind to these Jackpickers and their trade flourished until the tip became dangerously overheated and eventually caught fire. The pit officials were glad to get rid of the Jacks and would place wagon loads of them over the loading chutes of the Basin so that we could easily load them onto the boat. We then delivered the cargo to specially prepared sections of the towpath and laid them evenly as far as we could. As soon as possible we would then take a load of ashes and place these over the Jacks and we then had a very good towpath, well drained, level and durable. As was to be expected, the canal side dwellers soon found out about the Jacks and began to descend upon our appealing levelled cargoes immediately we left them and about half of them would be gone before we were able to cover them with follow-up cargoes of ashes. Authority, in the shape of the canal inspector, was not amused and soon we were taking cargoes of half Jacks and half ashes and sealing the Jacks immediately they were laid. This effectively settled the problem but a few die-hards still poked about among the newly laid paths.

An amusing glimpse of the frugal nature of the canal budget at that time was reflected in the working of the steam dredger. When the old dredger was low on fuel we would deliver a load of Jacks nearby and pick out enough combustible Jacks to bunker up the old vessel. When I see the new generation of canal maintenance men with a seemingly endless procession of vans, tractors, grabs, diggers and watch their onslaught on the bed of the old cut, I wonder how far they would get on a ton of Jacks.

Another company cargo detested but vital, was clay. The original builders of the canal used puddled clay to make a durable waterproof seal to their channel and as the pattern had not changed clay was still an essential commodity in the maintenance of the waterway. Nowadays an endless supply of interlocking metal pilings seems to be available for the places where the canal is banked higher than the land alongside and shiny neat lengths of sheeting are beginning to appear. In my day, clay was the only answer and the old lengthsmen knew of any suspect places where leaks could occur. One can imagine the consequence of neglecting the tiniest of trickles and so leak stopping was ever present. The danger time was usually after heavy and prolonged freeze-ups—a swift thaw after weeks of penetrating frost left the banks in a very soft and vulnerable condition. Any little seepage in the banks could be a recipe for disaster and to forestall this a constant eye was kept on known danger spots. Whenever a suspect leak was located the lengthsmen dug a slit-trench sufficient to the extent of the weep and would then fill it in with puddled clay and create an effective watertight wall underground and seal the danger spot. To make all this possible we used to supply and maintain

An unusual aerial view of the Albion Mill at Worksop taken from the local electricity boards generating station c1945. Two empty narrow boats are moored awaiting orders. Note the white road marking put down during the wartime blackout when several people fell into the canal.
(Roz and Ian Davies collection)

a number of stockpiles of clay at all danger points , putting four or five tons at a time wherever a lengthsman saw the necessity and make sure any emergency could be dealt with promptly. Our main supply of clay was imported and the dump created for us was at the railway viaduct just below Worksop alongside the locally famous Willows swimming hole of the thirties.

The viaduct was known locally as Nine Arches for obvious reasons and it was here that whole train loads of clay—hundreds of tons—were dumped simply by slinging the wagon loads of clay over the bridge parapet and creating a huge hill of clay adjacent to the two or three arches nearest to the canal. This clay mountain was our base dump, it settled and solidified, assisted no doubt by children playing at mountaineers, very dirty mountaineers, until it was a solid hump of clay from which we were to hack ton upon ton of the heavy sticky greasy muck and deliver it to sites as required. In bad weather, a detestable job—in times of thaw an almost impossible job; the only gleam of light on this dark cargo was the fact that it was so heavy that you didn't need huge quantities to make up the required twenty four tons. It was a difficult to get off the shovel as it was to get on and I seemed to spend all the time with a bucket of water and a scraper getting the spades clean—old hands would dip their spades in any handy water to make 'em slide. The boat became indescribably dirty and weeks of ensuing cargoes failed to wear off the clay stains on the insides of the holds. Other similar functional cargoes existed in the Company's requirements and sand, aggregate and suitable concrete making materials were regularly needed and these cargoes were usually the signs of an impending stoppage. Stoppages were needed when essential repairs were necessary and of such a nature as to require a halt in navigation. With the advent of these stoppages we had timely warnings in the form of stoppage notices posted on bridges, lock houses and such prominent places acquainting us of the exact time, duration and location of the operation.

The new inspector certainly had a wealth of ideas and prominent among these was, in my opinion, the repair of eroded banks of the canal and long continuous concrete copings began to appear at lock heads, bridgeholes and wherever the existing bank was becoming hazardous. These copings are still there in many cases and are a monument to hours of barrow and shovel work by my brother and I. The cement and shuttering timber was usually in the Norahboat and stayed on the job. The sand, limestone chippings and any other concrete making material was carried by us previously from the yard at Worksop or from a dump on the wharf at Retford which was called Crosslands Yard, situated between the lock and the winding hole. When major repairs were needed to locks, we could have bricks and copings to handle. Bricks, particularly engineer's bricks, were heavy concentrate loads and the 'canches' or 'tiers' of these had to be positioned evenly to spread their weight and avoid straining the boats. This was very important and I have noticed the unhappiness in the Old Man's eyes when a bit of careless loading was going on by some uninterested labourer to be replaced by a shocking invective riddled piece of advice to some 'Warp headed farmer who weren't fit to be on a bloody boort'. Bricks, engineering or otherwise were very hard on the hands; customarily they were handed two at a time, very casually by the experienced, very clumsily by others, and a form of hand shields existed made of leather and I have seem them improvised from lorry inner tubes. Whatever the source, they were welcome and essential. I remember a very dangerous cargo of stone we handled, it was the occasion when the lock-tail at West Stockwith was repaired. In preparation for the work, all the huge stone copings of the old lock-tail were to be removed taken on to some spare ground nearby and broken into handy sizes to be used as hard-core for a projected concrete edging to the towpath below West End Lock at Retford and immediately behind the girl's High School, in fact between the lock and Inkerman's bridge. The Canal Inspector decided he needed some of the larger blocks of stone for use on further improvements and so we had a cargo these mighty blocks of stone to be taken to the yard for use of the Company stonemason. They were used eventually to make the carefully shaped headstones where the lockgates fitted snugly into a seat and were held by a forged metal strap which was clipped to anchors set in the stone—hence the need for a sound stone block.

Now came the dangerous part of the operation, we used 'legs' to load the stone blocks, and these legs were simply that, just three legs forming a tripod of sufficient height to give lift clearance over the boats combings. Block tackle could be used on these legs and a winch was incorporated in the legs and this gave adequate muscle to the job. To actually hold the heavy stonework we used an appliance I called a stone-grab. This was a cross between calipers and scissors, two steel curved, pointed arms, crossed in a hinge similar to scissors and the inward pointed curved lower ends fitted into the sides of the stone block. A sling joined the upper arms of the scissors like grab, as the weight of the lift closed the upper part of the grab a correspondingly right pressure closed the claws of the lower parts and a balanced grip was obtained. The heavier the lift, the tighter the grip. I was always fascinated when watching the stonemason as he carefully eyed the block, assessed the best places to cut his gripholes in the stone's sides, and give a 'good hang'. I was of the opinion that this was another of those little jobs that looked easy when someone competent was doing it. You could rely on old Herbert Turner to cut the holes just where they did most good. The Old Man watched the whole operation like a Mother hen, each block was agonisingly lowered into the hold, each block was carefully 'seated' across one of the iron knees which joined the boat sides and bottom, spreading the clumsy, deadly weighted stones evenly over the hold of the boat. When the first layer was safely installed, the pressure was off—we could do little harm with them acting as a cushion for further blocks of stone. We had this nail-biting situation when we handled the concrete copings of the locksides but thanks to the competent eye of good old Herbert Turner, we never had a mishap.

Occasionally, a one-off, or way-out cargo popped up. For instance, we once flitted a lockkeeper from Misterton to Osberton and became furniture removers. Once, never to be forgotten, we shifted cargoes of the huge weed clumps at Gringley and Misterton locks and tipped them down the high banks of the 'puddle' at West Stockwith. To keep the lockheads clear of weed during the summer months, lengthsmen and helpers would drag the bright green clogging weed, along with any other debris trapped in it, dead animals, birds and fish etc., and would dump this in a heap at the weir head. Soon a large heap would accumulate and eventually need shifting. I vividly recall the messy disgusting work this entailed and although many years have passed since that long hot summer when we shifted the weed heaps, I will always remember with loathing, the indescribable stench which permeated the hold, and worse still, the cabin, for weeks after the filthy operation. Other catch loads existed, but these were usually carried by the other boats, Furleys and the few small operators could adequately cope with these loads. Coal to the paper mill at Retford was welcomed by the Furley's skippers who only too often returned empty to West Stockwith. Loads of 'smudge' were regularly delivered to the Sewerage Works at Worksop by the Chambers family who operated from Worksop Wharf. Smudge was the nickname for the very small type of coal used by the sewerage and was probably better known as slack by the lay public. I have handled this type of cargo when the Chambers family was busy. It was a good handling cargo—one could slide the pan shovel into the soft, loose mass of the smudge quite easily and this meant you could work downwards through the load and not have to sling the whole lot 'up from the shutts'. The load was carried away to the fireholes of the beam engine on a little railway in tubs similar to pit tubs. You could get unloadened just as quickly as you were prepared to work hard, we didn't quarrel with this situation into those days, we were paid by the load and any inconvenience needed to expedite this we accepted—never reasoned why— so to speak. Sometimes the Chambers family would deliver a load of smudge to the sewerage and if very busy at the time, would invite my brother Bill and I to unloaden it for them. Just a few shillings were involved but it was a welcome bonus—a bit of overtime you might say.

Another unusual by-load was turf. In those far off days the gardens at Osberton Hall were maintained in style and the clever old gardeners of yesteryear had their own ways of going about it. None of the present day patents existed. The modern, bewildering, lists of potting, seeding and cutting composts and mixtures had not yet arrived. Cultivations and compositions of the necessary textures existed in the brains of these of horticulturists and were often handed down from father to son. However the basic need for a good weed free loam was just as important as it is even today. To obtain good loam you needed well cut turf from suitable land. This had to be stacked and allowed to rot—thus at some future date you had a well rotted loam to 'push through the riddle' and form a basic ingredient upon which to build your potting soil etc. The mysteries of additives and sterilisation were the domain of the gardener, the supply of turf was where the boats were involved.

The Foljambe family besides owning Osberton, also had holdings along the Trentside at Sturton. These meadows at Sturton were occasionally flooded by the restless River Trent and during this event a layer of warp, that fine rich mud of the tidal river would settle and form a natural top dressing to the sward. In the drying clear days of Spring, the grass would eagerly grow through the layer and in a matter of time, with grazing, flooding and mowing an even high quality texture of stone free turf was formed.

A pumping engine shed and dyke nearby made a reasonable wharf at which to load this turf, hand-cut skilfully from the meadow. So, once a year, about twenty three or four tons of turf would be nearly stacked at the Osberton gardens, there to lay for another year as the gardeners used the previous year's cargo to make their composts. Now, of course, a lorry would arrive with many coloured plastic sacks of hygienic, super culture compositions. This doesn't bother the old gardeners of the 'turf years', they've gone before.

'Warp' was involved in another 'catch load'. It was a necessary ingredient in the brick-making industry which existed at Gringley, Walkeringham and Misterton. The old brick-yards were like the canal, in them also, time had stood still. The methods of their fathers and grandfathers were still being used by the brickmakers of the period of which I write. The demons of brute strength and ignorance ruled. The heavy clay had to be selected from its seams in the surrounding fields, transported to the sheds of the brickyards, pounded into a suitable texture for moulding into bricks, pipes and tiles of the old familiar patterns. When moulded, all these products had to be manhandled into drying sheds until they were sufficiently tough enough to be stacked in the kilns for firing. The title of Brickmaker was well earned by these latterday craftsmen who were not afraid to back up their accumulated skills and experience with some gruelling hard work. The boat's cargoes of smudge and cobbles were used in the drying and firing process where the kilns were kept at the correct temperature and for the correct length of time—(easy if you knew how). At a given time, the kilns would be sealed off, the fires drawn and the fireholes sealed up in order to allow the kilns to cool naturally. Quick cooling would undo all the hard work that had gone into the firing. Warp was the material used in the sealing up process. With a consistency akin to mortar the warp could be moulded into the fireholes along the kiln. There it would harden and form a seal and isolate the kiln during the natural cooling process. I was once thrilled when I was at the opening of one such firing. There on top of the bricks were the delightful figures of dogs and fishes lovingly sculptured in the soft clay and slipped in with the bricks. The warp was the cargo of the brickyard boats and the Hewitt family who had the concession knew the best places in the Trent to get this muddy cargo and bring to the brickyards. Several places for such loads existed at West Stockwith and Walkerith and on a suitable tide, the Hewitt brothers would extract heavy loads of the shining mud and of course the powerful, swirling Spring tides would replenish any excavation they made in the process. I dimly remember a couple of chaps who also handled warp, they were brothers I believe, and with an old narrow boat they extracted loads from the River Trent and took it an old mill near the site of the Chemical Works in the bight above Stockwith Lock. There they dried the warp in an old drying shed, ground it very fine and I was led to believe that this fine silica and sand laden dust was used in the buffing processes of the Sheffield cutlery factories. I think this was true as I can remember seeing bags of this product awaiting collection in the warehouse of the Old Mill and whenever I passed by the place their narrow boat would be laid there in various stages of unloading.

One cargo that was dwindling rapidly by the early thirties was one that the Old Man used to organise particularly well—manure. When horses were the main form of power for transport and similar heavy work, every town had a horse population and along with that, a bedding and manure problem. Also at that time, the 'cottage pig' flourished and along with outside toilets, outside wash-houses, we also had pig-sties, in fact just as today houses have garages, so houses were built with a pig-sty at the bottom of the garden. When one of these pig-sties was occupied, it was customary to collect all local household scraps and hopefully some of the neighbours would get a 'pig-fry' when the unlucky animal

The Albion Mill taken from the hose drying tower at the Fire Station. An AFS (Auxiliary Fire Service) lorry is seen loading hose reels. Beyond the corner of the mill is the furnace which the authors family kept stocked with coal and a horse and boat can just be discerned in the co-lateral basin top right.
(R. Allsopp collection)

was slaughtered. Schoolboys of my age can recall the terrified screams of the pigs when the slaughterman was busy for it was the custom for the butcher to wheel his lethal tools on his 'scratch' to wherever the pig was kept. With no refrigeration, most killing was done in cool weather and just before Christmas was a favourite time with a view no doubt to a seasonal feast of offal and all the many trimmings on the pig when it was cool enough to cut up. We kept pigs and I have memories of piles of chitterlings, 'chines', faces, chaps, spare ribs and home-made brawns and pork pies. We even ate the scraps of rendered fat sprinkled with salt, we devoured them greedily. I shudder when I think what such a rich diet would do to me now. All these goings on meant that all over the parish would be heaps of manure which the owners would be glad to be rid of. The Old Man had a cart and a dray and he soon accumulated enough manure from the back street stables and pig runs to fill a boat. This manure was welcomed by canal side farmers and the Old Man never had any trouble selling a boat load, and of course the price would be right. We had an old stable at the end of Garside Street and usually had two or three horses in it, also there was a spacious area where we could store our own manure and also any that the Old Man could acquire. We liked to locate enough manure for a cargo and load it directly into the boat, usually at Piggot's Bridge as this saved handling the stuff too many

The White Hart at Clayworth and one of Ginger, the horses' favourite stopping off places.
Here a narrow boat delivers cinders from the Kiveton area c1910.
The village roads in Clayworth were being stoned and surfaced at this time.
(Mrs Smith)

times. We made quite a bit of manure ourselves, particularly as we often brought loads of sweet smelling hay from the wide stretches of towpaths. This was cut, dried and cocked up by the obliging lengthsman, and easily loadened into the boat when we returned empty from some cargo. A lot of this hay was edible and we used it liberally and some was eaten by the horse and the rest soiled by manure became muck and money. No doubt a few shillings changed hands, a bonus for the obliging lengthsman and a bulging hayloft for us at the start of every winter. When I was very young I remember my father employing an old codger who slept in the hayloft when he was not away with the boat. This old man had an equally old lady who lived with him. The dubious morality of their relationship escaped me but my childish thoughts envied them. I thought it would be exciting sleeping in the hayloft with the winter gales rattling the pantiles, though I didn't include the lady in my plans. We had a very handy source of manure at the canalside stables of the local brewery and here also a good access by doors which opened on to the canal beneath which we could moor the boat. Being entirely horse manure it was not so wet and odorous as mixture with the sloppy sour pig muck in them and was much pleasanter to handle. We handled long-muck, short-muck and all varieties in between and muck forking was an art if such a procedure could aspire to that exalted description.

The uninitiated could 'towse their guts out' trying to fork it the wrong way from a heap but an old hand took it the 'way it went in' and the long strawy muck handled easier and instead of tugging away trying to get a huge fork-full they would build a 'pat' and lift it overside with skilful dexterity. It was often a steamy job, as the manure could be quite warm in the middle, so consequently in the absence of protective clothing and footwear, we improvised leggings and puttees with any material to hand. At the end of a day's 'muckin' your feet became soft and wrinkled through prolonged exposure to the warm steamy moistures of the manure. These one-off cargoes were called catch loads and were usually carried by owners who would 'forage' for work. I saw a bit of this trade, but the Old Man told me he used to have a good thing going with muck, but the inevitable end of this was already in evidence and so he was talking of the everlasting good old days of yesteryear. My recollection of the muck-trade was the really awful meal breaks we took, when we would huddle in the cabin on cold days and eat our meal, sometimes four or five of us, wet to the knees with manure 'juices', steaming around the stove and slurping and blowing the hot tea with which we washed down our thick sandwiches. The discomfort and the insanitary aspects of this I accepted—I knew no better—but I'll never forget the warm aroma of the cabin.

We had one cargo that needed very little brute strength to load or unload, this was the one cargo remembered so nostalgically by older Worksopians. It was difficult to believe that this particular voyage was so popular with the locals in these days of foreign holidays. I refer of course to the Greenmile Trip. It will be over sixty years since I took the last trip to Greenmile but even today I have older residents who are eager to tell me they went on 'Clarkies Greenmile Trip'. The occasion never fails to crop up when people talk about the time when 'boorts were on t'cut' and the event was quite something in its day. This unruly, uncomfortable, largely uncontrolled mixture of men, women and children, jammed in a boat made for carrying cargo only, was the only outing many local people ever got in these days of limited budgets, long hours and when hard work was a virtue.

Through the rose-tinted spectacles of time, the Trip to Greenmile was something of an 'I was there' occasion among the elderly people of Worksop, almost a status symbol, part of local history so to speak. In fact, these same people still say 'How do Boatie' when we meet. My memory of the Greenmile Trip is somewhat different, seen from the inside, as it were.

The trip was always a Bank Holiday affair and preparations to have a boat ready began during the previous week and this meant that the best boat had to be cleaned, swept, paintwork wiped down, all movables, with the exception of gear strictly necessary for navigation was stowed away. All spare planks were commandeered and with builders bricks converted into platforms in the hold suitable for small children to see over the combings or to sit on when tired of standing—no comfy lay back seats, no air conditioning, no services, no frills of any sort at all. The elderly and immobile passengers had the favoured seats on the decks fore and aft. The combined weight of the passengers gave the boat enough draught to be able to haul from the fore timberheads and thus avoid the hazards of a line swinging from the lutchet mast. My father was a man with a ready temper and his self control as he advised the children 'to mind your arms in the locks sonny' when the kids looked like getting their waving arms nipped as the boat listed when using the locks was a source of great wonder to me. It became more normal as his temper frayed and by the time the unruly assembly reached Kilton Lock he would be yelling at the top of his voice, 'Keep your bloody arms in you little varmints'. If during the voyage some eager child saw something of great wonder on his side of the boat and his excited cries caused the other kids to rush across to see the sight, then the boat would list alarmingly. The deck passengers would hang on for dear life and the Old Man used to go berserk. It used to amuse me and it was a sight never to be forgotten. Old Ginger, plodding away at the end of the rope would be twitching his tail and wondering what on earth he was pulling—I used to think the crafty old nag was even laughing. The trip was very much an 'off the cuff' affair although I can remember some trips arranged by the Salvation Army and the Fisherman's Arms public house. I believe these were run on Sunday and had to obtain special permission to 'pen' Bracebridge Lock during lock up hours. For the Bank Holiday trips the Old Man would 'gauge the weather' and if the signs were good he would engage the services of the cheapest advertising agency the town ever had—Tommy Ashley—well remembered by my generation as the Town Crier. This bewhiskered gentleman, complete with hand bell and details of announcement would, after a great peel of his bell, render in a loud voice, details of times, prices and anything else concerning a 'Twip to Greenmile in Metta Clark's boort'. By today's standards a rather primitive working class day's outing but it is still remembered with affection by a sadly diminishing generation of large ladies in flowery hats, kids in sailor suits and hairy gents with whiskers and large gold or silver watch chains. As a working boatman, all the trip meant to me, churlishly perhaps, was working on a Bank Holiday! I had possibly been past Greenmile once or twice in the previous week and scores of times in the previous year. Greenmile itself was just a bridge, a clearing, a couple of cottages and some splendid beech and Sycamore trees. Today's landowners would probably call it Private and not allow a flock of excited kids to yell, scream, create disturbance for a couple of hours while the elderly sat in the shade or supervised games and refreshed themselves with sandwiches, fruit and such. One of the cottage dwellers was very obliging, and knowing of the event in advance would have copper and kettles of boiling water prepared and hot tea would then be available and welcome. The crew, usually my family, would take the boat to the winding hole below Forest Top Lock, about a quarter of a mile or so downgate of the bridge. Having 'swung' the boat we would then lay in the filled lock and have our meal, laze on the grass or fish. Ginger would enjoy a spell with his gears off grazing on the lock side and being given a welcome tin of corn and a drink—in those days we dare use the canal water for that.

The return voyage was quieter, the elderly a little tired and the kids with limp bunches of bluebells, campions and moonpennies whichever flower was in season, were quiet and 'gone off the boil a bit'. As we drew nearer to Kilton Lock and Worksop, a bit of the original high spirits would return with greetings to friends

Morris's Chemical Works was situated on the upstream side of West Stockwith Lock.
Keels and narrow boats some with masts can be seen moored.
There was regular traffic from the canal to the works.
(R. Allsopp collection)

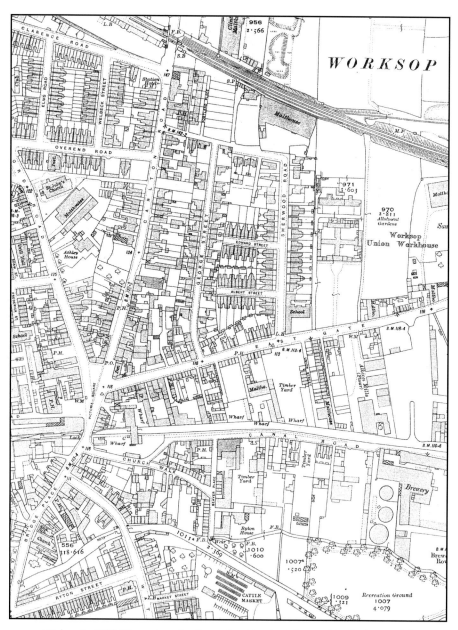

Worksop in 1920. The road crossing the canal and bearing left was originally the Attercliffe Turnpike leading to Sheffield. Smiths Albion Mill was built in 1906 on the north side of the canal opposite the Priorwell Brewery.

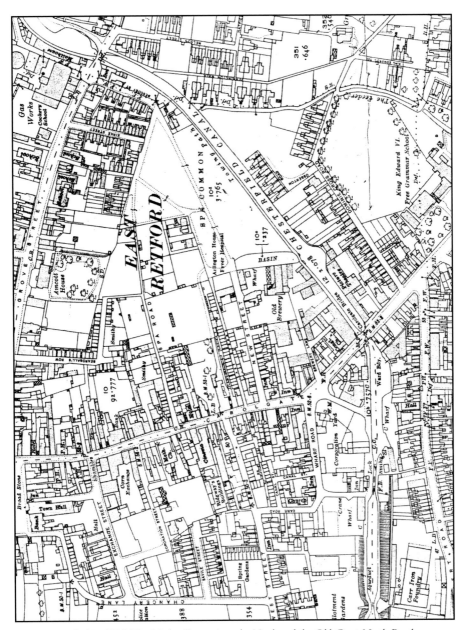

Retford in 1920. The Market Square is to the North and the Old Great North Road crosses the canal by Carolgate Bridge.

and neighbours and the familiar surroundings heralding the end of another 'Twip To Greenmile in Metta Clark's Boort'.

The Old Man told me that when he was young and before the collapse of the Norwood Tunnel, outings were a regular and accepted form of public holiday pastime. It is only reasonable to suppose that when the canal was used at full capacity and transport, particularly public transport, was very limited. The canal would be a handy ready-made addition to the few pleasures of the austere working family life. I was told of trips from Retford to Drakeholes and Wiseton and there is no doubt that the area about those places was amongst the prettiest on the waterway. I once visited Drakeholes and saw a vessel adapted for carrying passengers on pleasure trips, a sort of waterbus. I shudder to think of the stringent rules which must now be observed when carrying passengers.

White Hart, Clayworth

CHAPTER 4

DOWNGATE –
THE STOCKWITH TRIP

Bracebridge Lock

Cargoes were the reason for all the work and expense that brought the new artificial waterways into the transport system of our forebears. Chesterfield sat proudly at the head of its 'shining passage to the sea' and acclaimed itself an inland port. The country already had a waterways system in the winding, placid rivers such as the Thames, Severn, both Ouses, the Trent and all their tributaries. When the canals were built and became the threads in the web of natural rivers, we finally had a cohesive network: an inland waterways system. To the generations of boatmen skilled in the use of the swift tidal reaches of our larger rivers before the powerful engines of today came along, the still green peaceful waters of the New Cuts offered little challenge and so the original canal people came into being.

I have seen the present day imitations of the boat people as they come chugging up the cut in their elaborately painted narrow boats. It may be that they have done much for the present day existence of the canal and I do not criticise them. If today's seeming abundance of money and leisure must have an outlet, then there are many worse ways than the relatively harmless comings and goings of these new canal people. Long may they prosper. Their ardent desire to imitate the old narrowmen is a different matter; this they can never do. The missing ingredient is obvious; the original boatmen functioned for one reason, the utter necessity of earning a living. This cannot be imitated since a great difference exists between the search for a livelihood and the creation of pleasure. You can buy the most realistic traditional caravan and horse but it will not make you one of the wise, industrious old Romany Gypsies. Many of the new pleasure boat people try very hard and if they achieve a few of the better habits of the originals then this can only be admired.

My experience of life as a 'Boatie' was of the repetitive comings and goings on the restricted remains of navigable canal after Norwood Tunnel collapsed, leaving only about twenty eight miles of channel with Shireoaks Colliery Basin as the upper head of navigation. This meant we could have some nights at home and since most trips were only of two or three nights duration, we did not strictly live on the boats though we could survive quite adequately aboard for the time it took to complete the voyage. You may do well to remember that twenty miles from home is a long way when you average less than two miles per hour. Within the limits of local requirements however, the art of navigating the narrow boats about the canals remained basically the same over the whole system.

The particular knowledge necessary to navigate the horse drawn traffic of The Chesterfield Canal (my canal) was handed down to me by my father and his contemporaries, my older brothers, in whose hands I soon learned the many little things that went into make a good 'Chesterfield Canal Boatie'.

I always felt that a boatie had much in common with the old farm labourer. Far from being a music hall joke, the old 'farmer's boy' had an endless array of skills ranging from animal care, through to the knowledge of all the diverse forms of farm machinery coming along in increasing quantities in the nineteen thirties. We had a similar variety of tasks to perform and like the farmer's boy, became masters of many skills and far from being 'bumpkins' as is often mistakenly assumed.

I became a Boatie in the depression days of the thirties and I learned as I went on—or else. To adequately describe canal navigation is difficult. Perhaps the best way would be to give a detailed description of an everyday round trip, similar to the scores of trips I made as a boy and later as a young man. The particular trip I have in mind is one made regularly—a load of bank repairing materials 'downgate' towards the Trent and a load of grain to be picked up at Gainsborough on the return or 'upgate'. The boat would be our good ship 'Clarice' and would have been moored at Batty's Lock tail, Bracebridge on Saturday in order to make an early start possible on Monday. To 'hang on' or 'slack off' and start the voyage would be to over-simplify, for a working boat needed a variety of essential preparations before leaving on a trip. To try to describe boating in those bygone days, without describing the whole way of life would be incomplete, even incorrect. Boating was our whole life and any time left for social activities was a bonus. The trip in question was one of the longest we made (outside of being frozen-up in icy waters or delayed by waiting for cargoes or similar problems) and we would be away from our mooring from Monday until Thursday at least. Being responsible for the coal supplies of the Albion Flour Mill at Worksop, we had to be sure that the coal wharf was full even if it meant a few hours of shovelling on Sunday morning. We also had to make certain that the spare boat was laid nearby with a full cargo to replenish the pile of coal as the ever greedy 'fireholes' devoured the fuel.

The trip to Shireoaks for coal was a short one, some two miles with eight locks, one hour and a half upgate (towards Shireoaks) two hours downgate (towards Worksop) loaded. We decided the quantity of coal that we would load on the conditions we found going-up. We knew to a ton or less just the amount we would be able to carry on the water available. Of course, we could give ourselves a greater level of water in the 'short ponds' by 'flushing out' of locks and using plenty of water to 'come down'. In this we were fortunate to be travelling downgate when loaded—you cannot 'flush' going-up.

Flushing was illegal but widely practised. It was simple: all you did was wait until the horse had pulled the boat so far out of the lock, usually about a third of a length, and then we would draw up a 'top-slide' and the rapid inrush of water into the empty lock flushed the boat out of the lock and helped the horse quite a lot. In times of low water levels we sometimes drew both top slides and gave a considerably greater flush.

The Shireoaks trip was ideal for flushing but if several boats were in the Basin for loading, then irresponsible flushing by the first boats down could leave very little water for the later boats. However a sensible attitude usually prevailed and the needs of all boatmen were generally considered especially in situations of scarce water. In times of drought it was not unknown for the lock keeper to insist on all boats loading and waiting above the top locks until all the craft were clear of the basin which was rather shallow, particularly in the 'arm' which led into the basin. These situations did not arise below Worksop although we still gave the horse a welcome flush from the narrow locks down to Retford if no lock keeper was looking.

Sunday work was usually confined to a couple of hours in the stable; mucking out, swilling, brushing the horses with 'dandy brush' and 'currycomb'. It must have been very welcome to the horses, manger full of bran, oats and straw or hay 'chop' perhaps a turnip or a few carrots to clean their teeth on although that would depend on the season or what luck we had on our weekly voyages. The old horse like to gnaw at a swede, turnip or even a sugar beet and on Sunday it always seemed proper to give them a little extra attention—they certainly earned what little comfort they got. The Old Man, my father, usually made them a 'bran-mash' on these occasions; a bucket half full of 'broad-bran' with his own mysterious additives such as saltpetre, ground gentian, liquorice, linseed and other potions known only to himself. The whole mixture was scalded with very hot water and the bucket stood in the manger. The horses would sniff, snicker and impatiently try to eat the hot mixture while the Old Man said the clouds of steam did them a lot of good. I used to have a quiet giggle myself as I visualised the nags with towels over their heads and bucket as they inhaled under the severe eye of 'Dr' Clark in white coat and oversized horse stethoscope. What a vision! We hurried these chores, it was Sunday, we could use a little time off ourselves and breakfast was waiting. A final brush, 'hecks' filled with seeds, belly deep in sweet canal side hay, the horse would be all right until 'supper-up' time.

The trip began early on Monday morning, our starting time would be set by the estimated time we expected to arrive at our destination. As it was a Company load no help could be expected until Tuesday morning and so all we had to do was to get to where we had to go and get ourselves set up for a good start next day. The cargo this time was ashes for repairing the canal towpath and the site of the repair was at the start of Gringley Woods just below the 'getting off place' at the far end of Drakeholes Tunnel. When we used ashes it was usually to where the towpath had worn into a narrow single rut of a track and become muddy and waterlogged. Normally the canal labourers would be there on the day, prior to our arrival. They would cut the sides of the towpath to its proper width, lift off the overgrowing grass in turves and build low retaining walls with them, so providing a bed for the tons of ashes due to arrive.

Our preparations had been made on the previous Saturday. Enough coal was stacked on the wharf at the Albion Mills and a spare boatload was available nearby. This meant that my brother, Bill could manage the coal job single-handed whilst my brother Len and myself did the round trip. If we were held up, Bill could always fetch another load of coal in the then empty spare boat. The Old Man would help him or even my mother, who had stepped into the breech so many times before.

We had 'readied' our boat when we had finished loading it. The coal box would be well filled with 'nuts' if hard weather was likely. We always had a spare bag of coal 'in forward' and possibly a couple of huge lumps of 'Clowne Hards' which burned so well. (If we didn't need these reserves of fuel, we could always 'trade' with some canalside dweller). Water can full, supplies of corn and fodder stowed away forward for the old nag, Tiger. 'Gate-line' round the 'Parson'. The untidy heaps had been levelled and the boat 'trimmed' for hauling. The planks of the gangway (plankway) would now be neatly laid down the boat side, ends overlapping in one direction. Some skippers had planks cut to fit and these would lay 'butt to butt' with no step to trip over. This was a good idea where a regular 'sack trade' was carried on but we needed our planks for loading and unloading and a bit of extra length was an asset, also, cut to fit planks were not interchangeable owing to the varying lengths of the cargo holds. Cargo covers, neatly folded, were piled on the 'middle box', barrows, shovels and spare tiller laid on the even heap of ashes under the aft beam. The bucket, upside down with its 'lanyard' slipped round the 'windlass head' would be in front of the coal box on top of the cargo. The 'poles', 'hooks' and 'stowers' would be laid along the 'aft box', 'truck' on the 'windlass roller' for immediate use in an emergency. You never buried your poles! An extra long stower, used little, would probably be snugged down under the 'gunnel' (gunwhale); this would be much more important when we went in the Trent. The main tiller would either be laid in the curve of the aft deck or handily on the aft cargo. The 'hold brush' and mop filled any remaining space aft; and what a mop it was!

The mop was a real asset; you washed and dried your decks with it, you washed planks, beams and gunnels with it, you cleaned muddy boots with it, we even swept the chimney with it! A veritable maid of all work. These mops were usually home-made, none of your skimpy, stringy tiny shafted creations such as we see

One of Furleys narrow boats prepares to set off downgate from Bracebridge Lock.
This lock was closed on Sundays and overnight and boatmen would go through before
dusk to get an uninterrupted start the following day.
(B. Wilkinson)

today. They would be useless and anything useless and out of place was an anathema. The mop was a creation of the skippers; you could be approved or disapproved of by the condition of your mop. Strong, sturdy, well smoothed and painted 'shaft'—anything up to six feet long. It had to reach the water under any conditions and you sometimes pushed the boat away from a wall with it especially in confined spaces where the poles were too long. The head of the mop was a work of art—a long spike, squared at the point, and a large flat head would have a leather washer slid down it first and then the mop materials themselves. When a boatman's wife decided that socks, pullovers, jerseys, woolly underwear and such were beyond repair they were washed, cut up and became mop materials. The cut strips were then forced crosswise down the spike until it would hold no more and by varying the crosswise placings evenly, a huge fearsome mop was formed and a sealing washer inserted. The bottom of the shaft had a 'lead hole' bored and an iron ring around the end to prevent splitting (or 'spelching' as boaties called it). The squared spike would have its point inserted in the lead hole and then be driven in as far as possible, thus compressing the layers of socks etc., into a tight head. A mop is born. A well made mop could lift as much water as a bucket, swill and dry decks, dry covers and was a valuable all round asset. Some skippers could spin a mop dry with amazing dexterity— I was useless at it.

All 'top hamper' being 'snugged down', we could now think of the coming voyage. The cabin could be scrubbed out going down, there would be time enough. As we were going in the Trent, a long thick 'bass rope' would be evenly looped on the 'front box' because, who knows, some kindly tug or packet master on the River Trent might give us a 'snig' and we'd ride to Gainsborough in style. The heavy bass rope would be our tow rope, our life line, so to speak. The usual white cotton 'horse line' would be coiled in the 'fore peak' and all would be ready. The last decision was made, a five o'clock start was decided upon, and so we fetched Tiger and took the boat through the first downgate lock from Albion Mill, Batty's Lock (also known as Bracebridge Lock). All was ready to sail come Monday. The only preparation now required was at home.

I have come to realise just how important and largely unappreciated was a good home, the source of all well prepared departures and the ensuing homecomings, ruled by that willing slave, my mother. Always there, always taken for granted. This new world of ours has produced many wonders that have surpassed the wildest dreams of Jules Verne and his like, but it has not found a replacement for a good mother. Nor will it.

Clean sheets, pillow slips for the boat's bed, towels for the crew and cutlery, clean clothes (only clean clothes held any warmth), a mound of baking: jam pasties, scones, home-made bread, and all the old fashioned victuals for the 'snap basket'. All were there, never questioned, never doubted—hadn't we always had them? With the remains of the huge Sunday joint, meat pies, eggs, home fed bacon (full of fat), our snap basket needed to be large. Covered with clean towels, it was a veritable portable larder; we knew it would be ready, whatever the hour.

The five o'clock start meant rising at least by four o'clock. We came down to a warm fire, hot sweet tea, and breakfast already cooked. Churlishly, with eyes not yet fully open and minds still numb with sleep, we accepted these things. Our boots would be by the fire, our coats, caps and scarves waiting. Like ungrateful zombies we silently ate, dressed and got ready for 'going away'. As a very young schoolboy I was often awakened by these early risings and sometimes came quietly down stairs, thinking it all very exciting. With the nearest my mother ever came to being angry, she would steer me back to the stairs. 'Back to bed with you, you'll get more of this than you want someday'. Her words were timely, I was to find this out when I became one of the 'sleep numbed zombies', but she was still there.

We stabled at the bottom of Garside Street (or later at the Cross Keys public house). We had to feed and harness the faithful Tiger on the way to the boat. A tin of corn would be wolfed by Tiger whilst we yoked up. We didn't hurry this if possible, for we knew we would gain any few minutes we lost in the better performance of a well fed horse. One of us would usually go ahead at this time and put the snap basket safety in the dry cabin at the forend, pay out the horse line and light a fire in the stove with kindling, dry and safely store on either side of the cabin stove. All was ready. Soon the ring of hooves, the jingle of harness and the quiet words of command would herald the arrival of horse and mate. Another boatie's dawn had come, similar to hundreds of previous dawns and yet somehow all slightly different.

This morning was different, however, for on Saturday we had moored the boat's stern to a bank-ring against the stable at the locktail and allowed the head to lay free out in the channel. A couple of buckets of coal ensured us that the lock keeper would keep a friendly eye on our boat over the weekend. We would lock up the cabins fore and aft with 'hatch bars' which fixed the eye bolts either side of the hatchway and thus only the loose fittings spread on the cargo could be tampered with. The day of the vandal had not yet arrived and we had little or no trouble leaving the boat unattended. Fishing on Sunday was not allowed in the waters below Bracebridge Lock and a gate was locked shut across the towpath just below the bridge and so little was left to chance. If any boat was laid there, as in this case, then the Lock keeper would leave the gate shut but unlocked on Sunday night. Should any upgate boat stay there for the weekend, with crew on board, then the gate was left open. Some boats did stay at the lock over the weekend if a number of boats were at Worksop and the stables at the rear of the Royal George pub on Priorswell Bridge (Piggot's Bridge) were crowded. Then it was sensible to use the Company stables at the lock tail.

In those busier days, stabling was a prime necessity and the stables behind Bertie Probert's Royal George public house; the Company stables at Batty's Lock and the stables behind the Gas Tavern (now re-christened Canal Tavern) were all in demand. Two Furley Boats had arrived on this particular weekend; they sometimes did that when they had left West Stockwith on Saturday and had managed to clear Forest Lock on Saturday night. Then they would rest the horse in the Forest Lock stable overnight, slip up to Worksop on Sunday morning and would have to lie below the Bracebridge Lock until it was unlocked on Monday morning. On their arrival they could see at a glance the reason why our boat was moored there and they had moored their boats where we had been and then eased our boat downstream and moored us to their 'aft timber heads'. This meant that we could 'slack off' without disturbing their boats, although it

A double acting (geared) low gate slide at Bracebridge described by the author.
They were much safer and easier to work than the single lift type.
(Roz and Ian Davies collection)

was necessary to go along their plankway to reach ours. We avoided shouting and unnecessary stamping on their decks but, of course, they were used to such disturbances. Our horse, old Tiger, arrived and was carefully led down the curving lock tail and under the bridge, past the stable with its warm steamy smell of fresh manure—the unforgettable smell of an occupied stable. The horse man waited patiently at the head of the moored boats where he knew his mate would come along the gangplanks of the Furleys boats and hand him the 'key'.

The key was just that; the key to the locks, 'winch handle', just winch or even handle, call it what you may. A boatman always called it the key and with its curved crank it fitted comfortably around your neck and down your back secure under your braces—if you wore them—but in any case it would be there. Rarely did you see a boatman carrying a key any other way. We had a spare, of course, for emergencies, and a silly little square key for dropping slides but the best key was carefully looked after. Sometimes the man ashore would need the key and then it would be thrown to him from the moving boat. It was most important that it was thrown properly, it had to go through the air without spinning or twisting, just the right distance, just the right height. It had to be smoothly caught at the correct moment and deftly slipped on your shoulder and we acquired a real knack of doing it. If the key landed in muddy towpaths, it was a sin. If it landed on a stone and knicked the smooth well-worn handle it was a cardinal sin or even a crime. Many times was I called a 'bloody ham-fisted farmer' whilst I was acquiring the knack.

Key safely round the neck the horseman went down the bank and found the horse-line across the towpath where it had been thrown, the white cotton line shining in the dark. Slipping the 'hauling knot' into the 'strop' on the gaily painted 'cobble stick' of the horses 'long gears', all was ready. After making sure that old Tiger had taken the slack safely, the horseman would nip ahead to prepare Kilton lock—fill it if necessary and open the top gate. Back on his own boat again, the helmsman would swing the heavy wood tiller over the parson and slap it firmly into the eye of the hellum (helm). Easing the tiller to correct any 'falling away' as the horse took over, he would then coil and lay the aft mooring line on the cargo with its spliced eye around the windlass stump for immediate handiness, pay out the heavy gate-line in readiness and then take stock of things. He'd got his eyesight by this time and away from any artificial light, the human eye has a capacity for adjusting to the gloom in a manner that would surprise anyone who hadn't given it the chance to do so. A feeble gleam from the last quarter of the moon gave him all the light he needed. With the hatch nearly all the way over the hatchway to shield the glare of the friendly cabin fire, parson twisted to the wind, a friendly glow coming from it as the smoke escaped, the helmsman eased the boat into the tight inside bend where a tiny light flickered against the dim outline of the sewerage works buildings. With his back to the tiller as he held the boat into the bend, the helmsman could feel the list as the craft answered the helm and knew that more water had drained into the bilges and a snatch with the pump would be needed at the first opportunity.

A bit of good steering was needed now for the narrow aqueduct over the River Ryton followed by a nasty outside bend was the first test of the helmsman and had to be timed to a second to avoid stemming up (hitting the bank). The aqueduct was called 'The Narrows' by generations of Worksop's bathers and just below the aqueduct was the 'Sandy Bottoms', also a favourite bathing place, as also was Kilton lock. The youthful bathers used to run the gauntlet of Hunts Field to get to these places and Harry Hunt's excitement when he chased the frightened kids earned him the nick-name of Mad Harry. Bathing was illegal, and costumes in short supply, so when the lock keeper disturbed the young swimmers, they would scatter in their nakedness, hugging their poor bits of ragged clothing as best they could. There used to be a twinkle in old Batty's eye as he pretended to be angry, just as there was in the eye of Harry Campbell who followed him. The kids were usually poor working class kids who hadn't a penny for the Baths, and the angry red-faced lock keepers and the wild gesticulating Harry were perhaps more understanding than they appeared to be. No child was summoned, none were hurt and they did have many happy 'doshes' in the cut.

Kilton lock was an easy lock, not too deep, nicely sheltered by hawthorn hedge and the boundary fence of the Manton Sports Ground and here were had our first gate to catch. To ensure a swift passage through a lock, we first made sure that the lock was ready with top gate open and as we were downgate on this occasion, the top gate would be one to be opened first. The experience of boatmen was evident on these occasions and a simple effective and proven procedure would be used. The horseman, having opened the gate would then go to the inside 'low-slide' (we called the paddles that controlled the water levels in locks—slides). There he would stand, left foot on the gate, right foot on the coping and thus straddled across the angle of gate and coping he would fit his key on the slide and watch the approaching boat. This precarious balancing act was necessary when all low slides were 'single lift' and had to be reached from the lock side in this manner. Later on, a second part was added which extended the slide gear; the slides could then be 'drawn up' by the much easier method of having both feet safely on the lock side. We had very few accidents with the older slides, you got your feet firmly planted and the only danger was if the key came off a very worn slide and you over-balanced. Sometimes we had a situation where we needed both hands on the key to have sufficient power to turn the slides, which could be very stiff to begin with and we also needed to balance our wide-stretched legs. We had a golden rule for such occasions, you never start to draw up from the top. This means you never, under any circumstances, started to wind a slide by pushing at the key with the handle at the top as this meant that, should the key slip, you fell forward—into danger. You had to make sure the key handle needed pulling from the bottom, then if anything went wrong you at least fell backwards away from the danger of bruised ribs on the slide post or worse still, a swift plunge into the lock tail. Some oversure mates did ignore the rule just as some motorist still overtake blind and both were on a good 'hiding to nowt'.

Safely balanced, with the key correctly placed, the horseman would wait to draw up; too soon and the inrush of water might cause the top gate to close itself; too late and the swinging hauling line would foul the top gate and slide. At the correct moment the slide would be drawn, the stuttering clanging of the pawl indicating the speed of the wind-up. Replacing the key safely around his neck, the horseman would nip to the top gate to prevent any movement in the inrush of water and to clear the line safely over the gate as the boat entered the lock. Now the fun would start. We had the boat actually increasing speed into the lock, sucked in by water rushing through the low slide, with the horseman walking along the lock side at the same speed as the boat with the hauling line held clear and ready for 'holding her up'. Now it was all up to the helmsman— a shake to loosen the tiller, which was then taken out and laid along the deck with the handle on the coal box, nicely out of the way of the timber heads then the gate line was readied. (The gate line was the strongest line we used, except perhaps on the occasional times we had a tow in the River Trent and used the thick heavy Bass rope coiled on the forward box.) The gate line was securely fastened to a square forged stapled fixed in the head of the stern-post and to prevent undue chafing, a short length of chain was used between the staple and the rope-eye. As the boat surged into the lock the line was deftly dropped over the upright head of the lock gate, which usually stood about two feet or so higher than the 'balance pole' joint and a swift 'bend' round the timber head instantly secured the gate to the passing boat. The open gate sat in a recess in order to be flush with the sides of the lock entrance and as the gate line tightened, the lock gate was snatched out of the recess and immediately began to swing to the closed position with the pull of the low slide and the momentum of the boat. The boatmen could time this to a second, bearing away a bit to prevent a violent jerk which could snap the gate line and lead to all sorts of trouble. Now the gate would be closing by itself tight round the boat's stern in the grip of the inrush of water caused by the drawn low-slide and the second stage of the operations began.

The gate line was now slacked off the inside timber head and swung over helm and parson keeping it as taut as possible to prevent any slack loop forming and then swiftly bent round the outside timberhead just before the gate crashed shut. As soon as the gate closed the rush of water was checked and the boat swiftly slowed down, a lot of momentum remained however and this was why the line was changed over and wound round the other timberhead. With expert ease the boatman bears away a bit and the boat was finally stopped a few inches from the low gates, a neat way of shutting the gate, stopping the boat, and saving precious minutes in the time it took to 'pen the lock'. Of course, if you were clumsy and allowed a slack loop to get nipped in between the gate and the clapstone, you had to drop the low-slide, fill the lock again and release the trapped line and waste all the time you had striven to save.

The boat, safely checked swiftly sank in the lock. (They always dropped quickly at first with the full lock exerting maximum pressure and slowed down as the pressure diminished.) During this time, if not checked, the boat would drift astern in the lock and be in danger of hanging on the sills below the heel of the top gate damaging the rudder or even worse, spring the boat, as the water level dropped. To prevent this, the man ashore having kept hold of the hauling line would wrap a couple of turns round the head of the drawn inside slide immediately the boat reached the low gates. This was called 'holding her up' and the boat could settle safely in the lock and then the second low slide would be drawn up and the boat lowered even faster. The helmsman having 'caught the top gate' would walk down the far side of the lock to give a hand opening the two low gates when ready. One more danger remained, the rope holding the boat up would tighten as the boat lowered and needed watching and easing occasionally. If this wasn't done, the boat would be held tight against the low gates which could be very dangerous. Down the edges of the low gates were stout iron straps running the full length of the gates on the inside of the lock and these protected the gates from damage by the heavy iron stembars of the boats. If a boat was held too tightly up to these iron straps then the boat could wedge itself behind the edge of one of them and as the boat dropped the slight taper of the lock sides would cause the stern to hang to the strap. This was called 'hanging her up' and the boat would be in grave danger. Old boatmen, who should know, said that it was possible to break a boat's back by hanging her up and we were always very alert to this situation. We had remedies for this, and if we saw any risk of hanging up, the low slides would be instantly dropped and if the boat didn't ease herself clear then the top slides would be drawn up and this would remove any further danger. It sounds a bit complicated but it wasn't and we safely penned the locks with the effortless ease of long practice. We didn't flush out of this lock as we were both getting aboard and old Tiger would be quite safe for the next two miles.

So we headed down clear of the Manton Sports field fence, the sky paling ahead in the east, the hob nails of the night-shift at Manton Colliery ringing out clearly as they trudged homeward along the nearby road, a rooster or two crowing in the distance. Just another boatie's dawn. Now we had time to take stock.

Scores of voyages together had dried up all subjects for conversation, we had no need to discuss the job, we knew what to do, how to do it and when to do it, so conversation was a bit limited. On coming aboard, and after safely putting the lock key on the coal box, the horseman would plunge the mop head overboard, and drawing it up on deck near the drain holes of the 'screenings' would stamp his feet in the gushing water of the mop until all the soil and clay was washed out of the nails of his boots. A swift spin of the mop and then he would dry his boots and the deck and he would be fit to walk around the 'boort'. The scrape of a match and the sudden glare as he lit a Woodbine and then: 'How's she feel young un?' I would probably reply, 'She rolled a bit in't sewerage bends, ah reckon she's got a "sop" in'. A couple more puffs at the Woodbine, the tiny hiss as the 'nub-end' was flipped over board, the rattle of the bucket and he would set off down the plankway towards the middle pump. I had heard it all so many times— the thump as he gave the 'pump-sucker' a tap, upside down, to shake out any litter, the splash of the bucket as he drew some water, the throaty rush as he emptied it into the pump, the harsh rasping as a few swift pulls primed the pump and then the even gushing as he gave her a few snatches and finally the tell-tale gulping as the bilges empty. We were dry. Coming back aft, he would neatly replace the bucket and disappear into the cabin for his second puff of a fag, as he dropped out of sight, 'I'll trim her when its light'. In the dim light of a thin ring of moon, stars paling as the dawn began to show, we moved on past 'The Willows', Manton Bridge and under the nine arches of The Viaduct down towards the 'deeps' and Turnover Bridge. We were off to a good start.

As we rounded the outside bend above the turnover bridge, a couple of taps of a heel on the decking rouses the other half of the crew. With practised ease, a spring and a knee on the hatch carlins and then upright, stepping over the headledge, his stocky figure once again strides along the gangplanks now white with frost. As the horse reached the turnover bridge, where the towpath changed sides, it turns right over the span with its low, smooth parapets, the slack line dropped in the water and was gathered in and changed to the required side of the boat as the horse turned right again and made the steep turn under the bridge and so continued along the changed towpath.

The stocky figure came aft again, this was the 'Skipper' and my brother, eight or nine years older than myself. I boated with him for some years and he had

Single lift lowgate slides at Osberton in 1958. The boatmen had to straddle the balance beam to operate them or risk a ducking! Fortunately for the modern boatmen none remain in use today.
(IWPS/CCT collection)

always been a good Skipper. He took on many unpleasant and difficult jobs, which should have been mine, and uncomplainingly 'carried me' until I knew the ropes. He wasn't a big man, but he was skilled and untiring with barrow and shovel, and handling heavy cargoes. Even after the long hours showed no signs of distress. Sadly he died too young and even today I regret I was never able to repay his unselfish attitude. Like many young people, I only realised the full extent of his thoughtfulness when it was too late.

'I've got her', meant that I could have a break. We did this when we were passing down open reaches safe for the horse and when it wasn't possible to do much else until it was fully light. A brief spell in the cabin and we reach the trees and the approaches to Osberton with its two bridges and lock. I went ashore here at the head of the rock cutting leading to Long Bridge was a 'getting off place'. This meant that if we 'held in' and then swing hard over to 'hold out' the boat's stern would, for a brief moment, be near enough to jump ashore. With the key over my shoulder, a steady jog would get me to the horse in time to lead him through the low, dark and slimy Long Bridge. A good horse would safely negotiate such bridges alone, but with heavy cargo to pull, and the tricky half light of the breaking dawn, it was always best to lead the horse through safely. I liked this rather pretty part of the canal, the old bridges, the hall stable buildings and the fine hardwoods and evergreens which gave excellent shade in extremes of weather; it always had a 'privately owned' look.

My happiest memory of hereabouts was coming upgate in the early spring and gathering bunches of the fragrant sweet violets which I knew would delight my mother. They were one of her favourite flowers and in the sheltered banks of Osberton they competed with the cheerful celandines to be the heralds of spring. The lock at Osberton was approached downgate round a sweeping outside bend and the sudden end of the trees made it a delightful setting; then it was Wilkinson's Lock soon to be Batty's Lock.

Old Man Wilkinson was a bit dour but he swept the locksides, tended a fine rustic fence of climbing roses and was proud of his lock. His length was equally well maintained and the sweeping reaches of his lower length were always tidy; but so many sharp bends that we disliked it nevertheless. The bend at the lock-tail was silted badly but we didn't flush unless we were forced; then under 'Wilkie's' strict gaze, we did it correctly.

When flushing, as in a necessity such as grounding on a badly silted lock-tail, the boat would usually be just clear of the lock. Silting of lock-tails, when it occurred, was usually clear of the lock and the actual lock-tail was kept clear of silt by the regular emptying of the lock. The worst place was usually round about where the water of the weir emptied after its journey from the lock head. We like to have a 'good old fashioned flush' and this would carry the boat over any slight silting quite successfully but at an occupied lock we needed the permission of the Keeper and a 'correct flush' was then used. To do this we closed the low gates and filled the lock. Then we would swiftly draw up a low slide (or with some help, both low slides in unison). This created a miniature tidal wave which hopefully would float the boat off again, and only one lock full of water would be used unlike the greater quantity used when 'open gate' flushing. Of course, we broke all the rules if we thought we could get away with it as we were not supposed to draw any top slides when the low gates where open. It was supposedly the cause of low sills being fouled and preventing gates closing properly and the consequent leaking gates. We ignored this rule and when needing to fill locks quickly (as was the case when travelling light downgate) we would draw one or both top slides before running to close the low gates. The low gates would then only need 'starting' and the flush would swing them to. Sometimes when two top slides were used the volume of flush would ease the low gates out of their recesses and they would close themselves before we could get to them. This they did with a mighty crash as torrents of water drove them together. I could almost sympathise with the rule makers when their fine gates were so abused.

Clear of Osberton lock we had a chance to trim before reaching the notorious 'Chequer House bends' for which the long narrow craft needed to be in perfect steering trim. I would take a shovel and under the all knowing gaze of the Skipper, shift a bit of the cargo to one side of the boat or the other, as required, until she 'laid plumb'.

The boat now pumped out, was trimmed level and approaching Adam's Bridge where the skipper steered and I nipped ashore to cope with the tight bends, we now faced between here and Chequer House Bridge. We disliked this stretch, it contained some of the worst steering in the entire canal. First a tight inside turn behind Godfrey's Farm, then the wide outside sweep of Crabtree Turn, known to local anglers as Big Bend. A welcome respite as we went down past the Flashes, that wide, reedy winding hole and into another inside turn (approximately where a new A1 road bridge spans the canal) and then the really nasty outside bend where the old Retford road touched the canal as it passed through Ranby. It was really two bends in one having a short 'rack' in its middle, and when the local smithy stood on its far bank it soon became known as Blacksmith's turn; known and disliked. A few twists behind the houses and the Chequers Public House leads us to a vicious inside turn into Chequer House Bridge, the end of bends.

In the earlier days it was probably easier to negotiate these winding turns in the canal but the silting occurring as traffic dwindled left only a narrow channel between the muddy shoulders of a waterway that was narrow to begin with. The seventy-two foot long narrow boats needed just as much room in this channel as was needed when passing other craft and when rounding the bends. The boats kept the channel passable but we were increasingly losing the battle. The channel itself varied in relation to the nature of the bed of the canal and the amount of silting and scouring to make it wide enough to get around the bends. Good skippers knew the channel like the back of their hands and would skilfully ease their craft into the bends until the precise moment came to swing hard over and 'bring her round', then with any luck a clean turn would be made. Unfortunately, a narrow boat that could turn in a really tight loop when in clear water, became completely unsteerable if it touched the shoulders of the channel. The fact was that a boat could not cut across a bend, it could only go very wide and round the full sweep of a turn. The shoulder of the channel, at the apex of the inside of a bend, was called 'the point'. If you turned too soon and touched the point with any part of the boat, then it was quite likely you would stem up. When a boat failed to negotiate a bend and ran head on into the bank it was called stemming up; any other contact with the sides of the channel was called rubbing or hanging and so if you rubbed her or hung her up in a bend, the result was usually a stem-up.

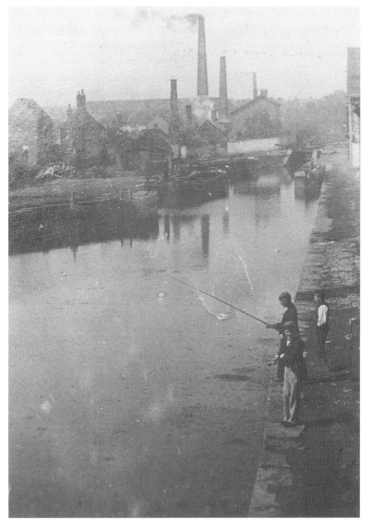

A rather indistinct but rare photograph of Retford Basin in 1899 showing a number of narrow boats moored. Spicers Paper Mill chimney is the tallest of several on view. The mill is still operational.
(Pegler collection/Bassetlaw Museum)

All this was why I went ashore at Adam's Bridge; the only other aid to steering, apart from the rudder, was good timing with the hauling line. We used to stop the horse pulling as we went into a bend and allowed the boat to slowly run into the eye of the bend. At a very precise moment, almost as it seemed the boat would stem-up, a vigorous swing of the helm, (some skippers gave repeated swings of the helm, almost using the helm as a fixed oar) coupled with a maximum effort by the horse, urged on by the man ashore, and a very tight bend could be safely rounded. We didn't like Chequer House Bridge downgate, the tight inside bend caused the line to drag the horses hindquarters towards the slimy edges of the underpass and it was a risky place to have the horse overboard. I remember several occasions when faithful old Tiger went in there.

Through the bridge we had a good section, from the tiny village school onwards and we had time to spend aboard again. I liked that little village school as it nestled on the canal side; I believe it is a private residence now. Nowadays I sometimes go fishing in this part of the canal, and a quite charming spot it is. The silence is no longer disturbed by the excited cries of school children at play, or punctuated by the compelling ring of the school bell—all that was in bygone years.

My own tender years had all the ingredients that seem often to be missing today, a comfortable home, well provided for by my father, with the day to day running in the able hands of my mother. If an infant needs a good mother, then I was indeed fortunate. Our 'Old Lady' was tireless, utterly and unselfishly dedicated to her family's well being. She is no longer with us, but my respect and gratitude for her increases over the years; it was well and truly earned. I was weaned away from all this at a small local school, along with children I knew, and in sight of my own neighbourhood. It seemed a most natural way to take the first steps in life, and the sight of empty village schools such as the one we were just passing makes me wonder if we are truly improving the quality of our way of life.

I got aboard at the bridge. Now we had time to perform odd jobs such as preparing a nose-tin of corn for the horse and bringing it aft, cleaning any mud and such from decks and walkways, and 'scutching' the cabin up, with the emptying of the ash-tin and shaking of the pegged hearthrug. We both knew that if any upgate boats of grain had reached Retford on Saturday, hereabouts would be the probably place we would meet them, and so we decided to have our 'first-bite' when we get below Forest Locks. For about a mile and a quarter we had an easy stretch, just two inside bends at each end of deep cutting. These two bends could be tricky, having the twin evils of a hard stony inside, and a wide muddy point; they were not as difficult as Blacksmith Bends but they did need a little extra care when steering round them. The top end of deep cutting was known variously to old boaties as the Barracks, or 'Diamond Skills'. I never knew how these names came about, but I do know that you could buy delightfully Pure Honey and large green duck eggs from the cottages there. We were both a little uneasy now, the chance of meeting an upgater meant it would be our turn to slack and then one of us would have to get ashore right smartly.

When boats met from opposite directions it was known as passing but when a boat overtook a slower craft it was call slacking. A few basic rules covered the situation when passing and slacking other boats. When boats were like, that is if both boats were laden or both were empty, then the downgate gave way and slacked for the upgate. Where one boat was laden and one was light, then the laden vessel gave way. It was the custom that the crew who were giving way would be responsible for a man ashore to pass the horses. If we had a situation where two boats met and the boat with the right of way had a man ashore already, then the rule was flexible and the horses were safely passed by the man already on the bank. This was accepted as a favour knowing full well that the favour would be returned on one of the many regular passings we had with each other. Also, of course, the safety of the horses was first priority and we had no silly 'who does what' attitudes.

When we rounded the inside at the bottom of deep cutting our fears were realised. Old Tiger's head came up with his ears enquiringly forward; he'd spotted something. We didn't waste time wondering, we knew one of us had to get ashore quickly, and sure enough we could now see a horse approaching from the trees at Half Moon Planting. A faint, hoarse voice shouted, 'Anybody off?' and we knew then that the coming boat had both crew members aboard and it was up to us.

When fully loaded, getting on and off the boat was restricted to locks, bridges and aqueducts and a few places where a bit of deep water lay under the bank. In this instance, we had none of these places and the only way open to us was to jump ashore. The place we were at precisely had wide muddy shoulders and it was impossible to edge her close enough to the towpath for a man to jump ashore, especially as the narrow deck gave no room for a run–up and so it had to be 'loping ashore'. This was simply a variation of a pole vault with a boat-hook for a vaulting pole which looked easy. The skipper took the boat-hook, I eased the tiller for a nudge as near to the bank as possible. With expertise the Skipper made a couple of exploratory prods to get the feel of the bottom. Deep mud was very bad for loping and you needed to know the feel of it. Then, deftly sliding the hook forward and downward, he waited for the upright position and swung himself in an arc safely onto the bank, swiftly retrieving the hook he passed it to me, truck foremost, and then ran swiftly to the converging horses. I washed all mud from the hook and replaced it in the aft box. Swift and effective, loping was the last resort when 'caught aboard'. One can easily visualise the stupid, comic situation where the man on a punt gets left hanging on his pole, that was for the funnies. We had a single golden rule for loping, you always laid your hook forward and down the side of the boat, then waited the odd second until the pole was upright; this gave time to set yourself for a spring. Because the pole was down near the side of the boat, the strong spring from the deck always carried you and the pole well past the centre upright position and you were in fact falling towards the bank—you just needed the knack! The rest was easy; the Skipper had passed horses hundreds of times. It could be tedious if the towpath was very narrow (and it was narrow in some places). All the horses had their own little habits; some would baulk, some would rush past and some weren't above having a nip at you. Our two main horses, Tiger and Ginger, had seen it all so many times and just looked bored. The actual passing was a well tried routine with few variations. The crew who were giving way were responsible for the man ashore to pass the horses. The helmsman who was giving way would hold his boat away over on the far side of the channel. The horseman held his horse as near to the hedge side of the towpath as possible and coaxed the oncoming horse past between his horse and the canal edge and then over the towing line which would be laid slack on the path. When the other horse had cleared the slack towline, the horseman would urge his horse forward to tighten up the towline. As soon as the line was tight he would stop the horse again, nip round behind the animal and uncouple the line from the strap on the cobblestick. Pulling hard on the line, he would take up the slack and swing the line into a nice straight position and then allow it to sink to the bottom of the canal, keeping a safe hold on the end of the line all the time. The right-of-way boat would be steered along the inside of the now nearly stationary give-way boat. The heavy cotton hauling lines sank quickly and the oncoming boat would usually pass safely over, then on its way unhindered. Sometimes however, the protruding lead edge of the rudder would foul the line and start to pull it from the grip of the man ashore. With a prompt grasp of the situation, the helmsman on the passing boat would swiftly reach for his short boathook, sliding this down the leading edge of his rudder and with line inwards he would push the trapped line below the rudder to safety. Sometimes this prompt action failed and then the helmsman of the stationary boat would have to go forrard and retrieve the line, and then throw the end ashore to the waiting horseman. In summer when weeds grew thick some obliging skippers would reverse the passing of the horses and carry the line over their boats instead of insisting on a sunken line. This saved the hauling line from being fouled with the heavy clogging 'flannel weed' and was appreciated by the 'give-way' Skipper. Empty boat skippers regularly allowed the 'carry-over' type of passing and this caused very little delay for either of the boats. In the few moments of passing I learned that as there were no more upgaters following; the lock at Greenmile would be full.

At Greenmile Bridge, the Skipper came aboard and I nipped ashore with the key, jogged on ahead of the boat and prepared Forest Top Lock. With gate open and inside low slide drawn, we were soon catching the gate and holding her up. Crafty old Tiger's knowing glances would be rewarded with his first tin of corn. The nose tin was hung on the horse's head and adjusted with a buckle and strap as the horse ate his way down the locks. Forest Locks were four in number; a Company stable and lock-house stands on the second lock downgate. This lock is actually called Forest Lock, hence the names of the other locks which are Forest Top Lock, Forest Middle Lock, and Forest Low Lock. Apart from a nasty inside bend below Forest Lock itself, this was a pleasant, uneventful stretch of the voyage. Safely below the locks we had a three mile pond and chance of getting a 'cup and a bite'. Kettle filled and stood on the fire, the heavy snap basket fetched aft, a quick mash, and we faced cold meat sandwiches, washed down with basins (we traditionally drank from basins, never cups) of hot tea laced with Nestle's milk. Usually we saved cooked meals for evening if we knew we would have enough time. Ladybridge, Botany Bay and Railway Bridge pass whilst we 'filled our Kite' and at the Cemetery Bridge, I had to go ashore to run ahead to Retford West Town Lock.

This lock is just below the road bridge into West Retford and on the far side was a wharf, Protestant Wharf. It was a deepish lock, with a really foul inside bend at the tail. A nasty lock to steer into upgate, but downgate we could manoeuvre quite successfully by waiting until the boat's stern was just clear of the low gates and then a good old fashioned flush would knock her round the bend. With a little care we could now negotiate the bend below Inkerman Bridge and three aqueducts where the canal goes over the River Idle and two small culverts. If we could hear the din of the old hand crane we would know a cargo was being unloaded into the company warehouse. Then the Skipper would lead Tiger carefully over the 'unloading board' which was a large wide wooden span laid across the towpath in front of the warehouse door to give a level platform for the 'running barrow' wielded by George Newstead, the silent unsmiling custodian of the warehouse. The hauling line was carried over the partially empty boat moored at the wharf and our boat had enough way on to glide slowly into the adjacent Retford Lock.

We exchanged friendly greetings with genial 'Fat-Jack' Hewitt and his mate Bob, they were hand balling (lifting by hand) the one hundredweight paper sacks of cement over the gunnel. Both were stripped off for the arduous task, having removed their waistcoats and heavy blue 'Boatman's Gansies' and tied their corduroy trouser bottoms with sack 'tiers'. With braces hung over their hips, leaving their trousers supported by wide, brass buckled belts and with the sleeves of their 'Union Jack shirts' rolled high, they were getting a 'lather on'.

The wharf was silted badly here and laden boats had very little room to adjust the position of their cargo holds to the jib of the crane or to the unloading board. If the loaded boat was downgate you had to commence unloading with the aft box and the boat could then be worked astern in the limited mooring, as the lightened boat cleared the muddy bottom. Upgate boats had to unload head first and this was the situation with Fat-Jack and his narrow boat 'Lena'. This old Skipper knew only too well the disadvantage of 'head-fost' lightening, his bilges would surely have been drained thoroughly to prevent any water running aft as the boat's head lifted and thus prevent any damage to cargo or cabin lino and carpets. This problem didn't occur with 'stern-fost' unloading because any water accumulations could be dealt with by the fore-pump in the corner of the foredeck.

The lock at Retford was a shallow affair, the top gate was a footbridge and part of a public right-of-way from Albert Road to Carolgate, and when we opened it we soon had an impatient knot of pedestrians queuing to cross over. We often had a bit of fun then—we would draw the low slides up to get a good pull and then delay the gate-catching as long as possible to build up a maximum slam as the gate crashed shut. The explosion of spray from the closure and the wet swinging gate line as we cleared it from the gate caused great alarm and despondency to the waiting pedestrians on the far side of the lock head and at times a little colourful language.

Bert Rossington was the lock-keeper at Retford, a kind, neat and obliging fellow. If we were laid at Retford and wanted to nip home on the bike, good old Bert would always care for the horse in the 'Navigation' stables next door. His wife opened her kitchen to any boatie needing drinking water and I well remember the old fashioned stone sink therein, impeccably 'stoned' clean, one cold tap, one tablet of carbolic soap and one tablet of Lilywhite Windsor soap; the place smelt clean. Old Mrs Rossington didn't know any other form of kitchen than in that primitive lock house of hers, but she didn't need any highly coloured television adverts to know how to keep it sweet and wholesome. With her home, children and husband, to me, she was typical of all that was best in the 'bad old days' or were they?

Below Retford Lock, at Crosslands Wharf on the far side, the company work-boat 'Norah' was being loaded with stone. Our deliberate flush from the lock had nearly torn them from the moorings and we were not loved—in fact we got a mouthful from the irate company men as we innocently slid by them. We would probably be unloaded by these same men tomorrow but all would be forgiven helped by a good mash or two. Through Carolgate Bridge was a 'crosscut' bridge in the towpath where an arm left the canal to the official Retford town

Looking downgate from Carolgate Bridge Retford common lies beyond the chimney on the left.
The co-lateral leads to White's Wharf. Little evidence remains of this today.
(R. Allsopp collection)

moorings, soon to be filled in and lost forever. This was Retford Common, home of fairs, feasts and sheep, horse and cattle sales. Our horses trod uneasily on these occasions, they were mistrustful of the shouts of auctioneers and the blast of steam organs. I crossed Retford Common recently but only had ghosts for company.

Gashouse Bridge takes us to a Malt kiln and wharf and a reed filled 'winding hole'. Skipper Jim Pettinger and his son were unloading barley. I believe their boat was 'Thomas and Mary' but I am not absolutely sure. For some obscure reason we called him 'Uncle Jim'. I believe my father, who was a Retford man, was a distant relation. The Skipper led Tiger over the uneven stones of the wharf and the hauling line was carried over the moored vessel. A pleasant winding section, past the Recreation Ground (the haunt of generations of Retford courting couples) we rounded into Claters Bridge and another Malt kiln. The canal hereabouts was a bit smelly from the effluent of a fellmonger's yard on the far side of the bridge and local legend spoke of huge eels in the drainage outlets! I shouldered the 'auger' many times hereabouts but I saw no evidence of these monsters. The Hop Pole Bridge was very bad to steer into upgate but we seemed to have little trouble downgate. The Old Hop Pole tavern has gone replaced by a road house of the same name and the bridge widened to road traffic. It was a narrow hazardous bridge in those days and regular accidents happened in the limited traffic of that time.

A steady sweep and we neared the first of the double locks of our trip, Whitsunday Pie Lock, known to all boatmen as 'Wisney-Pie'. Basically it needed much the same treatment as a single-pen lock and although we could still catch the topgate and we still held her up, a difference did in fact exist. The much wider lock meant that the powerful suction of the low slides was much less and having two top gates we needed to open one only. This also meant that all you could do when catching the open gate was to pull it nearly closed and then whip your gate line clear before the closing gate trapped it between its 'jaws'. This was quite satisfactory as the momentum of the boat was a fraction of that in a single lock and the strain of nearly catching the gate stopped the boat's headway sufficiently. We still held her up but this was also different. There was no danger of hanging her up by the stem-bar but in wider locks single boats tended to lay 'Katy cornered' and could still damage the helm if left uncontrolled. When we penned the double locks in pairs, the leading boat would enter through one inside gate and immediately it was inside the helmsman would push the stern of his boat across the lock as quick as possible and the following boat would enter the lock by the same single gate and ease down the side of the boat already inside. Two boats comfortably filled the lock but they still needed holding up. We could hold both boats up on one line if we wished, simply by slipping a tie round the matching timberheads of the two boats' aft decks.

Now we entered 'Nine-mile Pond', nine miles without a lock, and time once again to take stock. Soon we could expect to meet any of the Monday morning departures from West Stockwith; we could decide about a good meal; we would need to have a tin of corn ready for when we reached Clarborough Bridge; and we would plan for morning. We know we will have to 'bait' at Drakeholes tonight—we expected to get there around four or five pm. Old Tiger plodded on; he could be safely left to himself for he knew these towpaths from long experience. We ran parallel to the high railway embankment until we swung away through Bonemill Bridge and could feel the pull of the helm as Tiger eagerly headed for Clarborough Bridge. He would be a bit sulky if we didn't stop at the stable there but we had a nose tin ready for him and that would cheer him up. Landlord Jackson of the Gate Inn would make us welcome but we have a few more miles to travel yet.

Clarborough was not widely used as an overnight halt, but it had a good stable, a good pint, and was very handy at times. It was too near Retford for the upgate grain boats; the skippers and mates preferred to carry on for about another hour and a half, attracted by the picture houses and the 'chipholes' of the nearby town. It was a poor mooring, being shallow and stoney and a heavily laden boat needed a gangplank; also it was a very poor towpath there until the company built a concrete coping. An obviously reluctant Tiger, urged on by a bit of flowery language from the skipper, pulled us round Clarborough bend, a tight sweeping outside bend, into Clarborough Bridge.

Here I went ashore with his tin and with a swish of the tail and a bit of up and down with his head to get it comfortable, the old horse plodded on thinking about the nearby stables of Hayton and Clayworth.

The villages of Clarborough and Hayton had five bridges between them; they were easy bridges, Clarborough Bridge, Church Bridge, Lecture-room Bridge, Hayton Narrow Bridge and Hayton Bridge. Stabling was available at the Boat Inn at Hayton but not widely used as better moorings were available each way from here, at Clarborough and Clayworth. No navigation problems here, but it was handy for 'turning out' in the warm weather and I liked Hayton Bridge for that reason only. As we entered Hayton Bridge downgate we had to keep her wide to avoid a nasty stony shoulder just below the bridge on the inside. Old Tiger didn't hold much hope of stopping here and plodded on with Clayworth on his mind. Hayton Common and Clayworth Common were very open and exposed, bitterly cold places in winter and as we crossed through them I thought of the miserable loading place at Hayton Castle Farm. On one occasion a culvert collapsed and the fields were covered with mud and we took many loads of clay there to repair the 'bust'.

At about the place the disaster occurred we meet an upgater; fortunately a getting off place was handy, opposite Hunter's farm and I nipped ashore to slack as Jim Hewitt and the good ship 'Elsie' glided by us. Now I would have to walk with the horse to Clayworth bridge being unable to get aboard again until then.

Clayworth was a more widely used stabling than Hayton and genial Jimmy Greenan of the White Hart would welcome our custom and sell fresh hen's eggs from his poultry run nearby. It was a friendly pub and as a boy, I was fascinated by the old Gypsies who seemed to hang about this neighbourhood and frequent the pub. A lattice bridge stood at the head of a wide outside turn and an empty boat could be 'swung' there. I led a downright disgusted Tiger through the bridge. After a bit of reluctance he would now really swing the boat along as he figured that our destination had to be Drakeholes.

We knew we would have no more upgaters to meet today; old Jim Hewitt had told us he was the last, so now we could prepare for evening. The nose tin and halter 'chog' could be made ready, a pan of spuds peeled and put on the hob to simmer, the kettle filled in readiness, for we had no locks or such places where we could bump the boat enough to spill them. All was completed as we pass through Clayworth Low Bridge, Lord's Wood, Wharf Bridge and the picturesque village and bridges of Wiseton. On through Man-Face Bridge and into the gathering gloom of evening as we finally approached Drakeholes Basin, at the entrance to the tunnel, to the eerie cry of the early owls and the harsh cries of the pheasants looking for their roosts in the nearby coverts.

Tiger only needed one word of command to stop, he knew his way to the stable door at the Swan Hotel which stood dominantly on a hillside overlooking the canal at Wiseton and the wide acres of the River Idle marshes nearby. The skipper took the full nose tin and chog and followed Tiger. We would usually have a couple of extra feeds ready in a 'Chop-bag' as it was a very dark mooring in winter and we tried to save unnecessary journeys to the forrend. I would be very busy easing the boat into the wall, which formed one side of the basin and mooring, being careful to 'moor-in' or 'moor-out' to prevent the boat 'working about'. We never moored on lines that were at right-angles to the boat, the lines

Ladys Bridge or Old Man Bridge Wiseton. Wiseton Hall was the home of the Laycock family and the author recounts his chance meeting with Lady Laycock along the canal bank.
(R. Allsopp collection)

either angled towards to cargo hold (tying in) or angled towards the end of the boat (tying out). Both ends had to be the same—either both in or both out. At the stable the skipper would unyoke the horse and put a generous feed in the manger. A handful of straw would be used as an improvised brush to straighten out the scuff marks where the gears or harness had chafed the animal's sides, and the tired old nag would be left in peace with his grub. With an early tie-up we could have a relaxed meal and being the first night out, the basket would still have a wide choice to offer so a good solid meal would be enjoyed, making a satisfactory conclusion to the long winter day now drawing to its close.

Drakeholes Tunnel was reasonably straightforward to navigate. It had no towpath and the horse had to go over the top of the hill while the boat was taken through by manpower, that old and unquestionning solution to many of the problems of that time. The actual tunnel was high and wide with plenty of headroom and being perfectly straight we could plainly see the exit at the far end. The natural drift or flow of the canal helped the downgate passage and although in gloomy weather we had to feel our way a bit, we could easily manage to see in daylight hours. Going through at night time was different and then we did need a bit of light. The usual practice on these occasions was to have a cabin lamp on the foredeck; then we would rear (raise) the hatchcover against the windlass behind the light. This shielded the glare from the lamp and at the same time allowed the light to illuminate both sides of the tunnel. The helmsman aft could dimly see the outline of the tunnel, with the dark shadow of the boat just visible enough to keep her plumb in the middle. Empty boats could, and did, run about a bit when passing through, but when loaded, extreme care was taken to hug the channel especially a place just inside the tunnel top-end (upgate end).

At this place a fall of debris from the natural sandstone tunnel side had formed a hard shoulder on the outside of the channel and a loaded boat had to hold 'well in' as it picked its way through the restricted fairway. If was a nasty shock if you ran her on it without the help of a horse to ease her off again and could cause much delay. Advice sprinkled with filthy language would be given from the waiting horseman who, at the end of the tunnel, could see the problem but could do nothing about it. We had no demarcation problems as to who took her through; we were both equal to the task, loaded or light and we simply decided who was to do what as we approached the place. The traditional method of propulsion was 'launching', the boaties name for pushing boats along with a pole in a punt-like fashion. It was an easy, uncomplicated way of going through, although the deft skill of an experienced boatie probably made it look far easier than it actually was. The favourite pole on this occasion was the 'long-stower', a long, smooth pole with a 'truck' for the shoulder when pushing, a convenient hand-hold when pulling and a simple two pronged 'fork' at the business end. The fork of the stower gave a good hold when pushing and rarely slipped—with all the dangers that such an event could cause. We relied on the stower's 'bite' with absolute confidence and would 'lay our shoulder into it' right until the last second, leaving just enough time to shake it loose when retrieving. We had long boat hooks, but they had the depressing habit of getting fouled and we risked losing the lot when pushing with them; so we usually used them as they were intended—for pulling. The inside brick and natural sandstone walls of the tunnel held crevices and similar holds for the boatmen's stowers but I only used them when absolutely necessary, preferring the safer bottom of the channel for a reliable purchase. On the rare occasions I had to use the wall holds, I always gave a couple of testing jabs before I trusted myself to shoving. A few simple and sensible precautions and Drakeholes could be easily and safely negotiated; it was simply a necessary part of everyday boating. The only real boatmanship involved occurred in the actual approach and run-up at the entrances, for an efficient and business like entry was a saver of time and of great assistance to the helmsman who would be taking her through.

The downgate approach was the trickiest; here we had a full ninety degrees to turn in—about a couple of boat lengths. This was simple enough when empty, there being ample room to run the boat head right across the basin into the approach walls and yet leave plenty of time to 'swing her stern hard over' without losing much headway. The inside of the basin was itself a right angle and so the horse could do little more pulling when it reached the corner because of the angle of the horse line. It was all up to the horseman then; he would swiftly uncouple the horse line and hurry along the top wall with it, there he would speedily coil the rope in neat white loops and tidily drop the coils on the deck of the approaching boat. All he could do then was push at the passing boat for as long as possible to keep a good headway on. The helmsman would be getting set to start 'launching', the tiller would be loosened in the eye of the helm (This allowed it to rest on the 'Parson' and yet hold the helm straight) and the long stower would be unskipped ready for its purpose. I used to walk down a couple of planks, set the stower down the side of the boat and walk aft again pushing with shoulder set on the 'truck'; the steering could be corrected when I reached the deck, and the whole process repeated until we were safely through. This could not be done when a sheeted cargo was carried for the plank gangway would be down the middle of the boat; then you just had the length of the aft deck and a really long pole was an asset. Going through light and downgate was the easiest way of negotiating the tunnel. The Old Man used to say that a light boat would, 'Tek itsen through wi' a follerin' wind'.

When fully laden the operation was a bit more demanding. The heavy, deep laden boat could take no short cut across the entrance basin (as was possible when empty) and we needed to stop the horse at precisely the right time to allow the vessel to commence its right angle turn. The turn was difficult for a loaded boat in such a short space and we approached very gently, giving ample time for the horseman to coil his line and be available to fend-off if the boat's head looked like nudging the entrance walls, which was usually the case. All this was a ponderous and slower operation than the effortless entry of a light boat, and the helmsman would be working away with the stower in an effort to keep all the way on that he could—particularly as the actual tunnel archway was some distance from the end of the approach walls. The journey through when loaded was a slower, more exacting affair needing careful steering as well as more muscle power, but even then no real problem existed especially with the slow drift of the canal in your favour, it simply took a bit longer.

Where the boat emerged from the tunnel at the downgate end it was between two high embankments where the towpath was on a steep slope as it climbed up to the level of the lane which crossed over the top of the tunnel. The skipper and Tiger would come over, along the lane and await my arrival. The boat, now moving very slowly, would be placed nicely and give me time to nip forrard and cast the horse line ashore where it would be quickly coupled up to the nag and we would be under way with the long stower safely put away again.

Our arrangements for the second day of the trip were a matter of expediency. Our actual unloading place was just below the tunnel and only about a quarter of a mile below our overnight mooring. This meant we had to decide whether to hang the horse on and let him haul us the quarter mile down to the drop or leave the old nag in the stable and manhandle the boat for the short distance required. If we used the horse we would have to keep him tethered nearby while we unloaded and so have him handy for a prompt hang-on as soon as we were empty. This would be the easiest way for us and we knew that a nice sheltered corner, where Tiger would be tethered, existed at the getting-off place. The alternative to this was to leave the horse in the stable with an extra feed and have to walk back and fetch him when we needed him. I suppose the weather would determine the final choice, if it was a bitter cold day the horse would certainly be left in the warm stable.

In the event, the morning was cold but calm, and in the absence of cutting winds we knew old Tiger would be quite comfortable behind the thick sheltering hedge below the tunnel and so we decided to use the horse to take us down. Having decided, we could get the day's programme under way. No really early start was required, the company men could not arrive until the Lincolnshire Road Car bus brought them and that coupled with the walk from the nearest bus stop, could take some time. In fact, when the place of work was in an isolated place, considerable time was lost. The work force of the Company did not have the shiny selection of vans and such that we now see along the cut, the local railway and bus services were all they had. Being accustomed to early starting, the boat skippers found this type of delay very irksome. The Old Man used to go berserk when, after waiting, say a couple of hours, for the men's arrival, a breakfast halt would be taken. However, there was no alternative and so we had to put up with it. It always seemed worse to me when the few occasions arose where we were nearly unloaded and the men had to knock-off to catch the last available bus to get to their homes. We could be miles or hours away from our destination but the last bus was a real sacred cow and had to be caught—we were left holding the baby, so to speak. On this occasion we were fortunate, a bus stop existed at the tunnel head and long time wasting walks could be avoided. This still left us and the horse with ample time for a breakfast.

We were up well before daylight, a downgate empty boat had joined us at our mooring last night and the noise of its departure had roused us. The skipper would be keen to get through Gringley Lock when it was unlocked and collect another cargo for a fresh journey from the Basin at West Stockwith. My skipper would sleepily pull his clothes on, while coughing and choking from his first fag and then, without much to say, he would depart, Tiger's breakfast tin of corn slung over his shoulder. In the stable he would feed and water the horse, and then put its heavy collar on, to 'warm his shoulders'; old boaties were convinced it was best for a horse to start hauling with a warm collar. Having done this, the skipper would then get a 'scutch' of straw and wipe away any dirt on the horse's flanks that could be caused if the horse had laid in it's own mess. We used as much bedding as we could when 'suppering the horses up', but even then they always seemed to find some muck to lie in and this caused wet messy patches on flanks and hips which caked when dry and looked terrible if left untouched. At some lock-house stables, the bedding would often be canal side hay, cut, dried and collected by the lengthsman and carried to a stack near the stable in the little 'pompey' boats which most lock-keepers had in those days. This bedding was usually good herbage and the knowing old boat horses would often eat their own bed and then lie in their own muck. Still it meant that the lock keeper had a plentiful supply of good manure for his garden.

While the skipper was doing these chores, I had to get a cheery fire going, make a good strong brew of tea, get the basket fetched aft, if I had not had the foresight to bring it down the night before, and charge up (i.e., warm and fill), the heavy iron frying pan. The skipper was married and so, in theory, we were two separate units where victuals were concerned. We were also brothers, so we had no problems at all at snap-times. All food aboard was ours, not his or mine. Good home-fed bacon, very fat, and fresh eggs, hens or ducks, made a satisfying start to the day. We rarely used plates on these occasions, the pan, bulging with good hot fare, was placed in the centre of the cross-seat, and we sat either side with thick slices of bread and our 'eating irons' (knives and forks) and rapidly cleaned up the contents. The pan would be cleared complete, fat, grease, the lot. Call it nostalgia if you like, but looking back, the food seemed to have far more flavour straight out of the pan, than from today's detergent cleaned plates. Our morning tea could be a bit brutal by drawing room standards. We had a teapot on occasions, but most of my tea mashing was done by simply putting a measure of tea leaves directly into the boiling kettle. Fresh milk would not keep on board a narrowboat, so the eternal Carnation or Nestles was used. The finished product was 'hot, sweet and filthy'. The first basins of tea from the kettle would be lovely, the following top-ups would be less so from standing in the kettle; we had no supplementary hot water available and any third or fourth servings would be strong and stewed. As for food, we had little time for niceties—well cooked and plenty of it was all we needed. Long hours and plenty of fresh air provided ample sauce for the plain fare.

No time was wasted, I was taking the boat through and needed to be on my way. The skipper would have plenty of time to complete yoking the horse and bringing it over before I got the deep laden craft through the tunnel. Daylight was breaking, I didn't need the lamp forrard and accompanied by the echoing splash of the stower and the thump of nailed boots on the aft deck, I soon eased her through. When we emerged from the low end, I nipped forrard and cast the horse line ashore to the waiting skipper who promptly hung-on and soon old Tiger was snatching her downgate to the getting off place, while I replaced the stower and steadied the tiller. The corner below Drakeholes was a pleasant spot, a favourite with anglers and their wives in the 'dog-days' and well shielded from the icy blasts of winter. The skipper 'knocked off' and I let the boat drift in the channel until I could see our off-loading spot. The horse was tethered to the fence in the sheltered corner and a tin of corn was placed handy for him. His loins were covered with a thick cut open bran-bag (the large heavy bran bags were an excellent substitute for a rug) and over all this we hung a folded top cloth (the old worn sheets which we used to lay over the main covers to protect them from the wear and tear of nailed boots) which almost covered the animal except for his neck and head. Old Tiger would be comfortable and handy when we needed him. Now we 'set' the boat, with improvised stakes we 'moored-out' holding the boat as close in as the channel would allow. Next we rigged the planks, using the long planks borrowed from the Company for wheeling the ashes ashore and our own for cross-planks.

The formula for barrowing cargoes ashore was simple and well proven. We used the longest planks for a bridge ashore, then on either side of this wheeling plank, we placed two other planks across the boat, thus you could place your

Gringley Top Lock showing the winding hole which was silted up in the 1930s.
Today it has all but disappeared.
(B. Shaw collection)

barrow with wheel on the centre plank, and the barrow legs on the side cross planks. Wheeling the loaded barrow ashore was uncomplicated, all you needed was to keep your head up and match your steps to the bounce of the plank, bearing in mind that if by accident, or carelessness the barrow wheel left the plank, then you quickly let go of the barrow handles. Times many, the Old Man 'dinned' it into me, 'If the barrow goes in t'cut it's bad enough, but if the man goos in on't top of it, it's a bloody sight worse, so if you feel it gooing, let it goo!' It needed a bit of getting used to for you had to walk 'spraddled legged' on the separate cross-planks before you actually got on the wheeling plank. When we had to barrow a cargo on board it was more exacting. To begin with, it was uphill, and instead of cross-planks either side of the gangplank, we had both cross-planks on one side only. The skilful part of the operation was turning the barrow from the uphill sloping wheeling plank on to the platform of cross-planks and emptying its contents into the hold. To empty a loaded barrow from a narrow plank was simple if you knew how. All that mattered was to forget the natural way you would tip a barrow when on a wide, stable road or some such level place. On a plank you wheeled the barrow a little distance past the actual emptying point and then drew the barrow back towards you, lifting and tipping at the same time. This way the wheel hubs of the barrow would be safely on the plank even if the wheel rim edged off the plank, a combined leverage of handles and legs would easily right the barrow safely on the planks again. Simple and effective and done with unconscious ease by generations of boaties. Quickly

The Packet Inn at Misterton c1910, one time departure point for the Retford market boat, with a narrow boat probably working for Hill's unloading bricks.
(R. Allsopp collection)

we prepared for the arrival of the Company men. The kettle was swilled out and filled again, then placed on the hob to be 'singing' when the gang arrived. We always pretended we had just 'mashed' and they always pretended to be pleasantly surprised, and it made for a good start to a dreary job. We didn't just sit and wait when we had set the planks, we started unloading ourselves. This was better than hanging about and if we worked fore and aft simultaneously, the boat would be lightened evenly and also be easier to move about in when we had to spread the cargo. At last the Company men came into sight. We didn't always get the same gang so we watched with interest as they drew nearer to see who had come this time.

In common with working gangs anywhere, the canal workman had the usual mixture of attitudes to work and we knew by now the qualities of our gangs, ranging from good hard-working conscientious men, down to downright bone idle and couldn't care less types. In all fairness to them, I have to point out that they had absolutely no incentive to work any harder than necessary; no piece work, no special rates, no time bonus and in most cases they applied themselves to the job in hand with little urgency. In the total absence of any form of clothing provided by the Company, these gangs were a motley crew with garments ranging from sensible working clothes down to any cast-offs they could use and there were no two workmen dressed alike. The one thing they all had in common was the expectation of a cup of 'char' on arrival. On that day, we could count five men coming; the gang numbers varied with the requirements of other work on the canal at the time and five was a good sized crew. After a swift swig of tea, we got down to it. A gang of five meant we could have two barrows at work, with two Company 'fillers' to each and the fifth man could 'level' the cargo as we tipped it ashore. The two man crew of the boat would do the wheeling as was the custom,. The skipper and myself knew we had to empty the barrows quickly; the sooner we emptied them, the sooner they could be filled and the sooner the boat would be emptied. By dinner time we were doing all right, with the occasional interruption when we moved the boat and the men took a drag. Also a couple of Furleys empty downgaters came past, causing a bit of fancy line clearing and a bit of good-natured bad language. All in all, with the lovely rural setting and picturesquely attired gang and crew, the scene could have come straight from a Constable painting. Dinner break was a crowded affair. In rainy or cold weather, we usually invited the gang into the warm cabin and, cramped together, they would struggle with thick sandwiches and even harder with the powerful brew of tea which we offered them. The mornings work had lightened the boat considerably and, being higher in the water, we could now get snug into the bank. We could dispense with planks and barrows and the fillers would be able to throw the shovels full of ashes directly onto the towpath. While the last few hundred weights of cargo were being dealt with, I would set the gangplanks, clear the decks and pay out the horse line ready for the arrival of the skipper and Tiger from the sheltered corner. The old horse's whiskers would be 'tagged' with bran and sharps from his tins of corn and as soon as the last thankful Company man jumped ashore we would hang-on, slack-off and be away downgate; about two hours and a bit to West Stockwith.

The boat would be very untidy and our gear laid all over the place but would surge ahead nicely. Old Tiger knew where we were to an inch, he also knew that there was little chance of stopping at any other stable before we reached the Basin. He was a very good boat horse and the steady rhythmic swing of the hauling line showed he had settled down into a very good 'stroke'. We could take a last look back to the now distant Company men, scratching about, levelling the discharged cargo of ashes, as we slipped through Gringley woods. As I remember Gringley woods, I think of the lovely 'new nuts' we could gather from the canal far side in the approach to 'halfway house' (now a ruin). The media has, with cartoon-like coloured advertisements, elevated these humble nuts to 'rich protein filled hazel-nuts', but we called them New Nuts and gathered them by the handful in season.

We reached the lower end of the woods where they thinned out and allowed masses of primroses to dot the hillsides in spring. Here we passed the steam dredger, Joan, slowly and methodically ridding the canal of the massive growth of reeds and rushes which flourished here and severely restricted the channel. We greeted the engineer, Joe Gagg, and his helpers, they were doing a very good job but their efforts were very limited with the machinery at their disposal. Joe Gagg was a clean, tidy, independent sort of engineer, always wearing overalls, always clean shaven and although he was capable of smiling at any worthwhile joke, he managed to give me the impression that he would have been more at home on the footplate of a locomotive. An attendant used to sleep on the dredger when it was working, but the engineer and any other labourers would have the same inadequate transport as the gang who had just helped us unload our cargo. Sometimes, the evil looking black slime that was dredged out had to be taken to a suitable dumping ground in a couple of tenders, manhandled of course, but at this place the labourers were levelling any bushes and other growth and the mud was being deposited on the far canal bank.

We swept the hold, replaced the planks, dunnage and all loose gear in its proper place, swilled the decks and prepared to 'pen' the pair of Gringley Locks. At the Top Lock, was a lock house and stable. At the lock head was the overgrown remains of a winding hole and being the first lock for nine miles a large heap of 'rakings' from the lock head was usually stinking away on the head of the weir.

We passed the time of day with old Jack Green and his wife. We had, on occasion, been invited into his cottage when staying here overnight; the meagre, paraffin lamp lit, furnishings of that little living room made a change from our cramped cabin and a friendly game of whist could pass a pleasant hour. We were sure of huge mugs of Rowntrees Cocoa and a home-made bun or two as this generous couple liked to repay us for a few buckets of coal. Times must have been desperately hard for them on the scant lock-keeper's pay; they had so little to give but they gave what they had willingly, unhesitatingly, brooking no refusal; they were good people.

We had no time to waste; it was the wrong end of the day. Down below the lock-tail bridge we passed 'Lady Milton' an old narrowboat moored behind a small farm and owned by Fussy George Hewitt. In sultry summer days, we occasionally gave 'Old Fussy' a fry of eels; the canal hereabouts swarmed with eels and we took our toll of them with the sharp bladed auger. Old Tiger was by now really swinging along, through Middle Bridge with its cluster of cottages and round the outside bend at Hill's brickyard, into Gringley Shaw Lock. I'd delivered coal to the brickyard here and we got a friendly 'Good day!' from the yard foreman who lived hard by the lock. We penned the lock, and passed through the bridge into three mile pond. Now we completed the operation of cleaning the boat and the shades of oncoming night began to gather as we past Cocking's brickyard, Walkeringham Bridge, Narrow Bridge, Hodgson's Bridge and Fountain Hill.

As we approached Hill's Brickyard at Misterton Top Bridge, the lights were beginning to appear in the village. Round the sweeping Parsons Bends (some of us called it Howden turns), we pass the last brickyards, Misterton Bridge, Wharf Bridge, Middle Bridge and enter Misterton Top Lock with Hanson's Mill and Millpond at the far side of the lock-head. Next we had a very short pond and Misterton Low Lock. Old Tiger would now be very impatient, he could smell the stable.

We didn't let him stand at the lock-tail here, he was too restless; we kept him on the lock-side where we could control him. He knew only too well that below the lock tail road bridge was the Packet Inn, the railway bridge and almost a mile to the Basin as we entered Stockwith Puddle. We had to have a man

West Stockwith basin c1903, showing a whole variety of craft. Tomlinson's Boatyard is on the left. A narrow boat arrives from the canal direction with coal and the river lock is on the extreme right. In front of the coal carrying boat is a rare view of a tanker craft used for carrying gas tar from Retford Gasworks to Morris's Chemical Works at West Stockwith.

(Roz and Ian Davies collection)

ashore from the lock. The canal ran straight, raised on embankments at either side. It was a public right-of-way on the towing path between West Stockwith and Misterton and contained two swing-gates in its length where we had to open the gates and clear the line as the horse went through. Reaching the Basin bridge, Tiger stopped, he needed no bidding, the Skipper coiled the hauling line as the boat ran into the narrow hump-backed bridge; then, putting the neat coils on the foredeck he gave the boat a helping shove as it ran through into the basin. The horse waited impatiently, another swing-gate blocked the road into the bridge and with bit removed and reins loosened, the old nag was able to drink his fill at a little watering place just above the bridge coping.

There were two stables at the Basin, one at the Crown Inn on the bridge and one run by the Company actually on the basin-side. When the skipper and I crewed a round trip, it was customary to have 'baiting allowance'. This was the estimated cost of stabling for the trip and was based on the prevailing and accepted custom of sixpence for the stable and a bit of bedding and sixpence for a pint of beer when paying the stabling. This was the unwritten law and the landlords of the premises expected it to be put into effect. We expected to be away three nights and this meant that the Skipper would have the princely sum of three shillings baiting money given to him for the voyage. Imagine the vast field of monetary exploitation that would be open to him, the company stables were free and if we arranged to be at these places each night, well, we have money to burn. It seems a bit pathetic by today's inflationary standards, but at the time in question, the going rate for a mate was five shillings for a complete trip and his keep thrown in. We reckoned it cost one pound or perhaps one pound ten shillings ($£1.50$) to keep a horse for a week, depending on the quality of the feed stuff you used. My pay at this time was two shillings and six pence ($12^1/2$p) spending money per week. Of course I had good food, a good home, and sensible, if not expensive clothes thrown in; I was satisfied, although we nearly had a family crisis when I reached twenty years of age and demanded five shillings a week! Generally the pub stables were better accommodation than the those of the Company, with liberal bedding and we knew this only too well and so the skipper would settle for paying up and have a pint in the process. His condition when he came aboard sometimes made me dubious as to how many pints he actually did have.

Having taken the nose tin from the deck, the Skipper gave me a final push into the basin and disappeared with Tiger in the direction of the Crown Inn and its stabling. I barely had enough light to look for a mooring. Two loaded narrow boats lay just inside and I could just make out the names of them, 'Gerald' and 'Perseverence'. Their Skippers, old George Newton and his son Norman, would be going upgate very early in the morning. Old George had a heavy black horse called Paddy and true to his name he had an uncertain temperament. You had to allow for a possible nip or a 'cow-kick' when passing him on the towpath but he was a good old boat horse. Several keels lay in the basin and with the long stower I took our empty boat across the basin towards them. 'Dux' lay in front of the office, 'Energetic' lay in the 'idle-hole' and a fine 'packet' the 'Gainsborough Trader' was laid in front of the warehouse. Astern of the 'Trader' was a mooring, just in front of a moored fishing sloop which was the home of an ancient boatman who lived a hermit-like existence aboard the old vessel. It would take a bit of time to pay the stabling tonight, for the skippers would all be in the Crown Inn later.

Safely moored, a meal under way, and then a quiet word with 'Cock' Farr the lock-keeper who would know absolutely all there was to know relating to the tides etc., and when we could pen out into the tidal Trent to travel the 4½ miles to Gainsborough. We learned that the tides were 'on the make' and the morning tide was about 7 am, with a chance of a bit of a push from the Aegir size tide. This possibility meant we would have to 'lay' in the full lock until any turbulence was past, for old Cock Farr had no intention of taking any risk to the lock-gates.

There was little at West Stockwith in the way of entertainment but I always secretly liked being there. I was welcome in some of the local boatmen's homes and I had a real boyhood friendship with one two lads of my own age who lived there. The skipper would have company when he paid the stabling, for the skippers of the keels would be in the Crown. What skippers! Little Tommy Fines, 'Smiler' Sutton and 'Flaming' Herbert Barras. Such men as these were the old school of river captains, along with many more, and although I have lost touch with the River Trent, I don't think modern conditions will produce their equal again.

For detailed maps of the route, see Appendix.

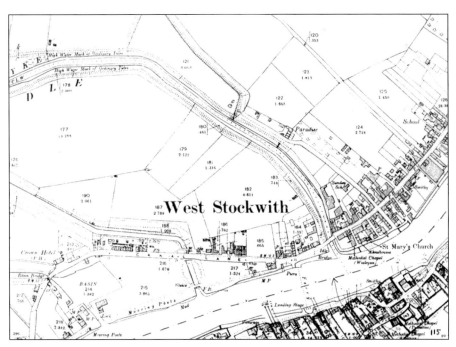

West Stockwith in 1890. The River Idle can be seen joining the River Trent on the right and the Chesterfield Canal joins via the Basin and Lock in the bottom left hand corner.

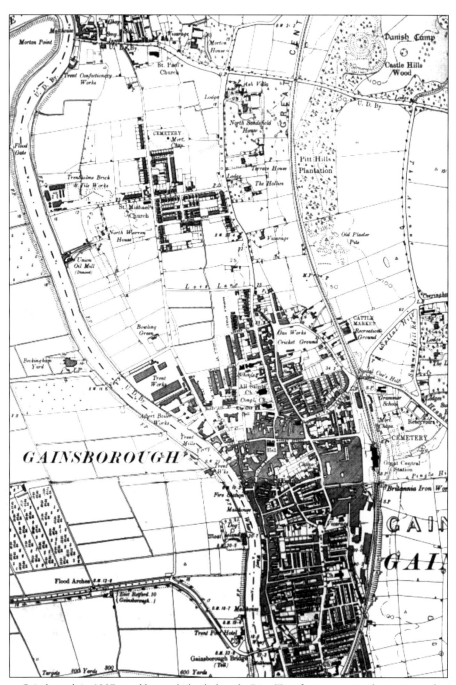

Gainsborough in 1907, an old port which relied on the River Trent for its prosperity during its growth years. The railways had an impact on the river trade but its wharves were still busy up to the 1970s. Even today commercial traffic passes through daily but few coasters or barges stop to load or unload there.

CHAPTER 5

THE TIDEWAY –
ON TO THE RIVER TRENT

Piggot's Bridge

One of the voyages which retained its interest for me long after the many repetitive trips up and down the canal had become boring with their monotony, was a trip in the Trent. This entailed passing through the Basin Lock at Stockwith and was a welcome change from the tight little channel we used most of the time. The River Trent hereabouts was tidal with all the moods of a free natural water. Placid muddy 'neaps' alternating with angry surging 'springs' and the noted 'Aegir' was only one of the many hazards; in fact we could never be sure of what we may encounter on the wide, deep, twisting river. In charge of the Basin Lock was a stocky, fussy little chap who knew everything, but everything, about the operation of this lock. We were told when to enter, what sort of tide to expect and with a check of strength and direction of wind, and an estimate of the amount of fresh water in the Trent, he would tell us to a few minutes just when the flood would arrive. His keen, searching eye noted our preparation for the trip. All our movable 'dunnage' aft in the empty boat to give the rudder more bite, long and short cratches laid fore and aft for the long oars or 'sweeps' which we used to steer the drifting boat. If anything wasn't to his liking or if we had forgotten something, he didn't come out and say so, he would observe and say, 'you'll not be taking the long chain, I see' or 'won't you need a fender then?' Whatever way he did it, you can be sure everything would be to his satisfaction before we left the shelter of the lock. We called him 'Cock' and I grew to value his help and friendship. He strutted about the lock-side and fully earned his nickname for he was a like a little Bantam Cock. He would always be waiting, and when you shouted 'lock ahoy' on your return to the lock he would be there to take your line and 'bring you up'. 'Little Cock Farr' was grievously injured when a wire hawser snapped whilst 'warping' a Humber Keel into the lock. His subsequent death left me with the memory of one of the real characters of his day. There have been other lock-keepers since Billy Farr, good ones no doubt, but the Basin Lock was never the same again without Little Cock Farr's quiet, acid, 'Gud Mawnin' young un'.

By boatie standards, 7 am was office hours and we had ample time to breakfast, feed the horse and leave extra corn for him. The skipper would probably take the horse into the basin-side Company stable, where kindly Cock Farr would keep and eye on him. To the sound of cocks crowing and all the noises of an awakening parish we would ready the boat for the Trent and our third morning under way.

It always appeared to me that no two trips in the Trent were alike; the changes of weather and tide were always ready to upset my calculations and when I first experienced these uncertainties I was fascinated and a little apprehensive, as the Old Man said, 'The Trent is no place for a numbskull'. On the canal we were at home; on the Trent, we were almost intruders. The powerful springs and feeble neaps, gave an unending variety of conditions and where we went, when we went, and how we went was dependent on the mood of this most unpredictable river. In the absence of any power of our own, the boats became dumb boats, reliant on using the natural forces of the river to navigate thereon. In my early experience, the most positive form of navigation on the River Trent was in the capable hands of the fleet of powerful tugs manned by expert skippers who knew every shoal and bend in the natural tidal sections of the waterway. On most tides, these sturdy work boats towed strings of dumb boats up and down the river in all weathers and seasons and to get a 'snig' from one of these passing tows was to me the very essence of navigation. To my canal weary eyes, laying behind one of these tows with a possible ten miles per hour or more and the turbulence of the leading boats spreading noisy, yeasty waves furiously up the muddy banks as we sped along, was poetry in motion—a glimpse into the jet age. Alas this only happened on a few occasions and usually the whole ritual of 'going outside' had to be endured.

In the absence of a tow, we had few options. The most likely would be drifting with the tide and maintaining a level of control of the boat with two large oars. These oars, one forrard and one aft, were mounted in heavy iron crutches fitted in specially sighted holes in the deck screenings. We placed 'short' crutches forward and 'long' crutches aft. We didn't actually propel the boat with the oars, what happened was that the boat had no actual headway to give a 'bite' to the helm. Skilful and energetic use of the oars were an alternative form of steering and holding the boat head-on, although we would often finish up athwarts the current when negotiating some of the wide loops of the river. A crude form of steering could be obtained by 'driving'. The old keelmasters were skilled in this form of navigation. They had plenty of practice. They also had a beautifully shaped hull, a large sensible rudder and an anchor, which could be dropped swiftly and retrieved with a powerful hand winch situated in the bows of the

A Humber Keel moored at Owston Ferry 3 miles downstream of West Stockwith
and another of the author's 'pick ups'.
(R. Allsopp collection)

craft. To such craft, driving was an art; to us, in our ill-proportioned narrow boat, driving was a poor imitation of the real thing but nevertheless we had to accept it. On big tides, the oars could be inadequate to control the narrow boat and then we needed the chain. The chain would be paid out until the heavier links were trailing on the river bed acting as a brake to the boat and the longer the trail of chain you used, the more effective was the braking. The Old Man hated chains, the rusty heavy iron links were cruel to his beautifully painted decks, screens and timberhead and left ugly scars in the woodwork. The effect of the chain was such that the boat would swing around on the 'drag' and drift along stern first, also the boat would be slowed down sufficiently for the faster flow of water to give a bite to the helm, and we would have a reverse form of steering. Crude, primitive, call it what you may, we could and did handle many cargoes in the Trent by these inelegant methods. We experimented with a home-made sail, but the inadequate nature of the gear made it of little use except during the few occasions the wind was practically 'up her arse', so we had little success to show for our efforts in that field. We envied the huge square sail of the keels with skilfully handled 'lee boards' to give a hold in the water against drifting to leeward and in the hands of the old keelmasters they were a cheap and effective form of navigation in the flat windswept reaches of the river.

We had entered West Stockwith Lock to await the tide. All was ready, any loose gear taken aft to help get as much hold on the rudder as possible, oars and crutches laid handy, chain coiled on the fore deck, heavy tow rope coiled hopefully

The River Trent at West Stockwith. One of the authors favourite craft a Humber Keel waits to enter the lock while the ferry boat can be seen moored on the Lincolnshire bank at East Stockwith.
(R. Allsopp collection)

in the fore hold with end looped around windlass stump for any eventual use, and decks cleared of any obstructions. As soon as the tidal push had passed, we dropped in the lock and as the huge low gates opened we left the tall, wet walls of the lock and with as much headway as we could get, passed out into the racing muddy River Trent. We had to get as far away from the side of the river as possible for the Trent made a wide turn hereabouts and the tide would set you into a jumble of jetties and piles in front of the old chemical works which stood on the river bank just above the bend. With any luck we would hold her plumb and as the tide veered to the Lincolnshire shore we could get her lined up to overcome the first obstacle.

When I was very young, the Old Man used to pay an old boatman to go with us on these Trent excursions and he taught us many skills which were useful to us later on. This old boatie was very tall, very thin, and very experienced and rejoiced to the name of 'Long Jack'. The Old Man paid him 'ten-bob' and he was worth every penny; he was never at a loss, saw and anticipated any snags and we profited greatly from his uncanny knowledge. His gaunt weather beaten face always held an intense, surprised sort of look and his dialogue was picturesque to say the least. All forms of breeze were called 'snarling winds', all cold mornings were 'cutting raw', big tides were 'cruel tides', little tides were 'lifeless'. He was one of a dwindling breed of river men and could have walked straight out of one of Lowry's paintings.

Today, however, we were on our own and having cleared the piles and jetties above the lock we were now all set for Gainsborough. The Trent had its own channel, the fierce tides cut and fashioned the river bed and generations of river men had to accept the natural conditions that this imposed upon them. Knowledge bred in families and handed down along with the skills of successions of boat builders, all accumulated to give us the ultimate in men and boats to navigate the river in its many seasonal moods; thus the legend of the Humber Keel was born. This fine functional craft was Queen of the River until the powerful steam and diesel engines challenged the rivers, tides and ebbs and the mighty dredgers of the sand and gravel industry and the Trent Catchment Board began to harness and control the waterway and the modern Trent navigation became possible. The hitherto inaccessible parts of the river became navigable and regular sailings were now possible using the timetable of the tides to greater effect than was ever dreamed of by the old drive and sail generations. The section of the river that I experienced was only the few miles between Gainsborough and Owston Ferry, with West Stockwith about in the middle of it. We usually collected wheat from the wharves and warehouses of Furleys, Gleadhills and Saunders at Gainsborough and from a warehouse at Owston Ferry. The wheat from the wharf of Furley & Co at Gainsborough was usually hard imported foreign grain, but the cargoes from the other warehouses were usually English wheat, grown locally and brought up by the farmers themselves to the warehouses for collection by barge.

On this occasion we were going to Saunders warehouse which was just above the old Gainsborough Toll Bridge and brought with it the hazard of having to 'shoot' the bridge to get there. We picked our way, trying to keep in the tide. Some old hands reckoned that floating driftwood indicated the main flow of the river but having seen the same driftwood hung in the willows of the riverside or on the shiny mudflats, I had my doubts about that and preferred to use what little judgement and control we had to keep in the flow. We knew it was time for the tugs to arrive, they usually came close behind the flood and although a powerless dumb boat had the right of way over engined craft, we were well aware of the urgent necessity of the long ungainly tows to be in the channel. There, they could find enough depth for the wide, deep laden string, and by so doing they had little enough room to manoeuvre if we were in the same channel. I looked aft all the time, the smoke plumes of the oil and coal fired tugs could usually be seem for miles when I was standing on the high banks of the river but from water level it was not so easy.

The Trent hereabouts is the boundary between Nottinghamshire and Lincolnshire. Just downstream, the river enters Lincolnshire and the Isle of Axholme. The wide marshy 'warpland', flat and exposed, allowed the river to wind and turn in a succession of loops, and in these waters the tugs could appear out of the blue, thus a good look-out was wise. I used to long for the appearance of these boats for a snig would mean an end of the back-breaking, slow painstaking progress we were making. Getting a tow, or snig as we called it was a fascinating experience. The tugs and their tows were always in a hurry; that was the nature of things. With a good tide under them they could travel fast and economically and naturally begrudged wasting any tide time at all. Slowing down was difficult and dangerous and any rapid slowing down was impossible. To get a snig was very uncertain but most tug masters were willing and left it to the narrow boat crew to get a line aboard the last boat of the string. This could, however, be something of a performance. It all depended on being close enough to throw the heavy noose of the towline to the crew of the end of the tow. If the skipper of the last barge was willing and if he saw our frantic signals soon enough, then he would ease the swiftly travelling craft as near as he could without upsetting the whole tow. My skipper would be awaiting the vital moment for a cast and the line he held would be carefully freed of any dangerous snags, for it would all happen any moment now. If the line was skilfully thrown, the passing crew would loop the noose over one of their timberheads and then it was all up to the skipper. The throw of the towline had to be accurate. The helmsman of the passing boat would probably have been at the tiller for hours; cold and fed up; he would probably be spragged (straddled) with his behind against the straining heavy tiller of the keel; and begrudge taking his hands out of his pockets to 'hang a bloody narrowman on'. A great number of 'probablys' and 'ifs' were involved when thumbing a lift behind the busy tows as they thrashed past and I was always thankful and surprised when we did get a hang on. The final act of the pick up was probably the most skilful and dangerous part. Although we were travelling with the tide ourselves, the speed of the passing craft almost left us standing and when the helmsman hung our noose on his timberhead the skipper would have to 'bear away' mightily to prevent the violent snatch on the line breaking the thick rope instantly. However, on this occasion, the skipper was equal to the task. Swiftly dropping a bight round the nearside fore timberhead he would take the line across the hatch and throw a bend round the fore offside timberhead and then return swiftly to the second nearside timberhead for a hold. The jerk of the pick up caused the line to fly round the timberheads but the loops acted as a brake and safety spring, the boat head would come to and a final hitch would secure the line; we were on! Now the tiller would be straining as our tiny boat bounced along in the turbulence of the towing craft. Towing empty was a lively affair, with the narrowboat vibrating to the strain of the towline. We like to tow with the heavy bass-rope; when the full length was used, the sheer weight of the line, as it rose and fell to the pull, acted as an excellent shock absorber and a delightful ride could be enjoyed.

On this end of a string we could simply follow my leader. The apparently aimless jumble of five or six keels on tow was very misleading indeed. The total length of the tow, and the often tight little bends of the channel, meant that all the skill of these shrewd helmsmen was called into play to prevent the tow 'crossing the point' or scrubbing the hard outsides of the turns; they made it look deceptively easy. A much easier tow would sometimes be available from one of the powered cargo boats that were appearing throughout the nineteen thirties in increasing numbers. If one of these craft came along without an accompanying tow it was quite simple for him to come slowly alongside and take our rope, receiving a few shillings for his trouble. This was simple and only

A superb view of the Trent steam tug Bowman hauling a string of craft past East Stockwith c1910.
The author recalls his attempts to catch a tow to Gainsborough on several occasions.
(R. Allsopp collection)

needed a captain who was willing to take us on. When towing behind a single boat we had to steer carefully, especially when loaded. If we lay immediately behind the vessel we got the full force of its powerful propeller wash and if we yawed too wide of centre we encountered the full force of the bow wave as the boat's stern pushed the waters aside. The only comfortable station was just out of line of the towing craft and in between the bow wave and the propeller wash.

That day we were unlucky, two tugs passed us: the Englishman and the Motorman, both hopelessly out of reach and we just got their swill. We were doing all right with a nice edge of tide and all we had to worry about was Morton Point and the Toll Bridge. Morton Point was a really nasty turn on the river as it flowed through the village of Morton. This hairpin bend was respected and hated by boatmen who called it 'No Man's Friend'—for obvious reasons— and here the river was a complex mixture of nips and slacks and very difficult for powerless craft. When we went down the Trent to Owston Ferry, we also had a mighty bend to negotiate and that bend was picturesquely called 'Jenny Hurn'. Boatmen called it 'Jinnyon' but it was nowhere as dangerous as No Man's Friend. We went round Morton Point, coming out athwarts the channel and almost spinning in the sucking boil which occurred on the village side; we were satisfied, a bit of pulling would line us up into Gainsborough Roads.

Watson's shipyard was the first group of commercial buildings and it stood on the Nottinghamshire bank. The working days here echoed to the clamour of rivetters' guns as they created the large iron lighters in the sheds. Gainsborough lay entirely on the Lincolnshire side and a long succession of petrol wharves,

The Aegir at Morton Corner near Gainsborough. To be avoided at all costs with a narrow boat!
(R. Allsopp collection)

mills, warehouse and general wharves glided past as we felt our way down. We often got some funny advice from keelmasters who found our tiny boat's efforts very amusing—but it was all good humoured and these same skippers would be the first to offer help if such was needed, knowing the limited capabilities of our small craft. Now we just had the three arched Toll Bridge. On big tides, a fall of six inches or more occurred as the water piled up against the restricting bridge. We chose the middle arch for on flood-tide the Lincolnshire side arch was a jumble of boil and slack water and this could be used as a holding water by boats that shot the middle arch and 'rounded up'. The warehouse where we were heading was a tall red brick building quite close to the bridge we had just passed and we had to pull with all our might to get the boat turning into the slack water and facing up the tide. It was the custom to enter moorings facing the current; to run in head-on was to invite all sorts of trouble and we never attempted to do it if any reasonable flow of tide was taking us. Once we had rounded up, the helm began to answer again and we could travel stern first and ease comfortably into the side. Old George, the warehouse foreman at Saunders was waiting for us and willingly took our line when we came near enough to throw it to him. Once this was secured we were soon safely moored.

We moored on long spring ropes holding us fore and aft and held her in on short 'warps' which could easily be adjusted when the water level altered to the tide; a number of iron rings in the warehouse walls made this possible, except on very low tides. Old George was a real character and we did things his way; it usually paid. The mooring was not a very handy place for getting ashore, except on quite high water and as George disappeared inside the building we knew exactly what to do. In preparation for loading we placed two planks athwarts the fore middle beam in order to receive the sacks of grain as they were lowered to us from the hoist box in the top of the building. Thus we would be able to load the fore box first and also the lutchet box, without having to alter our mooring. We waited patiently whilst all was made ready in the warehouse and then the long hoist chain came snaking down, empty. The unwritten rules now had to be obeyed, our collection note had to be safely folded and pushed into a chain link to be retrieved by George, who would carefully study it and decide what our requirements were. It was also the unwritten custom to hang a sack of coal on the chain as well, although there would no mention of this on our collection ticket. We knew, and Old George knew, that as the sack of coal disappeared into his little kingdom, the best of relations existed and no time would be wasted; this was very important, and, literally, in this case, time and tide wait for no one. If we missed the tide today it would not be for any lack of urgency on crafty old George's account. The first sack came plummeting down and posed exactly right for me to strike it, remove the chain and 'square the bag' for the strong shoulders of the skipper who would stow the load. This was the pattern; eighteen stones of English wheat to the sack, two sacks to the 'quarter', ninety six quarters to the load. We had one hundred and ninety two sacks to stow safely in the hold. Each sack had to be wheeled on a sack barrow to the hoist box, and then lowered down to us; there would be no time wasting tea breaks or no easing off for a fag. The bags would keep coming with steady regularity, it was a case of—square 'em, strike 'em, and keep your bloody thumb out of the chain when you 'knock the snotter off'. The tide surlily eased, paused and slowly began to ebb, and when at midday old George poked his head out of the hoist box traps and bawled 'Snap time', we only had the aft box to finish. The dinner break would be short, and we knew we needed every minute we could save, as we anxiously watched the now falling water. I nipped forrard and from the dark interior of the fore-end quickly handed out the top and bottom lashings, and as the skipper started stringing the bottom lashings I nipped aft and prepared a 'dish of tea' and some bacon sandwiches.

Sheeting down the cargo was not very easy unless you were in a lock, bridgehole or on a wharf. The dogs and hooks which held the lashings were in the gunwhale and the combing and were difficult to get at if you could not step ashore. The bottom lashings which supported the heavy tarpaulin were easy enough, you could walk on the cargo to get at the lashing dogs in the combing sides, but when the sheets were laid over the taut lashings, with the planks down the centre of the boat and then the bottom lashings over them, this formed a watershed for the covers. Ordinarily we didn't bother with the towing mast on these occasions and thus we could have a long uninterrupted gangway, from the windlass roller aft to windlass roller forrard.

After the brief dinner we soon completed loading, finished the sheeting and snugged everything down for the downtide trip. Decks cleared of all unnecessary hamper, long hook and long stower handily placed, crutches laid ready, heaving towing line coiled hopefully behind the fore windlass, and the heavy oars ready for instant use. The changed tide had taken away the slack water above the inside bridge arch and a nice easy glide invited us to a comfortable 'slack off'. So, with friendly wave to old George, we entered the Lincolnshire side span and started to get clear of the river edge and as the tide set about in the centre of the river we were soon drifting steadily past the long lines of keels which lay at the mills and warehouses of the busy Gainsborough Roads.

The broad stream of this reasonably straight section of river was just the sort of place where the tidal bore could build up and get quite a nice Aegir along here on the right tides. When the Aegir arrived; and all the skippers knew to a few minutes when it was due; the wharves and jetties along the roads would echo to the loud cries of 'Ware Aegir!' as the boatmen gave warning of the approach of the tidal wave. All that could be seen from water level as the Aegir drew near was the 'Aegir Shadow' and we soon learned to identify this after a few encounters. It was easier to spot the actual approach of the wave by following the moving turbulence in the river side, and the rise and fall of the moored craft when the Aegir lifted them as it passed below them. Today we were on a steady ebb and our slow groping progress invited further ribald advice from keelmasters and their mates who gazed in amazement at the 'Bloody Narrowmen'

At the bottom of Gainsborough Roads the tide set for the Nottinghamshire bank and we needed to hold her off or we could finish mixed up with the usual clutter of moored craft which lay off the shipyard, just below the town. We had a few hairy escapes from disaster hereabouts and were very wary of this accident zone. Safely passed the noisy shipyard we entered a deceptively peaceful looking reach where the channel wound through some shoals and back into 'No Man's Friend' or Morton Point. Many years ago I saw Frank Fox sail his boat around this bend and the degree of skill needed to handle a square sailed keel, with leeboards and all the old fashioned gear of the wooden boats, was a memory I still treasure. I believe it was the keel 'Wembley', a Lincoln boat which usually meant one hundred ton to five feet of draught.

We were running out of time now, we needed to get to West Stockwith with time in hand to make some of the canal journey homewards tonight. The long pull to Worksop was too much for one day except in emergency, and we avoided it at all times, preferring to get part of the haul completed and leave a shorter journey with a rested horse for the following morning. We had all these matters in our mind as we came out of Morton Point; the boat had held her course well and we were nicely placed, but the water was falling rapidly and the ebb was easing down. We pulled away, the Skipper aft and myself on the forrend. As I looked aft to the wide sweep of 'No Man's Friend' I could see a truly welcome sight: over the fields on the upper approach to the point I saw the foremast of a powered craft swiftly coming downstream. Very soon the bluff bows of the overtaking barge came into sight, and we could see the creamy, muddy bow wave as the powerful boat cleared the bend. The skipper and I were thinking alike, we knew we were in a very handy position for a snig, to have a powered

Gainsborough was the upstream limit of the authors trips on the River Trent.
Here barges unload cargoes at Richard Furleys wharf in 1962.
(Michael Jackson)

craft give us a tow would be the answer to all our problems. I could now make out the boat's name, 'Greendale'. We knew she was a fairly new cargo craft with a diesel engine and we could also see she was alone. I swung the noose of the tow line in the traditional signal and hoped for the best. When we were empty we could hang on to the tows as they passed by, then bear away and hold; but with a loaded boat this was almost impossible and we really needed a kind-hearted towmaster who would ease for us. I hoped the Greendale's skipper was a kind man and sure enough, the huge bow wave began to diminish and the barge came slowly alongside as its mate left the wheelhouse and came forrard to take our line. He thought Stockwith was hardly worth a tow but he took our noose, and a 'drink'. As the diesel engines began to pound we snubbed the towline across the fore timberheads and we were soon hanging on its full length as a lovely muddy wave built up round the stern—we were hung on.

To a canal boatie, particularly a horse-drawn canal boatie, surging and plunging along behind a powerful tug, with plenty of water all around us and below us was the complete opposite of normal activity. Now the boat vibrated, the helm needed full pressure from the tiller as we held our station. We rode firmly in the dead water between the prop wash and the widening bow-wave as it left the wide, strong prow of the Greendale. To my world of tiny decks and less than two

Chesterfield narrow boats on their way to Lincoln and the River Witham had to pass through the tidal lock at Torksey onto the roman Fosdyke navigation. Two empty narrow boats heading for home make ready for the tideway; one has a full mast; the other a shortened version with sail. Photograph taken c1911.

(R. Allsopp collection)

miles an hour when at full speed, the broad beam, sturdy hatch covers, windowed deck house of a fine functional powered craft such as the Greendale was the ultimate in waterway travelling. Such vessels made the Trent their servant with the powerful tides just being their timetable and being able to come and go when and where they wished. I had a love-hate relationship with the old Trent of pre-war days, I liked to get into the river and then was glad to get out of it again and I never became a proficient 'Trentman'. It was a humbling kind of situation, always liable to surprise, both kind and often cruel. When very young I was fascinated and at the same time apprehensive whenever I sailed thereon, and if anyone were to ask me to recall any highlights of my limited experience, then being in tow behind a good tug would be the top of my list.

The saddest memory of those occasions was the run of salmon on certain tides, and seeing these lordly creatures dying in the suspended mud and pollution in the waters they swam in. Their dead bodies stranded on the mud or hung in the fringe willows at the mercy of carrion, was a depressing monument to the days when salmon swarmed the river in their breeding migrations. Old hands told me that the suspended warp clogged their gills and slowly killed them, what was known as 'slotting' and the afflicted fish would sometimes feebly swim on the surface and be greedily hunted by all and sundry. I don't know if any of these lovely fish ever get up the river nowadays, but being an angler of many years standing I know the river has less pollution today. No wonder the Old Man used to say, 'The world must have been a lovely place before they put men on it'.

The skipper of the Greendale knew his stuff, he also knew our problem when we reached West Stockwith. We had passed Halfway Farm, Walkerwith Rack, Walkerwith Ferry and the derelict chimney stacks of the old chemical works were in sight; we were nearly there, soon we would be on our own again. At the start of Stockwith Bight, the tide changed sides again and set square into the moorings of the Northern Jetty and the old works. With fine judgement the kindly tugmaster knocked us off and we hauled in the heavy soaked towline as our boat headed into the bend above the Basin Lock. We had to round up, and we also had to slow down. The chain lay ready for such occasions and we paid the heavy rusty links over the side and as they bit, the boat began to come about and soon we were answering the helm again as we eased into the bank and shouting 'Lock Ahoy'.

Little 'Cock' Farr didn't need any warning, his stocky little figure was already coming along the river bank lane and he quickly took our thrown line and snubbed it around one of the posts placed for that purpose on the approaches to the lock-tail. Bearing steadily away we came to rest at the lock steps and got the muddy wet chain in; all we had to do was 'pen' in the lock and a glance at the water level assured us we had plenty of water in. On either side of the lock-tail stood a hand windlass and one of them would be used to square us into the lock. We took the windlass wire from the lock keeper, hung it round our aft timberhead and eased the boat downstream until its head was across the gap of the lock. We then pushed the stern out with the stower until the nose of the boat began to turn into the lock and the windlass wire tightened and began to haul the boat stern out square to the tide whilst the Skipper and I were easing the head of the boat into the lock tail and trying to prevent any twisting. Old Cock Farr was used to warping fully laden keels into the lock and our toy boat gave him no worries. We were soon in the lock and the tall gates closing behind us as we took our last glimpse of the muddy river through the narrowing gap as the gates met. A part slide was drawn, a full slide gave too much turbulence around our narrow hull and as the water level rose we were coming back to green water, the smell of weed and the narrow confines of the waters for which we were designed. The lucky tow had saved us a valuable hour or so and meant we could hang on and take the first few miles of our homeward trip. We needed a loaf of bread and a tin of Nestles milk; I launched the boat across the basin into the 'puddle bridgehole' and nipped down the village street to the little provisions shop in Chesterfield Terrace where I secretly hoped I would be served by the proprietor's daughter—all the boat lads hoped for that. Mr Redfern was a nice old gentleman, but his daughter Ruth was preferred when we needed serving. She was a pretty young lady and did eventually marry a boatman.

I recently met two fine young men in the Crown at West Stockwith and they introduced themselves to me. They were the sons of pretty Ruth Redfern and the last time I saw them they were little tots playing on the deck of their father's boat and as one would almost expect in the children of such nice parents, they were a credit to their family. It felt really good to be remembered by them.

Back at the bridge the Skipper and Tiger were ready, the old horse was taking a drink at the tiny drinking place above the bridge, he knew we would be going home. He knew it was little use sniffing at any of the stables along the upgate trip, we were going home.

Bracebridge Lock

CHAPTER 6

UPGATE OR GOING UP – THE TRIP HOME

Forest Low Lock

The skipper decided to walk; along the straight line of the puddle bank were two swing gates and these had to be held open for the horse's passage, also the hauling line needed lifting over the gate posts and so someone had to be ashore. As the basin bridge receded into the distance we turned our attention to the long haul home.

'Going up' was the boatman's name for upgate trips and the conditions when going up were less favourable than when going down. The steady natural flow of the canal was against you, no friendly drawn slide could pull you swiftly into the locks, and no time saving gate catching was possible. The poor old nag had to haul the boat almost up to the top gates of the locks and all that with the line chafing the copings of the lock side; in fact, we were against the fall of the canal and it was 'collar work' all the way. The time saved in the Trent meant we could clear Gringley Lock, which was closed to traffic at 6.00 pm. As we retraced our downgate journey we penned the two Misterton Locks, and had a mash and a jam pasty whilst passing the wide sweep of Oldham Turns and the Misterton brickyards. We had decided to push on as far as light would allow and have a good feed when we tied up. We washed away the last traces of Trent mud, checked the cargo covers which we had so hastily laid at Gainsborough and as we glided past Walkeringham and Fountain Hill, we had become a canal narrow boat again.

As we passed California Gate and neared Gringley Shaw Lock, the skipper took the key and jumped ashore; a scour on the inside meant we could hold well in and get ashore about one hundred and fifty yards below the lock bridge. The lock was empty and as we entered it the 'finishing bell' rang out from the adjacent Hill's Brickyard, where Foreman George Montague would be signalling to his labourers the welcome arrival of knocking off time. We could see the small group of workers leaving the sheds and kilns and I envied them their fireside and slippers as they departed. The thought of their lighted cottages and three valve wireless sets made our journey into the coming night seem very uninviting. The dusk began to gather as we went through Gringley Middle Bridge past old Paul Thompson's work sheds and cottage, with an Alberic Barbrier climbing rose on its porch, and on into Gringley Lock. The Skipper reckoned we had about enough light to make Drakeholes and I reckoned we could tie up at the lock and make an early 'hang on' in the morning. He was thinking of the pub at the tunnel, and visiting the pub to pay the baiting fee; I was thinking of my dinner, and a game of cards with a mug of cocoa in the little spartan living room of the lock-keeper's cottage. The Skipper, and common sense prevailed; after all, didn't the Old Man always tell us, 'An hour at night is worth two hours in the morning'. So we kept going.

We exchanged a few snippets of news with old Jack Green the lock-keeper, and his wife, for we hadn't seen a newspaper since the 'New of the World' last Sunday and then it was on our way. The Old Man used to read the 'News of the World' avidly, although it was a long time before I found out why he called it the 'Scoutmasters' Peril'. I eventually reasoned that the amazing adventures of lovely ladies and schoolmasters, parsons and scoutmasters, of 'innocent' girls and weird young men, together with all the suggestive details must have helped it to earn the title.

Old Tiger was really getting into his stride now, he knew what was on and whilst I lurked in the cabin preparing our meal, the Skipper thumped about on deck, a Woodbine in his mouth, steadying the tiller with his buttocks. On these occasions, he would sometimes sing. He wasn't a very good singer, usually well out of tune; he had a bit of difficulty with any but the most simple of melodies and if you allowed for an out of tune refrain, and a really weird ad lib of words, it wasn't too bad. I suppose the still of nightfall, and the echoing woods and hedges gave a sort of 'singing in the bath' quality. He knew a few Victorian music hall songs and a couple of hymns. I well remember the sad song about 'You're going to leave the old home Jim' and 'Her golden hair was hanging down her back'. These and 'The Miners' Dream of Home' were his limit but he sometimes got carried away and implored anyone within earshot to 'Count your blessings, count them one by one'.

By now we were near to the newly-laid ashes on the towpath where we had unloaded on Tuesday, the dusk was deepening and the trees emphasised the gloom. The Skipper got me on deck to get my eyesight. 'I'll take her through', he said, 'and we'll need the lamp'. We had some daylight left but the tunnel would be pretty dark. He took the old cabin cum stable lamp forrard and rearing the fore-hatch against the windlass he stood the lighted lamp in front of it. The feeble gleam scarcely showed in the half-light, but shaded by the hatch the light would be very welcome in the tunnel. With practised ease the skipper swung the boat's stern into the getting off place and I nipped ashore. I overtook Tiger and held his head as we climbed the greasy, stony slope up to the tunnel end. A post and rail fence enclosed the sheer brick walls of the tunnel arch and I urged the old horse on to give the boat a good start into the tunnel. At the last moment I stopped the horse and slipped the hauling line out of the strop. I climbed the fence clearing the line as I did so, and then, directly over the centre of the tunnel arch, neatly coiled the line and picking up the coils and deftly dropped the line on to the fore box covers of the boat, being careful not to disturb the lamp on the foredeck. We could very accurately place the line aboard with all the practice we got and the skipper could get on with pushing the boat through.

Tiger had gone—he knew where the stable was, but I hurried after him to lead him over the road in the poor light. We went straight to the stable and picked a clean standing, the heavy, long gears were removed, the cumbersome collar and harness slipped from his head and a good scuff down with a twist of straw, soon removed the rub marks of the traces and any mud from his legs. The Skipper arrived complete with lamp and nose tin, and I went back aboard to get the dinner completed. Another day was ending; pleasantly full of food from the now depleted basket, we lay on the side-seats, using coats for pillows and looking at the flickering firelight. After a fair 'lay down', the Skipper had a swill and a shave, a pan of hot water on the stove, bucket, towel and soap box ready. The Skipper didn't like shaving in the primitive conditions of the cabin, with the poor light and badly spotted mirror and left his beard until he looked a real villain. Tonight it was necessary; in the lighted tap-room with clean muffler hiding his soiled shirt, and his spare jacket on he would enjoy the company and the drink. He had never lived it up, fifty bob a week didn't make for a full social life and a glass with a few locals was his idea of a night out. I had a swill, scutched the cabin up, made the bed and then it would have to be sleep or an old Western magazine; usually sleep won. The long day and hot meal all added up to a good night's rest. We could be worse off, we were dry, warm and tied up. If the sky had been clear and freezing weather had been with us, then we would not have dared to tie-up early and would probably have still been hauling, cold and fed-up.

Somewhat later, a few bumps and a whiff of beer and baccy smoke, the skipper came aboard. He'd suppered old Tiger up and was soon in bed where we lay in inky velvet darkness with only the faint cry of a wild creature to disturb our slumber. We did not overlay; we were on the last day and just about eleven hours from home. We didn't need a modern computer to tell us that a five am hang on would, with good luck, put us into Piggot's Bridge by four pm.

The stillness and peace of a winter morning was around us when we awoke and we could see the glitter of frosty rime when we pushed the hatch back. When we moored at lock-tails or lock-heads, we had the characteristic hiss of water leaking through the gates under pressure, or the chuckle of clean water as it fell over the weir cill and gleefully hurried through the stones below. I say clean water deliberately for in the lower reaches of the canal we could, and did, dip the kettle overside for a fill-up when the water can was low.

On one never-to-be-forgotten occasion, when my mother was with us, we filled the kettle from the canal. At home my mother's sink was spotless, rubbing-stoned around the stonework, clean scrubbing bushes reared up to drain and dry and large red chunks of carbolic soap cut from the large blocks you could then buy. She immediately set about thoroughly cleaning the kettle, and when this was done to her satisfaction she said we would mash when we could get some 'proper' water. We were near to our destination, the slipway in Stockwith Basin, and when we moored there my mother asked a boatyard worker if he would fill the kettle for her. 'Certainly missus' said the obliging boatyard worker and carefully finding a space clear of floating weed, he dipped the kettle in the basin, swilling it out and then filled it. Handing the filled kettle to my mother he said, 'Here you are missus, you'll find that's the best watter for miles around here'.

In the stillness of moorings such as we were in at Drakeholes, you could 'hear the silence'. Conversations tended to be almost whispered and the thump of the hatch, or footfalls on the stone copings seemed to be magnified. When an empty boat was laid on a hard mooring any breeze would cause muffled bumps in the night, or when loadened, the protesting rubbing and creaking of the mooring lines made strange noises. Heavy raindrops spattering the deck timbers only seemed to make our spartan bed feel more comfortable and snug. These sounds were natural background noises, we would have found their absence more disturbing than their presence. The peace and quiet so eagerly sought after by people today was all around us in the 'boaties' dawn' and our first disturbance would be the crow of a barnyard rooster, who would in turn wake up the fields with the liquid notes of blackbirds and song thrushes.

In the little cabin the morning ritual began. We had an unwritten agreement: on cold days, one of us made the fire and mashed and the other went and yoked the horse, so when the skipper nudged me and said, 'What are you doin' then?' I knew I had the choice. Grudgingly I climbed out of the warm bunk bed, raked the stove, dry sticks and a shovel of coal were handy, having been prepared last thing along with a full kettle. A roaring blaze was soon going up the chimney with the help of the draw plate and I silently and sullenly dressed. The Skipper equally sullen joined me and I suppose he had a bit of a thick-head from the previous evening. Silently he dressed and then, pushing the hatch back, departed with the nose-tin containing a bit of extra good feed to get old Tiger in the right mood. I could hear the echoes of the Skipper's violent coughing and spluttering as he 'enjoyed' his first fag. Soon he returned and thankfully sipped a basin of traditional hot sweet and filthy tea while he gave the horse time to finish his feed and get his collar warm. Our conversation was very limited, 'I'll fetch him, get her head up' was my instruction. This meant the skipper was fetching the horse and I had to get the boat out of the right angle of the mooring and head her up the channel. We could let the horse heave the boat round whilst we bore away on the mooring line aft, but valuable time could be saved by manhandling her out and getting the line ashore ready. I would get my eyesight as I performed the task and be ready for steering the boat in the gloomy dark of the pre-dawn. Then came the jangle of harness chain and the snorting of the horse as he cleared his

West Stockwith Lock and Lock Keepers House in 1954.
(Bassetlaw Museum)

147

nostrils of the remains of the bran and oats of his recent feed, and as the Wiseton clock chimed 'five of a morning' we were all well and heading home as our night's mooring receded into the inky shadows

We now had to see Tiger clear of the Wiseton bridges and then it would be breakfast from our now sadly depleted basket. I disliked the first hour or two on these occasions, the darkness, the cold and the slow progress through the Wiseton Estate. It was much better in the summer when the dawn could be the best part of the day, in fact in June I actually, if reluctantly, enjoyed the awakening day, especially in reaches such as Wiseton, Gringley and Osberton, where the dawn chorus was a sound never to be forgotten. It is always a surprise to me nowadays when I actually meet people who have never heard of this delightful natural phenomena. Man Face bridge, Wiseton bridge and then Wharf bridge, the cold sound of Wiseton clock emphasising the darkness with its quarterly signals and the lights appearing in the windows of cottages and farmsteads, made the deck seem smaller and less inviting as I stood with collar up, hands jammed in pockets and steadied the tiller by putting my buttocks against it as I peered ahead into the gloom. Tiger would be all right now so the skipper got aboard forrard at Wharf Bridge and as he came aft with the snap basket, he said, 'Do what you can with what's left young un'. We had nice time through Lords Wood, Clayworth Low Bridge and up to Otters Bridge to have our breakfast. At Otters Bridge which stands in front of what is now Royston Manor, I nipped ashore with the tin and as Tiger had his breakfast, the dawn revealed Clayworth Village and the open sweeping marshes that stretched away to Daneshill and beyond.

The White Hart bridge Clayworth, formerly a swing bridge, the present bridge was built in 1890 when the Inn effectively lost one story behind the ramp of the new bridge.
(R. Allsopp collection)

Clayworth Bridge upgate needed careful steering for it was in a sweeping outside bend and we had to let the stern just clear the far side of the bridgehole before we gave her all the helm. Old Landlord Greenan was feeding his hens in the natural range below the bridge and he did manage a grunt in reply to our Good Mornings; he was a decent landlord but a bit dour. Through the bridge we faced Clayworth Common, a thankless place in winter, very exposed and very cold and with being able to see quite a distance ahead, it seemed to make our progress even slower than it really was. We expected to meet other boats along here, for it was about time for boats which had lain at Retford overnight to get below Hayton. Old Tiger spotted them first, head up and ears forward he could see horses coming and soon we had to get ready to slack. The skipper loped ashore and hurried after the horse. Two narrow boats came by us, George and 'Biddy' Wolfenden and their boats 'Elsie' and 'Pride'. With other news and bits of gossip, we learned that Albert Pettinger and his wife were not far behind them with 'Ruth' and a cargo of coal for Wiseton Estate. When we met them it would be their turn to slack for an upgate boat and as we went by Crowtree, we could see them approaching. Although in theory they should have been ashore to slack for us, in this instance we had a man ashore. Albert Pettinger was an obliging chap, so the skipper did the horse work and saw Tiger safely over the line whilst he held the head of Kit, the reliable mare that had pulled Pettinger's boat for as long as I could remember. More friendly greetings, more news and as the boats drew apart we approached Hayton weir and Hayton bridge.

Albert Pettinger and his wife with their old mare Kit were of the best of the old style boaties. Other husband and wife crews existed but I remember them most vividly for some reason or other. I remember tall, good humoured George Clifton and his fussy little wife Nellie, but when I think of them it is always of Nellie's home made wine, or the day she fell in the cut in front of the Albion Mill at Worksop. I also recollect Pierce Hindley and his wife Millie. Pierce was a very good man with boats and particularly good with horses but he had little patience and I remember him mainly for his quick temper when all was not to his liking and of course, his loud and extremely varied range of vocabulary on these occasions! Other brief memories exist of family crews but they require conscious thought to remember them. Not so with Albert Pettinger and his wife, even today after nearly forty years, I find my thoughts turn to them on occasions. Albert and boating seemed to be well suited, I never saw him excited or dejected at any time and I envied him his seeming air of contentment with his lot. He and his wife were my idea of a good crew. His wife was a very capable lady and I can only remember her with gratitude for her kindness to me whenever I was at West Stockwith over the weekend—where they lived. I was not asked out to dinner and tea—I was simply informed of the times of these meals and told not to be late.

The voyage on which we were engaged had reached what I used to call the 'dead stage'. We had met all our deadlines, delivered one cargo, collected another and all we had left to do was to get home. I unashamedly looked forward to tying up at 'Wossup' and that very fact made the last fifteen or so miles seem endless. The repetitive nature of our work seemed most frustrating during this end of the journey.

By now the day was well under way, the farmers and other canal side dwellers were appearing and we exchanged greetings and scandal whenever we could, often having to shout to do so. I was always impressed by the number of people who enquired after my father and it seemed to my youthful wonder that everybody knew 'Kingy' Clark. I marvelled at the number of privileges, the number of doors that were opened, simply because I was 'Kingy Clark's owd boy'. I was very confused, could we be talking about the same man? Could they really mean the loud-mouthed dictator, with little patience to speak of, who's one pleasure seemed to be finding fresh jobs for me to do, who commanded, never asked? Yet it was so. He was obviously well known, well liked, and I must have got my juvenile priorities and values all mixed up.

Old Tiger was quietly but effectively warming to his task, his stroke, never a bad one, was now definitely a 'let's get home' effort. Our boat, the good ship, Clarice, was one that would follow a horse and so with handy boat and willing horse, we were progressing in as good a fashion as was possible. We carefully evaded the hard stony shoal on the downgate inside of Hayton Bridge, carefully avoided twisting in Hayton Narrow bridge, quietly swept through Lecture Rooms Bridge and Church Bridge and confidently held in at the right moment to take the sweeping outside bend of Clarborough Bridge and then on past the Gate Inn. All the going hereabouts was easy, nice straight racks to steer along as we passed Bonemill Bridge and into the shade of the high railway embankment as we neared the last double lock upgate.

Above Whitsunday Pie Lock the channel was a tortuous procession of in and out bends which included a vicious inside bend approach to the Hop Pole Bridge. As we quietly lifted in the lock we put a tin of corn up for Tiger; this would slow the old nag down as he eagerly munched the contents and make steering that little bit easier in the coming reach. One hour to Retford, then six hours to 'Wossup', that's how we saw it as we carefully felt our way into Hop Pole bridge, eased her gently round by the Maltkilns, Claters Bridge, the Recreation Ground, around Gas-house Bend, through Gas-house Bridge, past the 'Packet' and on to Retford Common. We had no problems with our progress except for the occasional downgater and with the ease of long practice we took Carolgate Bridge with it's tight outside bend, and lined up for Retford Lock tail. Retford Lock was a shallow affair and we didn't want to hang about, for this narrow lock was the start of the last leg. We decided we had enough snap to do us, so we didn't need to visit the local shops. We got a bit of news, scandal and perhaps a laugh from George Newstead and Bert Rossington, the Warehouseman and the Lock keeper at Retford, whilst the usual impatient, amused or just plain curious, bunch of pedestrians waited to cross the footbridge of the top gate, which was a public right of way.

As we entered the first of the three aqueducts above Retford Lock, the chimes of the Town Hall clock rang out the hour. Ten o'clock on a fine dry morning, we were bang on time and as the Old Man would have put it, 'Piggot's Bridge afore four o'clock wi' the Grace of God, and a strong cramp'. The three aqueducts were tedious, their narrow passage hindered our progress, checking the boat as the water boiled and sucked its way round us in the little space available between the hull and the sides. We heartily hated such places and apart from the hindrance to laden craft, we had to be extremely careful when travelling light. It was not in the nature of an empty boat to travel in a straight line, in fact it often went considerable distances with a definite diagonal attitude. When narrow openings were ahead, such as bridges, aqueducts and lock tails, then we were obliged to run her head up away from the pull of the line, and at the precise moment drop her down straight into the gap. Failure to do this was the damaging 'twisting' that occurred when the boat was not into line. A collision could do varying amounts of damage, but most boaties thought twisting created a serious strain on the long, vulnerable sides of the boat. Woe betide anyone who twisted her when the Old Man was present.

The entrance to the low gates at West Town Lock were a fitting end to this pond, with its three aqueducts and a really tight inside bend made the lock tail very tedious. When upgate, we had no helpful flush to swing us round, and all we could do was inch our way in knowing only too well that if we went too soon we would catch the point or if we left it too long we would likely stem up; in short it was a cruel lock tail needing very precise navigation.

Above West Town Lock was a different world. The peaceful West Town Bridge opened on to a tree hung winding hole and the start of a very sheltered reach. A nice rack led us by the cemetery boundary and through a neatly built footbridge which served the burial ground. The inside bend at this bridge was misleading to the uninitiated for if you let her go too far in, you got a right solid shuddering bump as her stern hit the coping and probably laid her onto the inside shoulder for a length or two. All along here and through the sturdy Railway Bridge and beyond to Botany Bay with its farm and shading woods, the canal had a sheltered almost landscaped appearance. The Old Man used to reckon it was a 'Top-coort warmer here'. This effect soon disappeared as we entered the high embanked rack at Babworth, the scene of a disastrous burst when the culvert, which allowed a stream from Babworth Lake to pass under the canal, collapsed and let the canal empty itself into the meadows below. Beyond here we have a generous wide sweep of a bend; Babworth Turn and a nice run up to Lady Bridge, favoured haunt of fine fat Chub, and the many anglers who attempted to catch them. A deep wood shaded the far side for a short length and then we were in open country again. In times of gales, this was a noted black spot for empty boats, for the high winds which cut round the woods veered directly across the line of the canal and played havoc with the steering of the boat. An empty boat had a high, long freeboard and very little draught. If you let her 'get down' you could travel quite a distance grinding on the stones and gravel of the inside bank, also doing quite a bit of damage to the bottom spikes, besides possibly lifting the helm off. The only answer to a cross wind was to increase speed and thus give firmer steerage. I always found this very upsetting for we would have to whip the unfortunate horse into a lather to get enough way on. In most cases, the horse was a willing animal anyway, and it seemed especially cruel to have to abuse him further.

The four Forest Locks were handily placed, and apart from the time we begrudged losing as we penned them, they were reasonably easy. Low Lock and Middle Lock were on comfortable racks but Forest Lock itself had a badly silted inside bend, just below where an unusually long weir emptied into the main channel. This bend had the twin evils of a hard inside and a big muddy point on the outside; consequently the bed was treated with great respect by the helmsmen. Forest Lock had a lockhouse, a stable and a pump of lovely clear water where we could replenish our cans. In late spring, the smell of manure, weed and a bank of purple lilacs gave this lock an atmosphere of its own. As a very young lad, this was known to me as Wakefield's Lock, but now it was Wass's. Joe Wass was in my mind the tidiest, neatest lock keeper on the whole canal. The start and finish of his length were obvious to anyone who travelled thereon. The hedges were expertly and immaculately brushed with razor sharp hedge knife, the banks were regularly mown on both sides of the canal, no choking reed beds were allowed to develop and his slides were always well oiled. He was his own man and needed little supervision, a relic of the days when 'the job came fost'

Barnby Moor Bridge could be nasty. Great care was needed as the boat emerged upgate because of a very hard shoulder on an inside bend, and the narrow opening of the bridge made the positioning of the boat's approach to the bend very tricky, requiring fine judgement. Well-tended cottage gardens lined the far side as we passed a winding hole and entered Forest Top Lock. This lock, known to us as Greenmile Lock, had memories for me of the Greenmile Trips of childhood which I recounted in Chapter 3. This was where we swung the boat and rested in the lock whilst the boat load of trippers we had unloaded at Greenmile Bridge enjoyed themselves in the pleasant rural peace of the grassy space. Two farm cottages and some delightfully shading trees were there then. We weren't too worried about 'Clarkie's Trip to Greenmile' we had fed old Tiger up the locks and now we had time for our snap before we reached the heartily disliked Chequer House bends once again. We usually finished off all that we left edible in the basket at this, our last meal of the trip. Our healthy young appetites knew no bounds and if the remains of our victuals were not a culinary balance, well so be it, we were still in the happy times when we could 'eat owt and be glad of it'.

There were only two bits of fancy steering at each end of the deep cutting, otherwise we had a clear run to Chequer House bridge. The basket would be left aft this time and finishing our meal, in our turn, we faced going ashore and the last obstacle—the tortuous reach up to Adams Bridge. I went ashore, the Skipper's superiority was needed at the helm. I would handle Tiger in the necessary manoeuvres needed when deep laden in these difficult bends. With a mixture of skill, brute strength and some excited instructions from the skipper about handling the horse, we painstakingly crawled round the series of ins and outs, thankfully gliding into the shade of Crabtree Farm; the worst was over.

The run up to Osberton Lock is reminiscent of Wiseton with its park-like character; it was a nice feeling. We would soon be seeing Manton Pit chimney and again hear the nailed colliers' boots on Retford Road. Osberton Lock was 'Wilkinson's Lock' and had now become 'Batty's Lock'. Tall, lean and friendly Jack Batty was a good lengthsman, as was his brother Joe at Hayton. Both men were able to supply a few good free-range hen eggs and we tried to be especially nice to them. It was a pleasant unspoiled lock and lock-house then and in the winter gales we welcomed the shade of the stands of hardwoods and the brief respite from the buffeting of the open country downstream. It was a quarter past one with the Hall clock as we slid through Osberton Hall Bridge and the adjacent Long Bridge. We were well up on time—good old Tiger—the faithful old horse was now really showing his paces. He had been pawing at the ground and difficult to restrain at Osberton Lock and he could smell the stable. We had just time to get shipshape again, lines tidied, covers swept and if needed, washed, decks would get a really good swill, cabin and fore end tidied and a thoroughly tight boat would be ready for inspection if the Old Man happened to be waiting our arrival. He still had a keen eye and a ready tongue and we were very careful to arouse his hair trigger temper. All these chores saw us safely through Turnover Bridge and the Railway Viaduct along with the Willows Bridge and we eased the boat round the gentle bends in the shade of the delightful stackyard and sheltering elms of Manton Farm. Abreast of Manton Pit; Worksop people on the road; Tiger making the tiller swing with the urgency of his effort, I could

Retford Town Lock upgate from the basin c1920. The wharf and crane referred to by the author are on the left of the photograph. The toll house and lock keepers house is also on the left while the house on the right was occupied by the wharfinger. Also shown is the ex Manchester, Sheffield and Lincolnshire Railway Co's No. 1 dredger and a maintenance boat.
(R. Allsopp collection)

almost smell my mother's cooking. I unashamedly liked to get home again, to chairs and tables, clean dry clothes and being waited upon. I suppose we need Empire builders, giants among men, captains of commerce but I thought my Mother's remark about 'The simple pleasures in life are cheapest' fitted my requirements adequately.

At Kilton Lock we were both needed, one to watch the boat, and one to watch Tiger, who was by this time impatient of any delay. He was pawing the ground with his foreleg, lifting his head up, down and sideways as he registered his disapproval of the delay. 'Clarice' rose in the lock, she looked fine—almost all the rusty scuffs of the driving chain had been swilled away, her covers tidy, lashings taut, the mop had raised a nice clean look to decks and paintwork on bends, screens and fenders. As the boat left Kilton Lock, I pulled the gate halfway shut behind her. I had little time for more for I had to scramble after the horse and steady him at the difficult outside bend, which led into the narrows being the aqueduct over the River Ryton. Tiger had his head down and his tail up and in this mood he was capable of pulling the boat half way out of the canal.

Just clear of the aqueduct lay a boatload of coal moored to the sewerage wharf on the far side; the Chambers brothers, Jack and David, and their boat 'Ida' were unloading a cargo of 'Shireoaks Smudge' for the sewerage engine. Stripped to shirts, with sleeves rolled, they were tackling the job in their usual workmanlike manner. Jack said 'Hey up Mustard' (he had called me 'Mustard' since I was a

Bracebridge Lock showing the stable. Rowing boats could be hired from here
although they were not popular with the fishermen.
(M. Jackson)

154

schoolboy) and their teeth and the whites of their eyes stood out clearly from their coal-dust blackened faces; they were used to shovels, they earned their living with them for many year.

Now we glide gently past the moorings we left nearly four days ago, forgotten already was the load of wet, dirty ashes, the muddy, moody River Trent; the dark hours of our early start; we were in the last lock of the journey. I followed Tiger up the lock tail steps, round and over the bridge, keeping the hauling line clear of snags, clearing it over the lowgate footboard, pulling it along the lockside and keeping it clear of the windlass, I dropped it round the near timberhead and then giving the boat another heave from the more than willing Tiger, prepared to 'draw-up' Quickly the boat came up in the lock. Tiger was impatiently standing with head up and ears forward, he'd made really good time and almost seemed to be saying, 'How's about that then?' This then was the last lock home—Tiger walked smartly to the lines end and lay in the collar. He was eager, but even in his impatience to be rid of his gears he was wise enough to use his skill when taking the strain and get way on the boat. The long cotton hauling line was quite a weight and the length we used gave a spring effect with the usual natural sag. So the wise old boat horse used to take the strain and then literally lay in the collar whilst the weight of the line started the boat and, as the line sagged this would be repeated until finally a nice, smooth rhythm could be attained. Eager, inexperienced horses were often put out by this characteristic behaviour of the line and would tighten the line, then as they tried to take another forward step, the sag of the line would catch them off balance on a bad bank. We had some really hairy moments with horses new to the job for they were almost always troubled and excited by this unusual form of pulling before they finally got the knack.

The skipper stayed ashore—he closed the top-gate behind us and walked swiftly after the horse. At that period, the towpath here was badly in need of a new edge. The original sleepers had rotted and left the rusty iron nails and bolts, which had held them together, sticking out from the decaying remains of the timbers to form a nasty hazard for a close in empty boat and a snag for the line of a loaded boat should the horse stop and allow the line to drop. This part of the towpath was also used as a footpath by local pedestrians although it was an offence to take prams and bicycles and such on the towpath. Meeting a person with pram, bike or even barrow could easily cause the horse to stop and it was with this danger in mind that the skipper hurried after the horse.

From the start of the houses at Garside Street and along through the Piggot's Bridge, the canal contained an evil, black, gaseous mud bottom which became very bad in the Thirties and we had all sorts of trouble on occasions. We had to use 'snatch blocks' or even 'fetch water' from Worksop Lock to get through the black clinging slime, especially just below the bridge. We always approached this section hoping for the best but prepared for the worst. The disgusting sediment gave off a pungent odour and as we ploughed through it a most horrible smell could ensue especially in calm, warm days; how the inhabitants of the adjacent houses bore it was a mystery to me. Today I suppose this unpleasant state of affairs would provide many contented hours investigation for an army of neatly clad health authority officials and their supervisors, even more neatly clad, and driving official cars. These dedicated men (and women) would sniff, poke and investigate, waving impressive clip-boards and then they would audition the unlucky ratepayers. Then, eventually, even if they didn't cure the smell, they would label it and find an endless number of ways of compensating the nearby tenants. I have helped move some of this mud when it was finally dredged and I reckoned it was me that needed compensation. In the days when I had just left school and a few shreds of my meagre academic prowess still lingered, I pointed out to the Old Man that this smell was probably Methane gas and could be used for heat and light. The Old Man replied, 'Well then, I shud say we t'ev the warmest and best lit town for bloody miles around'.

Safely but slowly we passed this vile place and emerged from the bridge and on to Canal Road. Old Tiger had it all figured now. I don't know whether he counted his footsteps from the bridge or whether he recognised a particular coping stone but at a given moment he would stop at this regular spot. It was a special sort of stop, a stop to end all stops so to speak. You could almost hear the old animal say 'Get the bloody line off and my hip straps on'. (The hip straps were loops in both the rear back straps of the gears and allowed the heavy cobble stick to be held clear of the horses hocks as he walked to the stable). The Old Man, always slow to praise, used to say of this faithful old horse, 'I'd rather have an Old Tiger than a new mate'. On a few occasions we had upgate cargoes for the warehouse higher up at the 'Common End'. Then we had quite a performance from both Tiger and Ginger when we dared to pass the stopping place they were used to, for 'Unions have no fury like a horse's stopping place scorned!'

The Old Man was at Piggot's Bridge, leaning on his faithful old 'Wigfall's' bike. He slung the bike on the middle covers and stepped on deck as we ran along the roadside. The skipper followed Tiger in the direction of the stable, the large snap basket containing only soiled towels and empty pots, on his arm. I held the boat out for the empty mooring beneath the hoist box of the flour mill, carefully avoiding the moored coal boat in front of the boiler house. In the Old Man's reckoning, a voyage wasn't over until the cargo was unloaded and he said, 'It's nobbut fower o'clock, Owel Tommy will lighten us a bit tonight'. Old Tommy being Thomas Shelton, old, yes but still efficient and willing with the chain and ring hoist. I knew the mill would unload until five o'clock and laid the boat in the mooring with the aft box directly below the hoist. Bearing away with the after mooring line I took the way off the boat, and shouting to the Old Man who had the fore mooring, 'Tie out!' and we finally stopped; the voyage was over.

Quickly we removed all gear from the aft cover and started unlashing and removing the sheets. For me, the boat was no longer a warm, moving, living home, now it was just a container full of sacks of wheat that stood between me and home, the dubious delights of the pictures, billiard halls and whatever other attractions my limited time and budget would allow. The chain came down and the Old Man commenced hanging on whilst I started to get the fore cover off. The bags went aloft briskly with great clattering of trap doors and jingling of chain. The Old Man could hang a bag on with the best and he found time to light his evil pipe, grumble about his rheumatic joints and shout a few unnecessary instructions to me, for I was doing a job I could do blindfold. We were both aware that time would not allow us to unload the whole cargo tonight and so we lightened her fore and aft. We needed to leave the boat level in the water overnight with the remaining cargo; had we just unloaded one end, the boat would have laid with a steep fore and aft angle and heavy rain could have flooded the bilges at the low point.

By five o'clock we had emptied the aft box and the fore box and snugged the remainder down safely. The Old Man pushed the stern of the boat across the canal to allow me to get ashore and then he would tie up again under the hoist and use his old bike to come round on whilst I thankfully trudged home the short way.

Home again! This was the end of the voyage. It was not really the end of anything, we had to finish one voyage simply to be able to start another as quickly as possible and so it was not a full stop but perhaps the briefest of commas in the story of my Chesterfield Canal connection. Walking homewards in the gathering dusk, wrapped in plans for tonight, another trip completed, I fully expected I would be making the endless round of such voyages for the rest of my life. The thought gave me no surprise or regret, I was a boatie, it was what boaties did, and apart from any variety added by cargo or weather or such like, it was what I would be doing. I was not short of company, most firms closed at five pm and tired workmen made their way home on either side of the road; this was unique to me, to be finishing when 'normal' people finished was a rare event. I enjoyed the brisk walk through the town smells of fireplace soot and the mixture of Brewery and Gashouse fumes and I knew the sounds of footfalls around me were made by men who were thankful to be 'in work'. Thankful to be going home, thankful to be able to do another day's 'graft' tomorrow. Today's attitude of 'the world owes me a living' had not arrived—no-one owed anyone anything.

Gringley Top Lock

CHAPTER 7

ALL ON A
WINTER'S MORNING

Deep Lock

For more than a week, beneath heavy grey skies, a steady easterly gale had been blowing. Along the canal, the same bitter wind rippled the surface into wavelets and prevented ice from forming in the main channel. In the dank brown remains of the lush Summer margins however, ice had already formed and in some sheltered spots such as wooded or high banks, where the wind didn't touch, ominous skims of ice were already reaching out to cover the entire width of the waterway.

The boatmen knew the signs only too well—a mild spell lasting until after Christmas was heralded as a sure preliminary to a 'freeze-up'. Wise heads shook and talked of 'Ice in November to bear a duck, etc…' but there had been no November ice. The Old Man (my father) said, 'Any winter you don't get before January will be twice as hard after'. Some of his 'sayings' were very hard to interpret, but he was usually right. What was very sure, however, was that if the wind shifted, the heavy leaden skies would bring snow, and if the wind dropped then the ice would quickly seal the open water.

In the event, the wind dropped. In the stillness of the January night, the black, hard ice formed. The towpath, already hard from the freezing wind hardened even more so. The boats already splashed with ice where water had been spilled and hauling line as tight as a wire cable and thickened with an icy coat, through trailing in the canal, lay helpless at their icebound moorings. The grey fingers of light revealed all—it was a freeze up—a job for the ice-boat.

The ice-boat was unlovely, unhandy and disliked. Basically it was an improvisation using a short ugly LNER work boat, little more than half the length of a narrow-boat. Shallow, hard chined, with angled fore and aft, no curves, a floating orange box. You could tell the stern from the head only by the fittings to take the clumsy helm. Clamped with long bolts and cross pieces, three girders were fixed to the underside of the boat at the head, facing forward, one either side and one in the middle. These girders extended 10 or 12 feet beyond the stem of the boat, and were angled to appear out of the water at about 45°, the ends being firmly bolted to a sturdy cross-beam. Thus was formed a strong three-pronged ramp sloping upwards and forward from immediately in front of the boat. This was the cutting edge of the ice-boat. The boat had no decks at all, but for these occasions, a strong platform was fixed amidships, and the full width of the hull. Running fore and aft down the middle of this platform was a strong hand-rail about waist-high. The rest was simple, with an equal number of men either side of the handrail the boat was rolled from side to side as violently as possible. At the same time a number of horses hauled the craft as fast as it would steer. Thus, with an alternate up and down motion, the girders forward crushed down and through the ice smashing and chewing a channel as the boat swept forward.

The crew were a motley assembly. The Canal Company had no suitable horses available and so horses complete with handlers were hired. The company supplied the men to sally (i.e., rock) the boat and everyone would assemble, usually at the Company Yard at Worksop. All and sundry were under the Canal Inspector (an important man, complete with LNER waterproof coat, polished leggings and natty flat cap—and an enormous amount of theory which did not impress the 'old hands' or smash much ice either.) There really should have been a photographic record of the full muster. No protective clothing was supplied in those days. Thus every shape, size and gear was used. Leggings, puttees, home made sack aprons, scarves, all forms of head gear, macs, coats, First World War overcoats, all were there. No wonder the horses with their feedstuff on their backs in bags, and their cobble sticks hung in the hip straps stood patiently there with their ears forward in puzzled equestrian wonder. The next step was simple, all we had to do was haul the boat as fast as possible whilst the 'Sallyens' thrashed the boat violently from side to side and thus chewed, clawed and smashed a channel down the canal—a classic example of brute force and energy. Of course, nothing is perfect. The ice-boat only smashed a narrow channel, the floating ice very quickly knitted together again and so a primitive convoy system was used, the narrow boats followed the ice-boat keeping the channel loose. A real problem was caused when the ice-boat cut across corners, being short and light it could do this. The unlucky narrowboat men with much deeper draught and extra length could not leave the channel and were trapped on the larger bends, having to smash a wider channel for themselves with mauls and any other means at hand. This made the skippers love the ice-boat crew. It was in moments like this that the peculiar language associated with boatmen had its origins.

The coming of night brought its problems. We had to have stabling for the horses, this was essential. Alternatively hauling at full speed, or standing about at locks, awkward bridges or ice-jams, the poor beasts needed more than a swift snack from a nose-tin. They needed a snug stable, bedding of straw or hay and a good measure of the bran, chop and oats stowed away under the ice-boat's platform. This was a real problem. The ice-boat horses plus any more belonging to the narrow-boat convoy more than filled the pub or lock stables usually able to cope with three or four in normal conditions. However, we knew the area well and could eventually find shelter for all, most pubs and villages having stables available, stables alas, now acting as garages or cafes.

The human crew was another matter. The LNER men had an official finishing time and would hope to be near a bus-stop that could enable them to reach their scattered homes and comfort for the night. The horse handlers would usually split up and some go home with the Company men leaving one or two of their group to tend the animals. These unfortunates had to have somewhere 'to get their heads down'. I have been with both the ice-boat handlers and also the narrow-boat crews at various times and know only too well the discomfort that had to be accepted. If the stable was in good condition with a plentiful supply of bedding, a warm dry bed could be improvised therein—the horses kept the place quite warm as a rule. Alternatively a genial, kindly landlord would put you up, even if only on the seats in the taproom (usually for a trifle). The favourite solution for the unhappy handlers was to be invited to share the tiny cabin with a good Samaritan type boatman. The result was really unbelievable. The hard, small, inaccessible bed unrolled from its cupboard along the bulkhead had barely room for the boat's crew- especially if they were a bit on the heavy side. The answer was to sleep across the bed with your feet sticking out almost on the little coal stove (which was usually kept alight all night in the bitter weather). Can you imagine the situation? I'll always remember it vividly. The usual smells of paint, tar, bilges, mud, plus four sets of garments (often wet), four bodies, remembering that we never got a good bath unless we had one on the limited occasions we had a night at home. Add to all this tobacco, chewed and smoked, and on top of all, four soggy sets of boots and socks plus the feet which lived therein! I am now getting old but I can, and will I suppose, always remember the 'quaint smell'.

Thus, thrashing up and down the canal, with the help of the following narrow-boats, a channel could be kept open for a short period. When you think that no ice was removed, only smashed, to float in the channel, you can see that in prolonged freezing weather, say weeks of it, a gradual choke of ice would finally stop even the ice-boat. The answer then was a thaw, no other way existed.

At the onset of the freezing weather when the ice was thin and patchy, only bad in some sheltered spots, the boatmen, with help from lock-keepers and day-men provided by the Company, would keep moving by smashing the ice by hand. Like all natural things, ice was not consistent, it had its variability. After a still traditional night's frost, we found a black, clear ice that was the easier to cope with, the cracks obligingly 'running'. With cold grey skies and temperatures below freezing all day and night, we got a much tougher texture of ice, more reluctant to crack and needed more to be nibbled at. The really bad ice was 'snow-ice'.

Osberton Park where the author would get on or off the boat, to lead the horse and deal with the lock.
Osberton Hall has been home of the Foljambes for many years.
(R. Allsopp collection)

After prolonged, heavy snow-fall, a floating layer of slush would cover any water not disturbed by traffic. This layer only needed a light frost to turn it into a tough leathery ice which was well nigh impossible to break. It was possible to knock a hole in it, but only at the point of impact. It would not crack at all—something like thick frozen blotting paper. However, it disintegrated just as quickly in a thaw but was quite treacherous. Ordinary ice would bear a person's weight while it had enough thickness, even when a melting had taken place. Snow-ice reverted to slush quite quickly and while still looking thick and strong, would give way quite easily if it was stepped on.

Ice breaking by hand was a bird of a different colour. We had two types of hand breakers, not judging boat hooks and boat gear to be included under this heading. First we had the Maul—simply a long handled mallet, about twelve feet in length. These were ideal for breaking a bit of ice round a lock head or other such places. To break the ice in front of a moving boat was different, the maul head would often penetrate the ice and then need more effort to extricate it. This made the job very tiring indeed. When snow-ice was about, the mauls were useless. The favourite with the narrowboatmen was the home-made ice breaker. Next time you are by a stream or such place where the trees grow quickly, you may see a spot where a tree has been sawn or chopped down. The young shoots from the stump grow very quickly with all the energy of the root system available. In a few years you will see the old stump surrounded by a number of long straight, tapering new growths emerging from the old tree with a nice curve before reaching up for the light and air. Cut off close to the stump these were ready made breakers. The natural bend at the lower end and the long tapered growth, trimmed clear of snags making a comfortable shock proof handle. These home made breakers cut long holes in the ice and were quite easy to retrieve after each blow.

When hand breaking, we had to try and keep the boat moving and with the help of the mauls, etc., plus the boat itself, the thinner ice could be easily negotiated. The main problem was steering the boat. Heavy-laden boats had to hug the channel. It did not need much ice to make steering impossible and in the tight bends we needed someone with the horse and all the help we could get smashing a wide enough passage for the long boat to ease around the numerous turns. On these occasions, the human ice-breakers had to work from the foredeck—a slippery, tedious and tiring process.

The boat only had protective plating around the head, the stern and the sides were unprotected. This meant that after long hours of cutting, chafing exposure to the ice, long vicious raw cuts used to be inflicted on the wooden hull at the water-line. These were cut out and and faced with new timber when repair time came around. When the boat was light, it could be easier. The shallow draught allowed the vessel to travel close in the bank. Thus, the ice-breakers would smash a channel from the towpath. I saw a lot of this because we had to supply the Flour Mill at Worksop with two or more loads of coal weekly. This meant a two-mile, eight lock trip to the basin at Shireoaks Colliery and this short journey did not qualify for a full ice-boat turnout until the situation was really desperate.

All this was heartily despised by boatmen and company men alike, not forgetting the long suffering horses. The constant urge for headway, the frequent running aground, plus towpaths treacherous with snow, mud and ice, all added an intolerable burden to these important members of the team. When these conditions seemed likely, boatmen would have their horses shod with shoes with a bit of toe and heel plus extra holes cut in the shoe for future use. When this time arrived, you would seen the boatmen knocking 'frost nails' in the spare holes using the lock-key for a hammer. The frost nails were simply horse-shoe nails with wedge shaped heads instead of flat ones. These gave the animal a purchase on the treacherous banks when the shoes had worn smooth. I can think of a no more depressing sight than these willing animals, wet, tired, hungry, cut and grazed by slipping.

Of course, winters were not one long freeze-up. Then, as now, the really hard weather came in spells. We could go for long periods without ice, only getting a day or two below freezing when whatever little ice formed was dealt with by the boatmen themselves. In summer certain locks were closed to traffic from 9.00 pm to 4.00 am and in winter these times were 6.00 pm to 6.00 am. It was all handled in a very civilised manner for the most part. Lock-keepers were only human, and no-one wants to get out of bed at 4.00 am, come down and plod through cold grass or such to unlock the gates for some impatient boatman. Some of them left the key complete with its large wire ring and lump of cork large enough to float the key if it went into the canal, hung on his door knob. Some quietly unlocked the gate before they went to bed. The middle course was to open the bedroom window in answer to the boatman banging on the door in the dawn and throw the key down with a friendly 'Don't knock the bloody house down!' or 'Open the bloody gate yourself!' As I said it was all a reasonably civilized way of handling the situation.

The method of locking up was simple. One of the twin low gates was locked open with a chain and thus it was not possible to fill the lock, or some locked the low gates together thus preventing opening of the gates. This lock-up was only carried out a certain locks namely, Gringley Top Lock, Retford Lock, Forest Lock and Bracebridge Lock. Two gates were locked across the towpath at each end of the Company yard at Worksop for the weekends. The locks mentioned were closed all day Sundays.

In times of freezing conditions, the custom of locking-up was discontinued. Boatmen could keep hauling without hindrance if any danger of freezing up was present. It was quite common for a boat to travel all night in order to get to its destination before sufficient ice formed to prevent this. It may be hard to believe that these long boats could be navigated through narrow bridges, locks and the numerous tight bends in the dark winter nights, but it was done. It is hard to convince people who are used to well-lit homes, streets, shops, not to mention miles of illuminated motorways and such that once you get away from all the glare your eyes quickly adjust to the situation. Years ago, the only lights a boatman saw came from the smokey paraffin lamp, the friendly chink in a canalside cottage window, the red warm glow from a brickyard kiln or a distant glare from a nearby road as a car went along, not so common occurrence as nowadays. Without hindrance the eye could do its job very efficiently. A few stars, reflecting in the ripples of a breeze was enough for the steerman. A 'bit of moon' was a bonus—a full moon meant we could navigate as easily as in the sunshine, consequently we quickly learned the moon's phases. Woods, such as at Wiseton and Osberton caused problems on the poorer nights. Walking along in a lighted street, it is just possible to see the stars on a clear night. When you have steered a boat for some hours in the middle of the night, you see stars by the thousand, thousands more behind them and even thousands more behind them. Shooting stars are quite common on these occasions. Of course, there were conditions we had to accept that it was impossible to move, fog, rain and heavy overcast skies, we avoided travelling at night if possible.

Travelling after dark was usually for one of a number of reasons. To make up time lost by delayed starts; hanging on very early in the morning could mean some hours of darkness, or in very hot weather, night was the only time one could travel in comfort. Also, very often, the days were too short to complete a journey in daylight. These occasions were usually left to the boat skipper's discretion. Some did it often, some less frequently. In freezing conditions the choice was not so wide—you travelled or accepted the possibility of being ice-bound or having

'Joan' the 1929 dredger built at Worksop moored at Osberton Wharf in 1956.
A motorised maintenance boat and a small mud boat are moored alongside.
The authors family supplied coal and materials for the essential operations of this craft.
(M. Jackson)

the misery of ice breaking. I found it very depressing to be upwards of twelve hours journey from home, when a lovely Christmas card sun was low on the horizon; when the short winter's day was almost gone and you could feel the 'bite' in the gathering gloom. The flickering glow of a fire in the lock-keeper's cottage looked very comfortable and made the cold night air even colder. How envious we looked at anyone who, having done his day's work was making his way home to food, warmth, possibly the wonderful presence of the new craze, a wireless. I remember one night passing the cottages at Gringley Middle Bridge, just as someone entered. The shaft of soft light, and the unmistakable sound of Jack Payne's Band were swiftly cut off by the shutting door. The long, dark, cold, slow voyage before me seemed unbearable.

However, these were the low spots. Often enough, we reached our day's destination at a civilised hour, time to tend the horse as it should be tended, time to have a welcome meal in comfort. Plain food—but plenty of it—we had appetites. Faces glowing from hours of wind and cold, perhaps a pint in the pub if we had stabled at one, and so to bed.

We hadn't the sense to lay awake thinking of how much overtime we had clocked, what our 'overnight' money would be, or if the bonus for not being late for work that week would be paid. The flock bed, just big enough for two, about three feet away from the embers in the stove, was comfortable enough, when you had got used to it. Warm, dry and very welcome. In the depth of winter, we sometimes kept the fire alight all night in very cold weather, putting a shovel full of coal handy for the man on the outer edge of the bed to reach out and mend the fire if need be.

After four or five winter nights away with the boat, my bed at home seemed very large and cold and heated bricks and heavy oven shelves wrapped in brown paper were some of the methods to try and make it like the little boat bed to which I had become accustomed.

At least I could shut the door and listen in comfort to Jack Payne's Band, what more did I need? After all, tomorrow could bring a freeze-up!

EPILOGUE

Canal Road

Places and names of bridges and locks are having a revival through the canal Boat Clubs and of this I have no criticism. The new 'boaties' will never know of a certain lock keeper who kept his hedge and banks in park-like condition, who oiled his slides and straps every week, who would sit on the balance pole half the night talking—of another keeper who would help you all the way down his length. They would never have known of the lengthsman who like to 'bend his elbow', this unfortunate man had an amazing characteristic—when drunk he had difficulty walking and so used to run. How many times we saw this man jogging along the 'cut bank'. Old Charlie's been at it again. These new boaties will never need to wash in a bucket—get dressed up by putting on a clean cap, 'gansy' and scarf to go to the pictures at Retford, never have to live out of the 'snap basket' in the smoky lamplit Winters or the pitch-melting Summers. With their various shapes and sizes of boat they will push through more weed than ice and snow, and never be glad of a 'cup o' tea' in a basin.

The Old Man told me of many other activities in the hey-day of the canals— fly-boats, market boats, gunnel boats, lime, gaslime and nightsoil. Of these I know nothing, I can only write honestly of the times when I was there and this I have endeavoured to do. I saw the erosion caused by road and rail to the canal's necessity. Two hundred years ago the new cut must have been a remarkable innovation in comparison to the roads and transport of the day. One can easily imagine the many usages it offered as it looped and twisted its way from Chesterfield to the Trent. Today's marvels have diminished the achievements of the engineers of that time and of course, their navvies, but remarkable achievements they were. I saw the end of the canal in the terms of commercial trade. Trade was inescapably the life blood of the waterway and I watched this trade, eroded even when I was young, fall away even further. The skills, knowledge and advice of the Old Man and others, learned thoroughly, 'turned to ashes' and became useless to me but many of the virtues and basic understandings of that most formative time in my life have helped me, even in our 'grand new plastic world'.

About this time it became obvious that the Old Man was fading—along with the canal it seemed he had 'run out of cargoes'. To me it was almost a symbolical, natural thing, in the way that he and the canal should end together. The canal was definitely dying—the reasons for its being were rapidly disappearing, cargoes rarer and rarer and almost all the boaties I knew and respected were gone— dead, retired or in other occupations. Their descendants were accepting jobs 'ashore' and old family ties with the waterway were falling away.

I suddenly realised how much my father and the old canal had in common and what a change had taken place since he was known as 'Kingy Clark', as was his own father. Looking at him now, his old, tired sagging frame and weary trudging walk, it was difficult to associate him with the Old Man I knew, feared and respected as a young boatie. His sturdy erect figure with knuckles dug in his hips and elbows bent, whilst his temper was visibly increasing as he urged some 'knuckle-headed useless bugger' to get on with it—all this characteristic style was ended. His eyes, once so keen, so quickly grasping the situation, so promptly solving it, confident eyes, so full of life, were now lustreless and bewildered. His voice, that strong ringing voice, which had made us 'jump to it'so many times; which we had loathed when he bawled us awake in our warm snug bed in the cold small hours of a biting winter's day and which I though was incapable of whispering, was now a querulous mumble. The oft repeated saying of his 'come home to roost' with a vengeance. How often he said to me 'Owd age is rum stuff if you're lucky enough to have any'. He proved the truth of his sayings, faced with the facts that his useful life was over and the serious illness of my Mother, he gave up and died. My brothers all had regular jobs ashore and I was to join the workforce of the Albion Flour Mills. It seemed natural to do so having worked for them in one way or another since I had left school and now at last, there would be no 'Boatie Clark' on the canal. When Old Ginger, that most faithful of horses died and then Old Tiger, my feelings for the canal as a means of earning a living weakened and when the Old Man died, they ended. So be it.

I stepped over the threshold of my home. 'I'm home mam'. Never had so much meaning been in so few words. I sat at the table opposite the face I had always know, always loved and have always remembered. At home I never grew up, I was always her 'little lad'. The crude and unpleasant aspects of canal life never coarsened my mother, none of it was allowed in her living room and as I contentedly ate my first meal ashore, I little realised that I and my contemporaries of the canal were already passing into history.

The dying throes of the commercial Chesterfield Canal were now obvious, the reason for its being was finally disappearing. A few cargoes continued using the boats, a bit of brickyard coal, warp from the Trent, very little to hold a fleet together. The two hundred year old 'Lady' was fading fast. My feelings were mixed. How many times had I wished the 'bloody boat' would sink or ask why someone didn't make a road of it, fill it with concrete? How childish and petulant it seemed now. I experienced an almost embarrassing feeling of loyalty to the world of my adolescence and concealed a deep interest in its future.

The ruins of my boating days lay around me. Two of our boats were still moored in front of the Mill. I kept them pumped dry and lit an odd fire to keep the cabins aired. Soon these were gone. 'Lilian', named after my father's sister, lay sunk in the winding hold by the mill. 'Albion' lay on the bottom alongside Godley's Woodyard on Eastgate. 'Valour' stranded on the mud below Clayworth Bridge after we had sold her. 'Clarice' pride of our little fleet, named after my dead sister, was sold to a chap who was going to convert her, no doubt into one of the 'weird hybrids' we saw popping up at that time. In the event, 'Clarice' was taken to West Stockwith to get on with the conversion, unsuccessfully it turned out to be— soon she was sunk along with other hulks along the far side of the basin—her proud stem so lovingly painted bright red by the Old Man and so often mopped by my brothers and I, was now just a slimy weed covered protusion from the quiet waters of the basin. This was for me the real finale of the Cut.

What happened to Furley's fleet, I am not sure, they were mostly good boats. The last boat to be built, by Billy Tomlinson at West Stockwith, was called 'Ruth' and had unusually large cabin and a large rounded stem head—most unusual. I saw her with a cargo of Trent mud (warp) used at brickyards to seal the cooling kilns. This was the last cargo I saw, a sorry sight of the last of the fleet. I believe 'Ruth' was later shortened and converted into a pleasure craft by Ike Argent, a former boatman from the Erewash Canal.

This, then, was it—modern times would not allow the men, horses and boats to be viable in these expensive labour cost days. Now so many tons have to be carried so many miles, in so much time, at so much per ton. Quotas, norms and all the new fields of transport have turned our narrow boats into museum pieces. Now is the turn of the pleasure boat people. As commercial navigation slowed and finally ceased, a rapid deterioration of the waterways set in with silting of channels and neglect and decay of the works of the canal. Here we had the challenge for the canal enthusiasts and boating clubs. A challenge which we now know was accepted eagerly and which heralded a new community with new and remarkable boats, new language, new aims, new everything. But great as the change was, the same old canal dimensions remain just as they were for the old craftsmen who built the narrow boats and the old 'narrowmen' who sailed them. Once again we had a 'sailable' channel and a reasonable state of maintenance of locks and other works all the way from West Stockwith to Worksop.

I have visited West Stockwith recently and although the basin and the lock are still the same, a vast change has taken place. The sunken keels and narrow boats have been removed to make way for moorings, the filthy old earth toilet has gone (I heartily approve of that) and almost all traces of the old days have

All aboard for Greenmile. A Sunday school outing about to depart from Bracebridge Lock Worksop c1910.
(Roz and Ian Davies collection)

been erased. A few relics remain, the 'Idle Hole', the canal Company office still stands, and a few yards of the old mooring still exists between the office and the new Puddle Bridge. Gone is the old slipway, with its hand windlass high on the roadside; gone the jumble of sheds and workshops of Billy Tomlinson's boatyard; gone are the wooden keels and the new iron keels with all their masts, derricks and lee-boards; gone is the well oiled crane and the company store sheds and warehouses. No longer is there the smell of tar, linseed oil, pitch, 'charlico' and 'oakum' of the boat-builders and no longer can be heard the whine of a saw, the rhythmic thump of the 'caulkers' iron and maul', the sweet crisp bite of the adze and the crunching twist of the long handled augers. All these living sounds are gone, the skills and experience and the men who had them are lost to us. Today the modern bridge, the new concrete moorings and the weird and wonderful miscellany of craft of every shape and size, almost bury the basin. The only sound I expect to hear today is the ring of a cash register exploiting the amateur yachtsmen and the hire-craft sailors.

'The Crown' has been tarted up a bit and renamed 'The Waterfront Inn' and it is hard to find an old boatie in the company. So be it, if the old days are ended, a new issue of life may be open to old Brindley's cut in the hands of these modern crews.

The years that have passed since I was a boatman have, thankfully, given me an interest in the varied and interesting life which was abundant, but unnoticed along the canal years ago. Always a keen angler, I now have less desire to lure a fine fish on to a needle sharp hook concealed with a tasty morsel. When I fish now, I spare no effort to harm the fish as little as humanly possible. I have as much interest in the wild flowers and grasses, birds and butterflies as the float which I am supposed to watch. This interest grew with time, and I only hope some enlightened authority will realise the wonderful opportunity these old canals present.

On the Chesterfield Canal now, the efficient caterpillar tractored 'grabs' have ripped the rich mud from the canal and in many cases buried the old towpath under the spoil and miles of friendly sheltering hedges have gone. Along the far bank, these dredgings have been allowed to lie, dry and become the home of a prolific growth of rank weeds. Tall, smothering stands of docks, nettles, hairy willow-herb now flourish and the waterway looks more like a drain in many places. I feel the time has arrived to remember that we, the present generation, are in every sense of the word, just tenants. We do not own the world around us, we are not lords of all we survey. We are, just the present tenants who have followed previous tenants and can expect to be followed by new tenants in the natural course of events. We have criticised our forebears, and in the wisdom of their faults we should endeavour not to be found wanting when our turn comes.

Great and necessary deeds have been performed in our allotted span. The fantastic increase in traffic of all kinds has made the new motorways vital and many similar changes, necessary, but still needing valuable space in a small island where new developments need their share of a dwindling countryside. Therefore, some effort must be made to improve without destroying forever the inhabitants, animal, bird, insect and flora of our limited space. It may well be that the frustration of our choked highways has activated the return to the canals by our generation of leisure conscious people. This I heartily endorse. Given a safe supply of clean water, the water plants will flourish again, the fish will prosper and the birds and insects will have the basic requirements of their life cycle, their ecological chain, so to speak.

Here, at this point, our canal developers have a wonderful chance to hand. Preserve and maintain the towpath hedges, control the rank weeds, although even nettles have a vital part to play with a number of species of butterfly. Along this lovely old canal, we could have a vital haven for many of the wild flowers rapidly dwindling with the changes in agriculture and the all destroying sprays. In common with miles of inaccessible motorway banks, the inaccessible far banks of the canal could be the saviour of many of the rarer and disappearing types of the wonderful flora and fauna of which our pleasant land is so well bestowed. In these days of enlightenment it should be possible to assess our options, to pause in our rush to develop and improve and give a long look at the treasures we are liable to deny the future tenants, i.e., not to be 'weighed in the balance and found wanting'.

The Greenmile Trip

Note: *This hitherto unpublished story was written in 1977.*

GLOSSARY

1 BOATS

Adze	Woodworking tool for fashioning boat timbers
Barton Bulldog	Coastal sailing barge, sloop rigged, originally built at Barton on Humber.
Boort	Boatman's slang for Chesterfield narrow boat
Bends	The art of bending timber by heating in a steam chest to form the curves principally in the bow and stern.
Bottom lashes	The strings on the bottom cargo covers
Bulkhead	Forming the boundary between the hold and the fore cabin and cabin, they strengthened the boat athwarts or crosswise.
Carlins	Cross supports for the deck and beam, also the hatchboards
Catch or Ketch	A Trent vessel, related to the Keel, but with a square bilge and sometimes setting, in addition to the squat mainsail and topsail, standing lug mizzen.
Cog Boat	A keel or Sloop's boat or tender
Carvel	A flush jointed boat construction method
Clinker	A boat with over-lapping boards or plates
Caulker	One who seals the joints between a wooden boat's timbers
Combing	A type of weather board around the cargo space raised above deck level to which the protecting covers for the load could be fixed.
Combing irons	Iron plates carried by some boats to protect the combings when loading
Cleats	Usually fixed to the combings and headledges with which to tie the hold covers
Charlico	A mixture of tar, horse dung and oakum
Dumb-boat	Un-powered craft
Dogs	Square spiked hooks driven into the combing at regular intervals
Furley Boats	Boats sold to or owned by Richard Furley & Co of

	Gainsborough who bought most of the narrow boats which traded on the Chesterfield Canal.
Flare	Finely built
Forrend	Fore end or bow of vessel
Gunnel	The gunwhale or side deck of the boat
Gouge	A rounded chisel
Graining	A decoration similar to that used in domestic properties at the time known as scumbling. A cream base paint is allowed to dry and then varnished. While still wet, the varnish is combed giving it a streaky appearance.
Hard chine	Boat built with a square section, i.e., flat bottomed and vertical sides
Hatch bar	A bar for securing the hatch cover
Head	Bow or stem of the boat
Headledge	The cross timbers of the fore and aft bulkheads which extend above deck level
Ice plates	Plates lashed to the bows when cutting through ice. In some cases steel protection was a permanent feature round the bows.
Keelson or Kelson	The timber beam roughly 8 inches wide (200 mm) and 4 inches (100 mm) deep which was laid on the bottom planks and ran in scarf jointed sections from stem to stern.
Knees	The strong curved timbers in the bow (fore) and stern (aft) and also the 'L' shaped irons in the hold which secure the side of the boat to the bottom.
Keel	Family of Yorkshire and Lincolnshire river craft, decked over, often in sailing trim.
Lashings, Top	The strings on the top of the deck covers
Lashings, Bottom	The strings on the bottom of the covers
Leks	Water leaks
Lutchet	Mast step of a narrow boat or barge, sometimes known as a tabernacle. The normal hauling point for empty boat
Lee Boards	To stop sideways drift on a flat bottomed craft, under sail, with no keel. Can be raised or lowered according to prevailing conditions.
Maul	A type of long-handled hammer for breaking ice
Mast, long	Used for hauling when laden
Mast, short	Used for hauling when empty
Middlin of Water	Water in the boat, enough to warrant pumping out before loading or emptying cargo. To omit to pump out in these conditions would mean water rising above the floor (shutts) when the boat is unbalanced at one end or the other.
Narrow boat	A flat bottomed vessel around 70ft long and 7ft wide. Chesterfield narrow boats were 72ft long and 6ft 10 inches wide.

Parson	Wooden collar to cabin stove pipe chimney
Pen	To pass through a lock, a Trent boatman's term.
Pompey boat	A wooden work boat, flat bottomed, flat stern and vee shaped bow around 25ft long.
Registration	Boats had to register with the local Health Board under the Canal Boats Acts of 1877 and 1884. Chesterfield and Retford were the two 'Ports of Registry', later it became Retford only.
Scarf Joint	Tapered over-riding joint in the side timbers or strakes
Shutts	Planking in the bottom of the hold on which the cargo rested above any water lying in the bottom of the boat (bilges).
Steam Bending	Heating water to produce steam and passing the steam over timber until it becomes supple enough to bend to the required profile.
Strakes (strokes)	The side planks of the vessel.
Stem post	The substantial bow timber designed to withstand collisions.
Stern post	Opposite to the stem post and from which the rudder is hung
Sheer	The rake or angle of the hull—sheer sided would be straight sides.
Scantlings	Timbers lying parallel to the keels on and supporting the shutts
Shoulders	The widest part of the vessel reached after starting at the stem (bow) and where most of the 'knocks' would be taken.
Snugging down	Clearing the decks of 'top hamper' (qv) for safety reasons.
Tender	Small mud boat holding about 8 tons
Top Hamper	Removing all unnecessary boating equipment from the decks or walkways. See also, Snugging down (qv).
Timberheads	Used for towing when loaded under certain conditions. Also for slowing the boat down by putting a 'turn' round the timberhead and for mooring purposes. Two pairs of timberheads are situated at the fore end and one pair aft.
Tholes	The holes where the sweeps or oars, a type of rowlock, were located.

2 BOAT HORSE

Aims	The pair of metal chains either side of the collar to which the traces were attached
Broad bran	A coarse type of bran
Chop bag	A bag for straw and hay
Currycomb	Half round comb with teeth either side.

Cobblestick	The timber attached to the harness and to which the hauling line was secured.
Dandy brush	Soft bristle brush to finish off grooming
Hecks	Container for hay in a stable above manger bed
Hauling knot	A knot used on the end of a hauling line
Halter shank	A length of rope attached to the halter
Horse line	Hauling rope
Long gears	Harness from the collar either side of the horse to the cobblestick
Mucking out	Cleaning out used straw bedding and manure
Sharps	A fine type of bran
Strap	Loop of rope
Traces	Leather strap from the hook on the aims to the cobblestick
Tags	Dried manure on the horse

3 GENERAL

Arm	A branch of the main canal
Bait	Bed down for the night and wait to load/unload or for the lock to open.
Baiting Allowance	Allowance for stabling and nights away from home paid per trip
Bight	Loop or bend in the course of a river. Also the middle part of a rope.
Bearing away	After putting turns of rope round a timberhead or gate to slow the boat, letting the rope run through the hands would slow or check the boat. Also used to catch up a tow (qv) when getting a snig (qv) on the River Trent.
Boat Boy	Teenager working as mate on a boat
Bottom slide	The gate paddle attached to the bottom gate used for emptying the lock.
Basin	An area of water large enough to accommodate several craft at a time usually situated in importance places along the canal.
By-boat	Privately owned boat also known as a number one.
Cross cut	Branch canal usually at right angles to the canal.
Common End	The area of Worksop situated on the north side of the canal bank from Piggot's Bridge to the Town Lock.
Company	London and North Eastern Railway Company (LNER), owners of the Chesterfield Canal from 1923 to 1948.
Cill	The wooden block where the top and bottom lock gates locate. It is straight in the case of a single gate and vee shaped where two gates are fitted.

Catching the gate	Putting a rope round the head post of a lock gate to slow the boat and also close the gate.
Cutbank	Towpath
Clowne Hards	A type of coal mined in the Clown area of Derbyshire, good for giving out heat when burned.
Drive, to	To go with the flow of the tide, trailing the anchor or chain to give steerage way.
Drag	Slowing down effect caused by dropping the anchor or chain.
Dunnage	A boat's removable navigating equipment
Drawing a kiln	Removing the seals from the doors after baking the bricks to allow the oven to cool down naturally.
Dropping	Going down—steering towards the towpath side, falling away.
Demurrage	Payment made to a vessel when the cargo is held on board longer than agreed by the charter. To avoid deliberately slow unloading or using boats for additional storage.
Downgate	Travelling downhill through the locks
Draw, to	To create a flow or flush (qv) of water to assist a vessel or replenish water levels by raising a paddle.
Filling our kite	Eating our fill
Fellmonger	Hide and skin processor
Flush, to	To raise the slides or paddles to move the boat using the water's power.
Fresh water	Land or storm water raising levels. Term frequently used on the river to refer to the increased depth and flow.
Getting off place	A suitable deep spot to bring the boat close to the bank to go ashore.
Gansie	A boatman's jersey.
Gainsborough Roads	The straight length or river and moorings downstream of Gainsborough Bridge.
Gate line	A rope used for pulling the top lock gate closed behind the boat when travelling downhill. Known as catching the gate.
Going outside	Going out into the River Trent at West Stockwith.
Hang on, to	To attach the hauling line to the boat.
Holding her up	Keeping the boat forward in a lock when going downhill to avoid sitting on the cill or up against the top gate or rubbing board when going uphill.
Horse Marine	The horse's owner and driver
Idle Hole	The lay by on the upstream side of West Stockwith Basin, capable of berthing one keel.
Loping ashore	Leaping ashore
Lock head	Upper end of lock as opposed to tail (qv)
Lock Tail	Lower or downstream end of lock. Both the head and tail were outside the lock chamber.

Length	The section of canal entrusted to one maintenance man, a lengthsman.
LNER	The London and North Eastern Railway Company, owners of the canal from 1923 to 1948.
Nuts	A type of coal
Narrow Men	The keel skippers name for the Chesterfield Boatmen
Nowt	Slang for nothing
Paddle	A sluice or slide for filling or emptying a lock
Pick ups	Loading points away from wharves, usually isolated farms.
Pit top men	Colliery works who did not go underground to mine coal, were paid less, usually and known as Pit top workers.
Point	The point of a bend was on the inside and where the boat would go aground if the corner was cut.
Puddle Bank	The length from West Stockwith to Misterton where the canal crossed the River Idle/Trent flood plain on a clay puddle embankment.
Puddle Brighole	The entrance bridge at West Stockwith Basin leading to the puddle bank (qv).
Plenty of Water in	Enough water to float the boat over the low cill of West Stockwith Lock when the tide is running out.
Pen or Penning	To pass through a lock
Pound or Pond	Length of canal between two locks
Poles	Hooks and stowers on a narrow boat. The boathook was usually used for pulling in to the side or fending off or passing the hauling line of another boat. The stower was a long pole with a 'truck' a round wooden block, on one end (to stop it sinking into soft mud if used truck down). The other end was normally a tine or pointed hook.
Pit talk	The local miners or colliers 'flowery language'
Rubbing or Handying	Hitting the bottom or scraping along the edge of the channel
Rack	A straight reach or length on a river
Running up or going up	Steering towards the bank side, (the opposite to the towpath side)
Snig	A tow or a snatch. The thick tow or bass rope would be held up when a powered boat passed on the River Trent in the hope of getting a ride.
Snap basket	A type of picnic hamper or wicker basket
Shireoaks Smudge	Small coal or slack from Shireoaks Colliery
Scutching	Cleaning or tidying up
Slack off, to	To untie the mooring ropes
Sweep	A long oar for steering by rowing round bends when drifting with the tide on the River Trent.

Shooting the bridge　To get enough steerage to pass through the arch of the bridge as the tide attempted to pull the boat towards the bridge supports.

Snotter　A two foot length of light chain for lifting sacks with two inch diameter rings at each end, one attached to the derrick runner, the bight (centre) of the chain passing through the second ring to form a loop, put over the sack mouth and drawn tight.

Stower　Long shaft for poling the boat (shafting)

Sack trade　A cargo packed in sacks

Swilled　Swirled

Sheeting down　Covering the cargo

Stemming up　Going aground

Spraddle legged　Walking on two separate planks when loading or unloading the boat.

Single lift slides　Some of the gate slides in use at this time (1930s) were operated by standing on the lower gate walkway. They were not geared in any way and hence the term single lift. Geared slides were double lift and could be operated from the safety of the bank.

Top coort warmer　A layer of clothing could be shed—in other words it felt warmer or more sheltered from the elements.

Tine　The tip of a boat hook (point).

Top slide　The ground paddle at the top of the lock used to fill it.

Towpath　The path along the navigation to enable the horse to pull the boat.

Trimming　Spreading the load until the boat was level or plumb when moving.

Turning out　Putting the horse out to grass in summer instead of paying for a night's stabling.

Upgate　Travelling uphill through the locks or upstream on the river.

Warp　Mud or silt deposited by a fast flowing river.

Winding hole　A wide place on a canal where a boat may be turned or 'winded'.

Wad and a cup　Sandwich and a cup of tea. (Coffee was relatively expensive in the 1930s and not drunk by as many people as today).

Wossup　Slang for Worksop

Wireless poles　Early form of radio aerial used before reception improved. A wire strung between two poles.

4 TIDES

Aegre　Also spelt Aegir or Eagre. A tidal wave known as the Bore on the River Severn.

Agre Shadow	The effect created by the tidal wave which broke the reflection on the water.
Falling off	Decreasing from spring to neap conditions and all tides in between.
Making or Mending	Increasing from neap conditions to spring conditions and all tides in between.
Neap tides	The smallest rise and fall with little flow and no Aegre.
Spring tides	The largest tides of the year, usually at the Spring and Autumn equinox. Very fast tides accompanied by an Aegre wave.

APPENDICES

Weights and Measures

Grain   63lb – 1 bushel of wheat
60lb – 1 bushel of maize
60lb – 1 bushel of rye
56lb – 1 bushel of barley
42lb – 1 bushel of oats

8 bushels = 1 quarter

504lb – 1 quarter of wheat
480lb – 1 quarter of maize
480lb – 1 quarter of rye
448lb – 1 quarter of barley
336lb – 1 quarter of oats

20tons – 89 quarters of maize
20tons – 93 quarters of wheat
20tons – 93 quarters of rye
20tons – 100 quarters of barley
20tons – 133 quarters of oats

Metric Conversion:
A narrow boat would normally carry 20–22 tons with summer water levels and up to 26tons on good winter water levels.
20tons = 20.320tonne
26tons = 26.416tonne
1 quarter of barley – 202.6 kilogrammes
One hundred weight (cwt) = 112lbs = 50.85 kilogrammes

Coinage:

£ p	£	s.	d.
£1.00	1	0	0
50p		10	0
25p		5	0
12 1/2 p		2	6
10p		2	0
5p		1	0
2 1/2 p		0	6

Linear Measurements:

Narrow boat	72ft long (21.950 metres)
	7ft wide (2.135 metres)
Trent size keel	74ft long (22.559 metres)
	14ft 4ins wide (4.370 metres)
Lincoln size keel	74ft long (22.559 metres)
	14ft 4ins wide (4.370 metres)
Sheffield size keel	61ft 6ins long (18.595 metres)
	15ft 6ins wide (4.720 metres)

List of Narrow Boats working on the Chesterfield Canal in the 1930s and 1940s *(referred to in the book)*

Reg No.	Boat Name	Captain	Owner
E Retford 58	Clarice (named after the Author's sister)	Henry Clark	Henry Clark
E Retford 51	Lilian (named after The Old Man's sister)	Henry Clark	Henry Clark
		Henry Clark	Henry Clark
E Retford 27	Albion (formerly Doris)	Henry Clark	Henry Clark
E Retford 57	Valour (formerly Evelyn)	Henry Clark	Henry Clark
E Retford 43	Gerald	George Newton	Furley & Co
E Retford 59	Perseverence	Norman Newton	Furley & Co
E Retford 48	Ruth	Albert Pettinger	Furley & Co
E Retford 53	Lena	Jack Hewitt	Furley & Co
	Thomas & Mary	Joe Beeston	Furley & Co
		Jim Pettinger	
E Retford 14	Lady Milton	George Hewitt	G C Cooper
E Retford 47	Lord Milton	Chris Hewitt	G C Cooper
E Retford 55	Elsie	Jim Hewitt	Furley & Co
		George Wolfenden	
E Retford 44	Pride	Biddy Wolfenden	Furley & Co
		George Clifton	
		Pearce Hindley	
E Retford 46	Ida (originally Coronation)	Jack & David Chambers	Alfred Chambers
E Retford 48A	Mavis	Bob Hewitt	Furley & Co
E Retford 56	Joan	G. Lelyton	Furley & Co
E Retford 52	Edna	Ernest Hewitt	Furley & Co
E Retford 45	Norah	John Pettinger	Hill Bros

NOTES:

Ruth, built at West Stockwith in 1930, was the last Chesterfield boat to be registered. She was acquired by Ike Argent, Section Inspector on the Erewash Canal in the late 1950s and taken to Trevithick's Boatyard at Nottingham to be cut in half before being converted into a pleasure craft by the new owner. She was last seen at the Boat Museum at Ellesmere Port but is not sadly on display. All the carrying boats listed were built at Tomlinson's Boatyard, West Stockwith, with the exception of three boats:

Reg No. 55 – Elsie

Reg No. 56 – Joan

Reg No. 57 – Gerald

These boats were built at Thorne. No. 57 Gerald built in 1925 was too wide for the narrow locks above Worksop and could not therefore reach Shireoaks Colliery for return loads of coal.

Two maintenance boats, the dredger No. 59 Joan built 1929 (not to be confused with No. 56 Joan) and Norah built 1930 (not to be confused with No. 45 Norah) were built at the LNER Company maintenance yard, Worksop. Neither boat was full length both being little over 60ft (18.29m).

The above are brief details of the boats and owners only and more information is contained in the Canal Boat Register for Retford dated 1880–1929.

Details of a Chesterfield Canal Narrow Boat

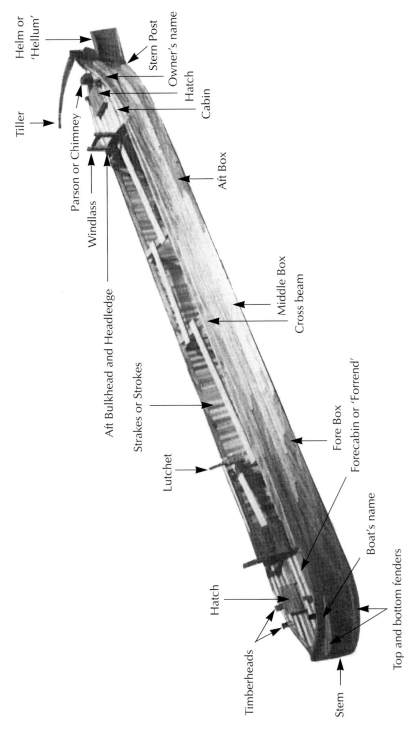

Tiller

Helm or 'Hellum'

Stern Post

Owner's name

Hatch

Cabin

Parson or Chimney

Windlass

Aft Box

Aft Bulkhead and Headledge

Middle Box

Cross beam

Strokes or Strokes

Fore Box

Forecabin or 'Forrend'

Lutchet

Boat's name

Hatch

Top and bottom fenders

Timberheads

Stem

Note: The coal box (not shown) stood between the aft bulkhead and the hatch

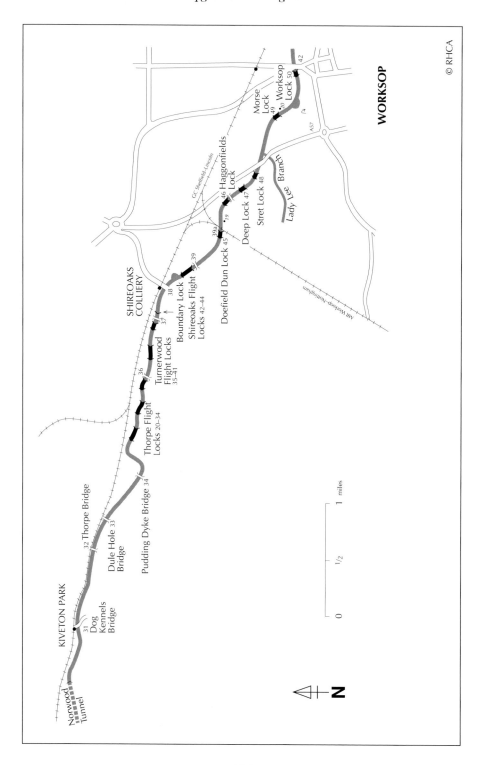

© RHCA

WORKSOP

Worksop Lock 50
Morse Lock 49
Haggonfields Lock 46
Deep Lock 47
Stret Lock 48
Lady Lee Branch
Doefield Dun Lock 45
GC Sheffield–Lincoln
SHIREOAKS COLLIERY
Boundary Lock 37
Shireoaks Flight Locks 42–44
Turnerwood Flight Locks 35–41
Thorpe Flight Locks 20–34
Pudding Dyke Bridge 34
Dule Hole Bridge 33
Thorpe Bridge 32
KIVETON PARK
Dog Kennels Bridge 31
Norwood Tunnel
MR Worksop–Nottingham
A57

N

0   ½   1 miles

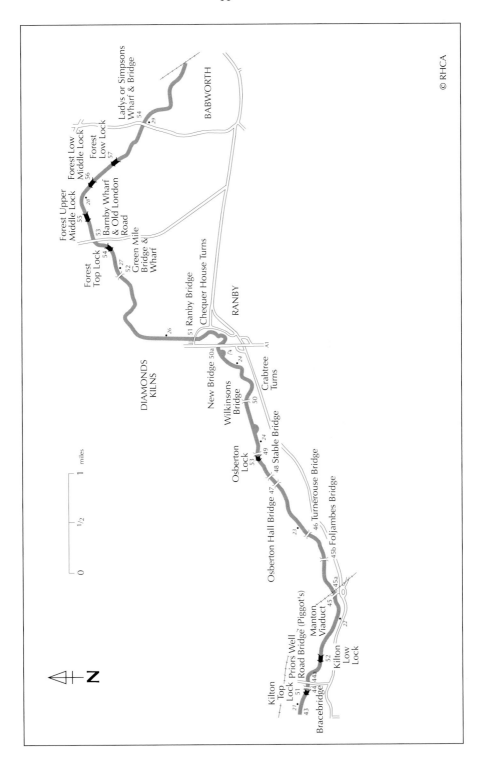

© RHCA

N

miles
0   ½   1

Ladys or Simpsons
Wharf & Bridge
54
29

BABWORTH

Forest Low
Middle Lock
56
Forest
Low Lock
57

Forest Upper
Middle Lock
55
28
Barnby Wharf
& Old London
Road
53

Forest
Top Lock
54
27
52
Green Mile
Bridge &
Wharf

Chequer House Turns

RANBY

51 Ranby Bridge
26

DIAMONDS
KILNS

New Bridge 50a
24
Crabtree
Turns
A1

Wilkinsons
Bridge
50

23
24

Osberton
Lock
53
49 48 Stable Bridge

Osberton Hall Bridge 47
23
46 Turnerouse Bridge

45b Foljambes Bridge

45a

45
27
Manton
Viaduct

Priors Well
Road Bridge (Piggot's)
52

Kilton
Top
Lock
51
23
44
44
Kilton
Low
Lock

Bracebridge
43

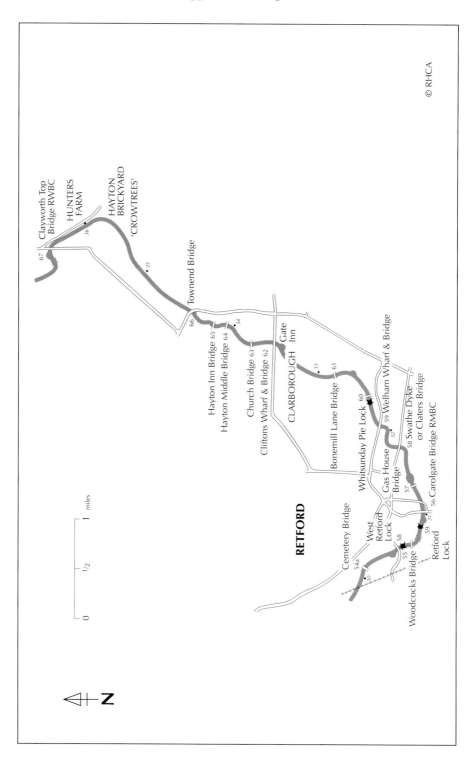

© RHCA

Clayworth Top
Bridge RWBC

HUNTERS
FARM

HAYTON
BRICKYARD
'CROWTREES'

67

36

35

Townend Bridge

66

34

Hayton Inn Bridge 65

Hayton Middle Bridge 64

Church Bridge 63

Cliftons Wharf & Bridge 62

Gate
Inn

CLARBOROUGH

33

Bonemill Lane Bridge 61

Whitsunday Pie Lock 60

59 Welham Wharf & Bridge

Gas House
Bridge

32

58 Swathe Dyke
or Claters Bridge

57

56 Carolgate Bridge RMBC

West
Retford
Lock

Cemetery Bridge

RETFORD

54a

55

58

59

37

30

Retford
Lock

Woodcocks Bridge

N

0   ½   1   miles

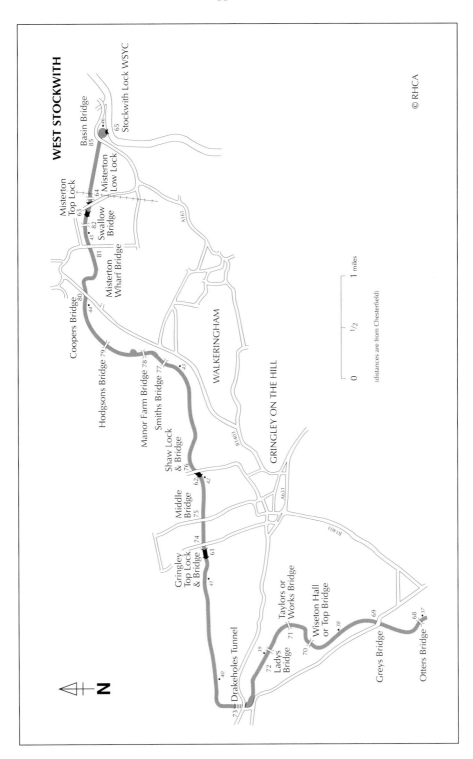

WEST STOCKWITH

Basin Bridge
85
Stockwith Lock WSYC
65
46

Misterton Top Lock
63
64
Misterton Low Lock
82 Swallow Bridge
45
Misterton Wharf Bridge
81
A161

Coopers Bridge
80
44

Hodgsons Bridge 79

Manor Farm Bridge 78
Smiths Bridge 77
43

WALKERINGHAM

Shaw Lock & Bridge 76
62 42

Middle Bridge 75

B1403

GRINGLEY ON THE HILL

Gringley Top Lock & Bridge
74
61
41

A631

Taylors or Works Bridge

Wiseton Hall or Top Bridge
71
38
70

B1403

Drakeholes Tunnel
40

Ladys Bridge
39
72
73

Greys Bridge
69

Otters Bridge
68
37

© RHCA

0   ½   1 miles

(distances are from Chesterfield)

N

ACKNOWLEDGEMENTS

The publication of this book would not have been possible without the help of a number of people and I wish to record my thanks to all of them even if they are not referred to individually.

Particular thanks are due to my daughter Sandra who prepared and typed the original manuscripts and has been a constant source of help and inspiration.

Also the following who have provided financial backing and support in various ways:

The Retford and Worksop (Chesterfield Canal) Boat Club
David and Helen Dawson
Barrie Littler
Harry and Lucy Richardson
John and Barbara Lower
Michael Jackson
Richard Allsopp

The grateful loan of maps, photographs, etc., are credited individually but I would also like to acknowledge assistance from:

Bassetlaw District Council Museum
Janet Robb, Worksop Library Archivist
Christine Richardson; Mike Taylor; Dr Christopher Whetton; Ralph Durham
Pauline Climpson and the staff at The Hallamshire Press

Finally special thanks are due to Lucy Richardson who transformed the manuscripts to computer discs, Neil Bangham for the extended free loan of a lap top computer and Harry Richardson for arranging the distribution and sales. Also to Richard Allsopp who proof read the manuscripts and provided many of the maps, photographs and drawings and convinced me that the book should be published.

FURTHER READING

The Chesterfield Canal by James Roffey. 1989 Barracuda Books ISBN 0-86023-461-4

The Waterways Revolution 1768–1778 by Christine Richardson 1992. The Self Publishing Association Ltd. ISBN 1-85421-161-7

Minutes of the Chesterfield Canal Company 1771–1780. Edited by Christine Richardson 1996. Derbyshire Record Society. ISBN 0-946324-20-4

Walkers' and Boaters' Guide to the Chesterfield Canal and Cuckoo Way by Christine Richardson and John Lower 1994 Hallamshire Press. Available from IWA (Sales) Ltd., PO Box 114, Rickmansworth WD3 1ZY. ISBN 10874718-25-3

The Chesterfield Boat Registers 1795 and 1878. Derbyshire Records Office, Matlock. ISBN 1-872776-48-5

The East Retford Boat Register 1878. Bassetlaw Museum, Retford. ISBN 1-872776-48-5

The Gainsborough Boat Register 1795. Lincolnshire Records Office

The Lincoln Boat Register 1795–1804, Lincolnshire Records Office.

The Retford and Worksop Boat Club, Clayworth Wharf, Clayworth, Retford, Notts. publishes a monthly newsletter '*Lock Key*'

The Chesterfield Canal Trust publishes a quarterly magazine '*Cuckoo*'.

Approaching Misterton Wharf Bridge.
(M. Taylor collection)